A BEGINNER'S NEW TESTAMENT GREEK GRAMMAR

Sakae Kubo

UNIVERSITY
PRESS OF
AMERICA

LANHAM • NEW YORK • LONDON

Library of Congress Cataloging in Publication Data

Kubo, Sakae, 1926-
  A beginner's New Testament Greek grammar.

  Includes index.
  1. Greek language, Biblical—Grammar. I. Title.
PA817.K8   1983   487'.4   80-64247
ISBN 0-8191-0761-1 (pbk.)

FOREWORD

This grammar is written primarily for the college student but is also adaptable for the Seminary student. For the latter in many cases two lessons can be taken at once. Because it is primarily directed to the college student, the one dominant goal of this grammar is simplicity. The author has taught Greek for over twenty years and is convinced that Greek can be taught so that any ordinary college student can learn it adequately.

Some of the features of this grammar are presented below:

1. In most grammars one lesson is usually too much for the college student to take for one day's assignment. This grammar is arranged so that each lesson is suited for one assignment. There are 123 lessons. The grammar section goes up to Lesson 53. With Lesson 54 reading from 1 John begins, alternating with a general review of grammar. While it is possible to take 123 lessons in a year with four class periods a week, it is not necessary to do this, if there are fewer class periods, since one can easily stop after reading through 1 John or up to any chapter of the Gospel of John.

2. The lessons are arranged so that one builds upon the previous lesson. Thus the future follows the present, the second aorist follows the imperfect, the perfect follows the first aorist, the subjunctive follows the indicative.

3. After every four or five lessons a review is provided. After the review a reading is provided utilizing the vocabulary and grammar learned primarily in the previous four or five lessons, but including other matters learned up to this point. We have mentioned that after the grammar has been dealt with alternating with the reading from the NT a general review is also provided. In the reading section from the NT, grammar is also reviewed and matters of syntax discussed.

4. The section of readings from the NT is coordinated with my Reader's Greek-English Lexicon of the New Testament which handily provides vocabulary for words which the student has not yet learned. By providing vocabulary and thus cutting out the time-consuming task of looking up words, the student will be able to take a larger section of reading. Exposure to a large amount of Greek leads invariably to repetition of forms, vocabulary, and structure that helps considerably in the learning process.

5. Emphasis is placed on the recognition of individual forms and their translation rather than the memorizing of paradigms. The teacher needs constantly to keep in mind that the goal of his teaching is not memorizing paradigms but learning how to translate Greek into English. Too many learn forms without being able to translate them in a sentence. They can recite the paradigm but cannot recognize one of the forms when it is looked at in isolation. For this reason recognition exercises are provided and translation of forms is stressed.

6. The middle voice is not found in English. Therefore its introduction is delayed as long as possible. The deponent form when it is introduced is, therefore, associated with the passive form instead of the middle.

7. The masculine and neuter forms are placed beside each other rather than separated by the feminine since they share certain forms, and this can be seen more readily when placed side by side.

8. The rules have been kept as simple as possible. However, more detailed and comprehensive explanations are provided either in the appendix or in the notes. Syntactical matters which do not occur frequently are treated as they appear in the reading of the NT. Some syntactical matters such as all the various uses of the cases, especially the genitive, the tenses, the participles, and infinitives, would be more appropriately treated in the second year of study.

It is the hope of this author that this grammar will help many to desire to study more deeply the actual language in which the Gospels and Epistles were written.

My heartfelt thanks go to the following for suggestions that have been made to improve the book and especially for their willingness to use it for their Greek I classes: Ellie Economou, Lucile Knapp, and Beatrice Neall. My Greek I class at Andrews University during the 1977-78 year deserve special thanks for the inspiration they provided by their enthusiasm in learning Greek from this grammar. To Douglas Clark and William Richardson for many valuable suggestions I stand in debt. I owe much also to Mrs. Virgil Bartlett for her expert typing of the original draft.

College Place, WA
February 1979   Sakae Kubo

TABLE OF CONTENTS

LESSON 1

THE ALPHABET

Capital Letters	Small Letters	Name	Pronunciation	Transliteration
A	α	alpha	a as in father or as in cat	a
B	β	beta	b as in bat	b
Γ	γ	gamma	g as in gone	g
Δ	δ	delta	d as in dog	d
E	ε	epsilon	e as in set	e
Z	ζ	zeta	z as in daze	z
H	η	eta	e as in obey	$\bar{e}$
θ	ϑ	theta	th as in thing	th
I	ι	iota	i as in sit (short), ee as in feet (long)	i
K	κ	kappa	k as in kitchen	k
Λ	λ	lambda	l as in law	l
M	μ	mu	m as in man	m
N	ν	nu	n as in new	n
Ξ	ξ	xi	x (ks) as in axiom	x
O	ο	omicron	o as in obey	o
Π	π	pi	p as in peach	p
P	ρ	rho	r as in rough	r
Σ	σ (ς)	sigma	s as in slow	s
T	τ	tau	t as in talk	t
Y	υ	upsilon	u as in universe	u

1

Φ	φ	phi	ph or f as in phone	ph
X	χ	chi	ch as in loch	ch
Ψ	ψ	psi	ps as in slips	ps
Ω	ω	omega	o as in note	ō

1. Ordinarily γ is pronounced as a hard g but if it is followed by another γ or κ, χ, and ξ, it is pronounced as an n. Thus εὐαγγέλιον is pronounced euangelion.

2. Notice that there are two forms of the sigma. ς is used only at the end of a word while σ can be used anywhere else. Thus ἀπόστολος.

3. It is important to learn, recognize, and pronounce the letters of the alphabet as soon as possible. The student should make this his immediate object since he will be handicapped and begin to fall behind if he does not know them by the time the next lesson is taken up. It is especially important to recognize the small letters. Since the capitals are used for proper nouns and usually at the beginning of paragraphs, it is still necessary to learn them but not as urgently as the small letters. In learning the Greek names of the letters one picks up the pronunciation of them since the beginning sound of the name of the letter is the pronunciation of the letter; thus beta is pronounced as a b, kappa as a k.

4. Certain Greek letters look like English letters but should not be confused with them. Thus the η is not an n but the long e, eta; ν is not the v as in vine but the n as in name; ρ is not p but an r; the χ is not x but chi; ω is not w but omega. Spend some time on these letters so that you will not confuse them.

5. α, β, δ, ε, ι, κ, ο, σ/ς, τ, υ not only look but are pronounced like their English counterparts so they should not cause any problem.

6. After you have studied closely the letters referred to in Number 4 and eliminated those in Number 5, concentrate on the rest of the letters: γ, ζ, ϑ, λ, μ, ξ, π, φ, ψ. Once you have equated γ (g), ζ (z), λ (l), μ (m), and π (p) with their English equivalents they should be easy to learn. The others are double consonants and are equivalent to two English consonants: ϑ (th), ξ (ks), φ (ph or f), and ψ (ps).

7. Every vowel that begins a word must have a breathing mark. The rough breathing (ʽ) is pronounced as an h; thus ὁ=ho.

The smooth breathing (') is not pronounced; thus ὁ=o. The initial υ in a word always takes the rough breathing and this is the case almost always for ρ, though it is not a vowel.

8. υ is transliterated as a y except when it is used as a second letter in a diphthong (two vowels sounded together as ου).

9. Every Greek word (with a few exceptions) takes an accent. In some instances it may take two accents. These accents are called acute ('), circumflex (~), and grave (`) and were used to indicate different types of musical pitch accent. No attempt is made to follow this. The student can consider these accents simply as signs indicating what syllables to stress.

Exercises

A. Read aloud and transliterate the following Greek words into English letters.

1. ἄγγελος	15. φωνή	28. καύχησις
2. ἄνθρωπος	16. ἐξουσία	29. ζητέω
3. διάβολος	17. ἀγάπη	30. παρουσία
4. καρδία	18. θλῖψις	31. συγκατάθεσις
5. προφήτης	19. ἀμήν	32. ἡμῖν
6. χρόνος	20. βαπτίζω	33. φόβοι
7. ψυχή	21. θεός	34. πρῶτον
8. χάρις	22. πόλις	35. σάρξ
9. ἐκκλησία	23. ὑποκριτής	36. ἐπαγγελία
10. ἀδελφός	24. ψευδοπροφήτης	37. ὑπέρ
11. ἀπόστολος	25. σπέρμα	38. μετάνοια
12. ἥλιος	26. ἐπιστολή	39. δυσφημία
13. πνεῦμα	27. ἐδέξασθε	40. ὡς
14. σῶμα		

LESSON 2

DIPHTHONGS, BREATHING MARKS, AND PUNCTUATION

1. Writing the small letters. The number 1 indicates where one should begin writing and 2 where the second stroke should begin, etc. Notice the words that are written above or below the line.

2. Recognizing the capital letters. The student should have no difficulty recognizing A, B, E, Z, Θ, I, K, M, N, O, Π, P, T, Φ, X, Ψ, since they look like their corresponding small letters. Do not confuse the P and X with the English letters that look like them. The student should concentrate on Γ, Δ, H, Λ, Ξ, Σ, Y, Ω. Do not confuse the H and Y with the English letters that look like them. These can be mastered quickly.

3. Diphthongs are sounds produced by two vowels pronounced together, the final letter being either ι or υ. These and their pronunciation are:

αι	as in aisle
ει	as in eight
οι	as in oil
υι	as in quit
αυ	as in maul
ου	as in soup
ευ, ηυ	as in feud

4. Improper diphthongs. These are sounds produced when an iota subscript (a small ι) is written beneath α, η, or ω (ᾳ, ῃ, ῳ). The iota subscript is disregarded in pronunciation. They are pronounced as though they were simple α, η, or ω.

5. A diaeresis (¨) is occasionally placed over the second of two vowels to indicate that they do not form a diphthong and are pronounced separately, e.g., Ἡσαΐας.

6. Breathing marks fall on the second letter of the diphthong; thus αἱ, οὐ, etc. If the initial vowel is a capital, the breathing mark and accent stand in front of it; thus Ἄ.

7. Punctuation marks. The comma and the period are the

4

same in English and in Greek. The student should especially learn
the Greek question mark which looks like a semi-colon (;). The
English colon and semi-colon are represented by the raised period
(·) in Greek.

8. Article. Greek has no word for an indefinite article.
To indicate indefiniteness the definite article is omitted.

9. Vocabulary

ὁ the (masculine article)   καί and (sometimes also trans-
Ἰησοῦς, ὁ Jesus   lated as also, even)
θεός, ὁ God   κύριος, ὁ lord
*ἐστι(ν) is   λόγος, ὁ word
ἄνθρωπος, ὁ man   υἱός, ὁ son

10. Exercises

a. Capitals.   Read aloud and transliterate.

1. Σιλῶαν   11. Πέτρος
2. Ὕπαγε   12. Λώτ
3. Δαυίδ   13. Ὗιός
4. Ἡλίας   14. Ῥούθ
5. Ῥαββί   15. Ὡς
6. Γαλιλαία   16. Ξένος
7. Σίμων   17. Χριστός
8. Ἡρῴδης   18. Δός
9. Λάζαρος   19. Ὠμέγα
10. Ζακχαῖος   20. Γνωρίζω

b. Diphthongs.   Read aloud.

1. λέγει   7. αὐτῷ
2. ἄνθρωποι   8. ἀγαπᾷ
3. εὐαγγέλιον   9. ἀρχῇ
4. αὐξάνω   10. λύσει
5. λύουσι   11. λῦσαι
6. υἱός

c. Translate.

1. Σίμων ἐστὶν ἄνθρωπος.
2. ὁ Ἰησοῦς ἐστὶν ὁ λόγος καὶ ὁ κύριος.
3. ὁ Ἰησοῦς ἐστὶν θεὸς καὶ ἄνθρωπος.
4. θεὸς ἐστὶν ὁ Ἰησοῦς.

*Certain verb forms in the third person usually take what is
called a movable nu at the end. Ordinarily when the third person

5

form ended in a vowel and the next word following without a punctuation also began with a vowel, the movable nu was placed at the
end of the verb. However, this rule is not always followed. The
movable nu is found many times even when the next word does not
begin with a vowel.

LESSON 3

SOME CHARACTERISTICS OF GREEK

1. The gender of nouns. In Greek all nouns have gender, i.e., every word is masculine, feminine, or neuter. The articles, ὁ (masculine), ἡ (feminine), and τό (neuter) indicate the gender. Generally, obviously masculine objects (such as man and son) are masculine in gender and likewise obviously feminine objects are feminine in gender but otherwise the gender of a particular object (such as house or heaven) is difficult to determine otherwise. Thus ὁ ἀπόστολος is masculine, ἡ γυνή (woman) is feminine, but τὸ αἷμα (blood) is neuter, ἡ ἁμαρτία (sin) is feminine, and ὁ θάνατος (death) is masculine. The student should learn the noun with its article to learn its gender.

2. Cases. In English the form of the noun changes very little. The plural forms usually add an s (boys) or change their form (men) and the genitive forms add 's or ' (boy's, boys'). In Greek nouns always change their forms according to their use in the sentence. Thus the form for man is ἄνθρωπος when used as a subject (nominative case) but ἄνθρωπον when used as a direct object (accusative case). Nouns that end in ος are called second declension nouns and they follow a basic pattern of endings. The nominative singular ending is ος and the accusative singular ending is ον.

3. Verbs. In English we say, I <u>eat</u> but he <u>eats</u> indicating agreement between the verb and the subject. <u>Eats</u> in English indicates third person singular. While in English the verb form does not change except for the third person singular, in Greek it changes with every person both in the singular and the plural. Because each form is different and indicates what person is doing the acting it is not necessary to have the pronoun as subject. Thus λέγει means "he says" and λέγουσι(ν) means "they say." The ω at the end of the verb indicates first person singular, the ει, the third person singular, and the ουσι(ν), third person plural.

As in English verbs have tense, voice, and mood. Tense in Greek in contrast to English indicates kind of action rather than time. However, in the indicative mood (the usual mood), tense indicates both time and kind of action. The active voice (the usual voice) indicates the subject as the one performing the action of the verb. The forms given above are both present active indicative forms.

4. Word order. Since the form of a noun indicates its function in a sentence it is not necessary for Greek words to be arranged in a certain order to be intelligible. In English correct word order is an absolute necessity for intelligibility since there are basically no difference in forms. "The man eats the fish" is not the same as "The fish eats the man." In Greek, however, it is possible to shift the order of the nouns or even the verb without change of meaning. ὁ ἄνθρωπος λέγει τὸν λόγον is the same as τὸν λόγον λέγει ὁ ἄνθρωπος or λέγει ὁ ἄνθρωπος τὸν λόγον or λέγει τὸν λόγον ὁ ἄνθρωπος. The ending ος tells you what the subject is (ὁ ἄνθρωπος) and ον tells you what the object is (τὸν λόγον).

5. Accents. The accents are important in distinguishing certain forms. Otherwise for reading purposes they are relatively unimportant. The following is provided for information sake.

a. The accents can fall only on the last three syllables.

b. These syllables are called ultima (the last syllable), penult (the next to the last), and the antepenult (the one before the penult).

c. The acute accent (´) can fall on all three syllables, the circumflex (~) on the last two syllables only, and the grave (`) only on the last syllable.

d. In the verbs, the accent will go as far back as the rules allow while in the nouns the accent will generally remain where it was in the nominative singular form unless the rules forbid it.

e. The basic rules of accent are:

(1). The circumflex can stand only on a long syllable.

(2). If the ultima is long, the antepenult cannot be accented and if the penult is accented, it must be an acute.

(3). If the ultima is short, a long penult, if accented, must have a circumflex.

(4). A long ultima can have either acute or circumflex accent.

(5). An acute on the last syllable always changes to a grave when followed, without intervening punctuation, by other words in a sentence.

f. The vowels η and ω and all diphthongs except final αι

8

and οι are always long. The vowels α, ι, υ may be long
or short and must be learned by observation.

The student should not try to learn all these rules at this
point but may refer to them if he finds some accent puzzling. A
more comprehensive set of rules governing accents is found in Appendix 1.

6. Certain words do not ordinarily take any accent. These
are called proclitics and enclitics. Proclitics go so closely with
the following word that it takes no accent. In this class are the
articles ὁ, ἡ, οἱ, αἱ. Enclitics, on the other hand, go so closely with a preceding word that they normally do not take an accent.
In this class are the present indicative of the verb to be, except
for the second person singular, and the first and second person
singular personal pronouns μου, μοι, με, and σου, σοι, σε. Accent
rules for these are given in Appendix 1.

7. Vocabulary

λέγω I say, speak
λέγει He speaks
λέγουσι(ν) They speak (The ν is usually found but may be omitted)
ἄγω I lead, bring
ἀκούω I hear (takes accusative and genitive object)
ἔχω I have
υἱός, ὁ son

πιστεύω I believe (takes dative or εἰς. . .)
οὐρανός, ὁ heaven
τόν the (the masculine accusative)
εἰς into, in (with accusative)
διά on account of, because of (with accusative)
πρός to, toward, with (with accusative

8. For those teachers who feel that they can include it within their program (about 5-7 minutes daily), it is recommended that
a verse or two at the beginning but more as the students become
more acquainted with the Greek from either the Gospel of John or
I John be read in class from this point on. Naturally at the beginning the teacher must explain just about everything. He should
concentrate on words or forms that occur frequently. Vocabulary,
case endings of nouns, and verb endings should be pointed out.
The student should not be required to learn these forms but will
learn them by repetition. He should also be encouraged to make a
little notebook of pertinent information, those especially emphasized by the teacher. This inductive approach long with the tradi-
tional approach of the grammar will correlate the rather objective
study of grammar with the actual use of it as observed in the New
Testament. It will also make learning of the grammar easier since
more and more the student will find that parts of the grammar to
be learned have already been met in the reading. It will serve
also as a review of what has been covered in the lessons.

I would highly recommend this approach.

Exercises

A. Read and translate

1. ὁ ἄνθρωπος λέγει τὸν λόγον.
2. λέγουσι τὸν λόγον.
3. ὁ υἱὸς ἄγει ἄνθρωπον εἰς τὸν οὐρανόν.
4. ἄγει τὸν υἱὸν εἰς τὸν οὐρανόν.
5. ἀκούω τὸν ἄνθρωπον.
6. ἀκούει τὸν λόγον.
7. ἀκούουσι τὸν λόγον.
8. ἄγουσι τὸν ἄνθρωπον εἰς τὸν οὐρανόν.
9. ἔχει τὸν υἱόν.
10. ἔχουσιν τὸν κύριον.
11. λέγει ὁ κύριος τὸν λόγον.
12. πιστεύει εἰς τὸν κύριον.
13. ἀκούει ὁ υἱὸς τὸν θεόν.
14. διὰ τὸν κύριον τὸν λόγον ἀκούουσιν.
15. ὁ ἄνθρωπος πιστεύει διὰ τὸν υἱόν.

LESSON 4

SECOND DECLENSION NOUNS.   PRESENT ACTIVE INDICATIVE VERBS

1. The genitive case and the plural forms of the Second Declension Nouns in the nominative and accusative cases and their
corresponding articles.

	Singular	Plural
Nominative	ὁ ἄνθρωπος	οἱ ἄνθρωποι
Genitive	τοῦ ἀνθρώπου	τῶν ἀνθρώπων
Accusative	τον ἄνθρωπον	τους ἀνθρώπους

Notice how the article ends in the same way as its corresponding noun forms. The genitive plural ending for all nouns is
the same regardless of declension (ων). In English the nominative
and the accusative forms are translated the same, <u>man</u> in the singular and <u>men</u> in the plural. The genitive, <u>if without a preposition</u>,
is translated usually by "of . . ." But if a preposition precedes
the genitive, it will take precedence over the "of" form. Thus
ἀπὸ τοῦ κυρίου is translated "from the Lord," not "from of the
Lord."

The nominative case is used for the subject and predicate
nominative. The main use of the accusative case is as the direct
object. The genitive case has various uses. One of its uses is to
indicate possession or some kind of relationship which can be translated by the "of . . ." phrase. Specific uses of this case will
be indicated as they are met.

2. The second person forms and the first person plural of the
present active indicative of the verb λύω (I loose or destroy).

		Singular		Plural
1	λύω	I loose/am loosing	λύομεν	We loose/are loosing
2	λύεις	You loose/are loosing	λύετε	You loose/are loosing
3	λύει	He looses/is loosing	λύουσι(ν)	They loose/are loosing

The third person singular is <u>he</u>, <u>she</u>, or <u>it</u> but to save space
only <u>he</u> will be given in all the conjugations. Also in the present
tense only the first form will be given with the second form understood, i.e., <u>I loose</u> instead of <u>I loose/am loosing</u>.

3. The indicative mood (the most common of four moods) makes
a statement or asks a question. The present tense in the indicative
mood usually indicates action going on in the present.

4. Vocabulary

ἀδελφός, ὁ brother
ἄγγελος, ὁ messenger, angel
γινώσκω I know
ἀπό from (with genitive only)
ἐκ, ἐξ out of, from (with genitive only; the second form is used before a word beginning with a vowel)
οὐ, οὐκ, οὐχ not (the second form is used before a word beginning with a vowel with smooth breathing, the third before one with a rough breathing, the first with words beginning with a consonant; used with the indicative mood)

γράφω I write
κόσμος, ὁ world
οἶκος, ὁ house
διά through (with genitive)

Exercises

A. Recognition

1. γινώσκεις
2. γράφετε
3. ἄγει
4. ἀκούομεν
5. ἀκούεις
6. ἀνθρώπου

7. ἀγγέλων
8. κόσμον
9. οἴκων
10. γινώσκετε
11. ἄγουσιν
12. κόσμους

B. Translate into English

1. ὁ ἀδελφὸς τοῦ ἀνθρώπου ἄγει τὸν ἄγγελον ἐκ τοῦ οἴκου.
2. γράφεις λόγους.
3. οὐκ ἄγομεν τοὺς ἀγγέλους ἐκ τοῦ κόσμου.
4. γινώσκετε τοὺς λόγους τῶν ἀνθρώπων.
5. οὐ γινώσκεις τοὺς ἀδελφοὺς τῶν ἀγγέλων.
6. οὐκ ἀκούομεν τοὺς λόγους τῶν ἀνθρώπων.
7. ἄγουσιν τοὺς ἀγγέλους πρὸς τὸν κύριον.
8. ἄγει τοὺς ἀνθρώπους εἰς τὸν οἶκον.

C. Translate into Greek

1. The man hears the word.
2. We hear the words of the Lord.
3. You (s.) lead the messengers into the house.

LESSON 5

THE DATIVE CASE. SECOND DECLENSION NEUTER NOUNS.
PRESENT INDICATIVE OF εἰμί

1. The dative case. The most common use of the dative is
to indicate to or for whom anything is done, what we call the indirect object and the dative of advantage or disadvantage. The
forms in the singular and plural of the second declension respectively are ῳ and οις.

	Singular	Plural
Nominative	ὁ ἄνθρωπος	οἱ ἄνθρωποι
Genitive	τοῦ ἀνθρώπου	τῶν ἀνθρώπων
Dative	τῷ ἀνθρώπῳ	τοῖς ἀνθρώποις
Accusative	τὸν ἄνθρωπον	τοὺς ἀνθρώπους

One example of its use is as follows:

γράφει τοῖς ἀνθρώποις. He writes to the men. It is used
here to indicate an indirect object. Other uses of the dative will
be explained as they are met. The dative, if without a preposition,
is translated "to or for. . ." But like the genitive, if the preposition precedes, it nullifies this translation. Thus ἐν τῷ οἴκῳ
is translated "in the house," not "in to the house."

There is another case called the vocative (the case of
address), but since it is infrequent and when used is easy to recognize, it is not necessary to spend time learning it. In the
sentence, "Tom, come here," Tom is in the vocative. In the second
declension the vocative is ἄνθρωπε in the singular and ἄνθρωποι in
the plural. Frequently the vocative takes the nominative form.

Some grammars include the ablative (with the same forms as
the genitive), the locative, and the instrumental cases (these last
two with the same forms as the dative). However, the leading
grammars do not consider these as separate cases but only different
uses within the respective cases. If we determine case by function,
we would have more cases than the additional three. It would be
better to go by form and indicate the different functions within
each form.

2. The second declension neuter nouns. These nouns have
the same endings as the masculine nouns in the genitive and dative
singular and plural. Another thing to remember is that the nominative and accusative forms in the singular are the same and likewise

for the plural. Thus one needs only to learn the forms for the
singular and plural nominative.

	Singular	Plural
Nominative	τὸ τέκνον	τὰ τέκνα
Genitive	τοῦ τέκνου	τῶν τέκνων
Dative	τῷ τέκνῳ	τοῖς τέκνοις
Accusative	τὸ τέκνον	τὰ τέκνα

3. In almost every instance the neuter plural subject will
take a singular verb. Thus τὰ τέκνα ἀκούει rather than τὰ τέκνα
ἀκούουσιν.

4. We have already seen the present indicative third person
singular form of the verb <u>to be</u>--ἐστι(ν)--he is. The rest of the
forms are listed below. Note the similarities with the regular
verb in the plural forms.

	Singular		Plural	
1	εἰμί	I am	ἐσμέν	We are
2	εἶ	You are	ἐστέ	You are
3	ἐστί(ν)	He is	εἰσί(ν)	They are

5. Frequently in Greek you will find a noun, θεός is a good
example, and especially abstract nouns such as life, love, peace,
etc., which take the article but in English we would not ordinarily translate the article. This is also true of proper nouns.

6. Postpositives are conjunctions which cannot stand first
in a clause, even though we translate them first in English. They
are usually in the second position. Example: ἄγω γὰρ τὸν ἄνθρωπον.
For I lead the man.

7. Vocabulary

γάρ for (postpositive)
ἐγώ I
σύ you (singular)
εἰ if
οὖν therefore, then (postpositive)
ἀποστέλλω I send
ἐσθίω I eat
ἐν in (with dative)

εὑρίσκω I find
λαμβάνω I take, receive
ἔργον, τό work
ἱερόν, τό temple
νόμος, ὁ law
σημεῖον, τό sign
τέκνον, τό child
ὄχλος, ὁ crowd

Exercises

A. Recognition

1. ἀνθρώπῳ
2. τέκνοις
3. ἐστέ

4. εἶ
5. ἀνθρώπους
6. ἐσμέν

14

7. τέκνα
8. ἐστί
9. τέκνον
10. εἰμί

11. εἰσί
12. ἄνθρωπον
13. ἀνθρώπου
14. τέκνων

B. Translate into English

1. γράφει σημεῖον τοῖς ὄχλοις.
2. ἐγὼ ἀποστέλλω τῷ τέκνῳ τὸν νόμον.
3. ἐστὲ γὰρ τὸ ἔργον τοῦ θεοῦ.
4. λαμβάνει οὖν τοὺς ὄχλους.
5. εἰ ἀκούετε τὸν λόγον, λαμβάνετε τὸν νόμον.
6. ἄγουσιν οἱ ἀδελφοὶ τὰ τέκνα τῷ κυρίῳ ἐν τῷ ἱερῷ.
7. εὑρίσκομεν ἔργον τοῖς τέκνοις.
8. εἶ ὁ λόγος τοῦ θεοῦ.
9. τὰ τέκνα ἐσθίει ἐν τῷ οἴκῳ.
10. ἐσμὲν σημεῖα τῷ κόσμῳ.
11. σὺ εἶ ὁ υἱὸς τοῦ θεοῦ;

C. Translate into Greek

1. For you (singular) are the child of heaven.
2. He eats in the house.
3. We are God's messengers.
4. The children receive the word.
5. He sends a law to the crowds.

LESSON 6

REVIEW OF LESSONS 1-5

1. Review the vocabulary of Lessons 1-5. Write the words
on cards and then see how many of these words you know. Concentrate on those you do not know till you have mastered all the
words.

2. The alphabet. If you have not learned the alphabet yet,
you are already finding it difficult, almost impossible to learn
the vocabulary and to read, translate, and to learn the conjugations and declensions. You must master them. Give the Greek
names, the pronunciation, and transliteration of the following:

γ, ζ, ϑ, λ, μ, ξ, π. Γ, Δ, Η, Λ, Ξ, Σ, Υ, Ω.

3. Breathing marks, accents, punctuation marks, diphthongs.

a. What kind of breathing marks are there?
b. Where are they placed?
c. Give the pronunciation of the following: ὁ, ὀ, οὖν,
οἱ, αἱ.
d. What kind of accents are there? Name the following:
΄, ῀, `.
e. On what syllables are the above placed?
f. In a word beginning with a capital letter, where is
the breathing mark and accent placed? Which comes first
when they come together?
g. What is the Greek question mark like?
h. What is a diphthong? How do you pronounce αἱ, εἱ?
i. What is an improper diphthong and how does it affect
pronunciation?

4. Characteristics of Greek

a. What do we mean by gender? How are Greek nouns
different from English in this respect?
b. What do we mean by case? How do Greek and English
differ here?
c. Is there any difference between Greek and English
verb endings? How are they different?
d. Is word order important for intelligibility in Greek?
Why?

5. Review the second declension masculine and neuter nouns
in Lesson 5. Compare the endings of these carefully.

16

a. What is the difference between the masculine and neuter noun endings?
b. What is characteristic of the neuter nominative and accusative endings?
c. Are the article endings always the same as the noun endings in the masculine and neuter nouns? Where are they different? Where do you not have the τ before the article?
d. Give the endings of the second declension masculine and neuter nouns.

6. Review the regular verb endings of the present active indicative in Lesson 4. Give the person and number of the following active endings and translate them with the verb, I hear.

ομεν	ουσι(ν)	εις
ετε	ει	ω

7. Review the present indicative of the verb εἶναι <u>to be</u>.

a. Where are they similar to the regular verbs?
b. Translate the following:

εἰσί(ν)	ἐσμέν	ἐστί(ν)
εἰμί	εἶ	ἐστέ

8. Translation and Recognition.

a. Verbs

γράφει, ἀποστέλλω, ἀκούετε, εὑρίσκομεν, ἐσθίουσι, ἐσμέν, εἶ, ἄγουσι, λαμβάνετε, ἐστέ, ἀκούεις, γινώσκεις, ἀκούομεν.

b. Nouns

τέκνον, ἀνθρώπους, ἔργῳ, σημεῖα, τέκνα, κύριον, τέκνοις, θεοῦ, ἀνθρώπων, ἀδελφούς, ἀγγέλοις.

READING 1

A.

ὁ λόγος ἦν[1] πρὸς τὸν θεόν. καὶ ὁ λόγος λέγει αὐτῷ.[2] ὁ θεὸς ἀποστέλλει τὸν λόγον ἐκ τοῦ οὐρανοῦ εἰς τὸν κόσμον. οἱ ἄνθρωποι τοῦ κόσμου οὐ λαμβάνουσι τὸν λόγον. οὐ πιστεύουσιν εἰς[3] τὸν λόγον. ὁ λόγος ἐστὶν ὁ υἱὸς τοῦ θεοῦ. ἀλλὰ[4] Πέτρος[5] ἀκούει αὐτὸν[6] καὶ πιστεύει εἰς τὸν υἱόν. ὁ υἱὸς λέγει αὐτῷ· ὁ λόγος εἰμὶ

[1]was
[2]to him
[3]in
[4]but
[5]Peter
[6]him

17

καὶ σὺ εἶ ὁ ἄγγελός μου.[7] Πέτρος ἔχει ἀδελφόν, εὑρίσκει [7]my
αὐτόν, ἄγει αὐτὸν πρὸς τὸν υἱόν. οἱ ἀδελφοὶ λαμβάνουσιν [8]because
αὐτὸν ὅτι[8] γινώσκουσιν τὸν θεὸν καὶ ἀκούουσιν τὸν λόγον [9]his
αὐτοῦ[9] καὶ ποιοῦσι[10] τὰ ἔργα αυτοῦ. λέγουσι τοῖς ὄχλοις[10]they do
καὶ γράφουσιν τοῖς ἀνθρώποις ἐν τῷ κόσμῳ. διὰ αὐτοὺς[11] [11]them
ἄνθρωποι ἔρχονται[12] εἰς τὸ ἱερὸν μετὰ[13] τῶν τέκνων [12]go
αὐτῶν.[14] ἐν τῷ ἱερῷ ἐσθίουσι τὸν ἄρτον[15] τοῦ οὐρανοῦ [13]with
καὶ εὑρίσκουσι σημεῖα τοῦ οὐρανοῦ ἐν τοῖς οἴκοις αὐτῶν, [14]their
ἄνθρωποι γὰρ τοῦ θεοῦ εἰσί. [15]bread

B.

    ἐσμὲν τὰ τέκνα τοῦ θεοῦ. ἀκούομεν γὰρ καὶ [1]his
λαμβάνομεν τοὺς λόγους τοῦ υἱοῦ αὐτοῦ[1] καὶ πιστεύ- [2]peace
ομεν εἰς τοὺς ἀγγέλους αὐτοῦ. διὰ τοὺς λόγους τῶν [3]gives
ἀγγέλων ἔχομεν εἰρήνην[2] ἐν τῷ κόσμῳ. σὺ οὐχ εὑρίσ- [4]to them
κεις σημεῖον ἐκ τοῦ οὐρανοῦ, ὁ γὰρ θεὸς οὐ δίδωσι[3] [5]of love
σημεῖα τοῖς τέκνοις αὐτοῦ. ἀποστέλλει ἀγγέλους [6]They teach
αὐτοῖς[4] καὶ λέγουσιν καὶ γράφουσι λόγους ἀγάπης[5] [7]them
τοῖς ὄχλοις. διδάσκουσι[6] τοὺς νόμους ἐν τῷ ἱερῷ. [8]bread
ἄγουσι αὐτοὺς[7] εἰς τὸ ἔργον τοῦ κυρίου. τὰ τέκνα [9]of life
τοῦ θεοῦ ἐσθίουσι τὸν ἄρτον[8] ζωῆς[9] καὶ ἐν τῷ ἱερῷ.

LESSON 7

FEMININE NOUNS OF THE FIRST DECLENSION
PRESENT PASSIVE INDICATIVE

1. All feminine nouns of the first declension end in α or
η. Feminine nouns make up the vast majority of this declension
with a few masculine nouns. The pattern of the plural endings of
all the first declension nouns are identical including the masculine nouns which will be taken up later. There are three different
patterns for the singular but since recognition is the important
thing the student should learn only that these nouns take either
the α or η in the singular with their regular endings. The feminine nominative singular article is ἡ. As in the masculine it adds
the τ before the non-nominative forms and its endings are the same
as η feminine nouns of this declension. The declension of ἡ
γραφή, writing, scripture, follows:

	Singular	Plural
Nominative	ἡ γραφή	αἱ γραφαί
Genitive	τῆς γραφῆς	τῶν γραφῶν
Dative	τῇ γραφῇ	ταῖς γραφαῖς
Accusative	τὴν γραφήν	τὰς γραφάς

The first declension pattern of endings is basically the
same as that of the second declension. The main difference is the
use of α/η instead of ο before the final letter. Keep in mind
that the genitive plural endings for all nouns are the same and
that first and second declension nouns always take the iota subscript in the dative singular.

2. The other two patterns in the singular (the plurals all
have the same pattern of endings) follow: ἡ ἡμέρα, day; ἡ δόξα, glory

	Singular	Singular
Nominative	ἡμέρα	δόξα
Genitive	ἡμέρας	δόξης
Dative	ἡμέρᾳ	δόξῃ
Accusative	ἡμέραν	δόξαν

Note with ἡμέρα that the genitive singular (ἡμέρας) is identical with the accusative plural (ἡμέρας). The article and/or context will determine the case and number.

While it is not important to learn the rules for the differences in the endings of these nouns in the singular, they are
accounted for by the following rules:

19

a. If the noun ends with an η in the nominative, it keeps the η throughout.

b. If the noun ends with an α in the nominative, it keeps the α throughout if it is preceded by ε, ι, or ρ as in ἡμέρα.

3. The passive voice indicates that the subject is being acted upon by someone else in contrast to the active voice where the subject is the actor.

Examples: Active: I hit the ball.
          Passive: The ball is being hit by me.

You have already learned the present indicative active forms. We present now the present indicative passive forms of λύω (I loose or destroy).

	Singular		Plural	
1	λύομαι	I am being loosed	λυόμεθα	We are being loosed
2	λύῃ	You are being loosed	λύεσθε	You are being loosed
3	λύεται	He is being loosed	λύονται	They are being loosed

These forms should be mastered.

4. Vocabulary

ὅτι that, because
ἁμαρτία, ἡ sin
βασιλεία, ἡ kingdom
γῆ, ἡ earth
γραφή, ἡ writing, scripture
δόξα, ἡ glory
δοῦλος, ὁ slave
τίς, τί who? what? which? (The first form is masculine and feminine, the last neuter. The neuter is translated "why?" as well.)

ἡμέρα, ἡ day
καρδία, ἡ heart
βλέπω I see
βάλλω I cast, throw
εἶπον I said
ὑπό by (with genitive),
     under (with accusative)

Exercises

A. Recognition

1. βλέπεται
2. βάλλῃ
3. λυόμεθα
4. ἡμέρας

5. γραφῆς
6. γῆν
7. δόξῃ
8. ἡμέραν

9. βάλλεσθε
10. βλέπονται
11. ἡμέρα
12. καρδίαι

B. Translate into English

1. βλέπεται ὁ δοῦλος ὑπὸ τοῦ ἀνθρώπου.
2. αἱ ἁμαρτίαι βάλλονται ἐκ τῆς καρδίας.

20

3. εἶπον ὅτι λαμβανόμεθα ὑπὸ τοῦ κυρίου.
4. ἀκούεσθε ὑπὸ τοῦ κόσμου.
5. βάλλῃ εἰς τὴν γῆν.
6. τὶς πιστεύεται ἐν τῇ βασιλείᾳ;
7. λαμβάνει ὁ υἱὸς δόξαν ἀπὸ τοῦ θεοῦ.
8. γράφεις ἐκ τῆς καρδίας.
9. γράφομεν τὰς γραφὰς ἐν ταῖς καρδίαις τῶν ἀνθρώπων.
10. οἱ υἱοὶ τῶν βασιλειῶν βάλλονται ἐκ τῆς γῆς.

C. Translate into Greek

1. Sin is being seen in the hearts of men.
2. The words of God are being written in heaven.

LESSON 8

FIRST DECLENSION MASCULINE NOUNS. ADJECTIVES

1. We have already indicated that the majority of second declension (o ending) nouns are masculine with a few in the neuter. The neuter differs from the masculine slightly in the nominative and accusative forms. While still fewer in number than the neuter, feminine nouns also are present in this declension. However, their endings are identical with those of the masculine. They are distinguished by the feminine article. Thus ἡ ὁδός (the way).

2. While the great majority of first declension (α, η ending) nouns are feminine, a few are masculine. Their endings are identical with the feminine except in the nominative and genitive singular. Since their nominative forms (προφήτης, νεανίας) are like the genitive singular of the feminine nouns, the genitives take the second declension endings (προφήτου, νεανίου). The article also distinguishes them from the feminine. Thus ὁ προφήτης, ὁ νεανίας (the prophet, the young man).

	Singular		Plural
Nominative	ὁ προφήτης	ὁ νεανίας	οἱ προφῆται
Genitive	τοῦ προφήτου	τοῦ νεανίου	τῶν προφητῶν
Dative	τῷ προφήτῃ	τῷ νεανίᾳ	τοῖς προφήταις
Accusative	τὸν προφήτην	τὸν νεανίαν	τοὺς προφήτας

The plural endings of νεανίας are the same as those for προφήτης.

3. Since the adjectives modify nouns, they must have gender, number, and case to agree with the nouns. The endings are the same as those of the nouns which you have already learned. The masculine and neuter adjectives have the same endings as the masculine and neuter nouns of the second declension (o ending). The feminine adjectives have the same endings as the first declension (α/η ending) nouns.

	Singular			Plural		
	M	N	F	M	N	F
N	ἀγαθός	ἀγαθόν	ἀγαθή	ἀγαθοί	ἀγαθά	ἀγαθαί
G	ἀγαθοῦ	ἀγαθοῦ	ἀγαθῆς	ἀγαθῶν	ἀγαθῶν	ἀγαθῶν
D	ἀγαθῷ	ἀγαθῷ	ἀγαθῇ	ἀγαθοῖς	ἀγαθοῖς	ἀγαθαῖς
A	ἀγαθόν	ἀγαθόν	ἀγαθήν	ἀγαθούς	ἀγαθά	ἀγαθάς

Remember that the feminine adjectives following the first declension nouns may have α or η in the ending. This is all one

needs to keep in mind since recognition is the important thing.
The rule is that it takes an α if it is preceded by a ρ or a vowel.
Thus δικαία, μικρά instead of δικαίη or μικρή. The α is kept in
all the singular forms. Thus μικρά, small, takes α throughout.

N   μικρά
G   μικρᾶς
D   μικρᾷ
A   μικράν

4. Adjectives in Greek, like the article, must agree with
the noun they modify in number, gender, and case.

Examples: ὁ ἀγαθὸς ἄνθρωπος   τὰ ἀγαθὰ τέκνα
             τὸν ἀγαθὸν ἄνθρωπον   ἡ ἀγαθὴ ἀδελφή (sister)
             οἱ ἀγαθοὶ ἄνθρωποι   αἱ ἀγαθαὶ ἀδελφαί
             τὸ ἀγαθὸν τέκνον   ταῖς ἀγαθαῖς ἀδελφαῖς

5. "The good man" can be expressed in two ways, but the
adjective must always be preceded by the article.

ὁ ἀγαθὸς ἄνθρωπος
ὁ ἄνθρωπος ὁ ἀγαθός

6. "The man is good" can be writen ὁ ἄνθρωπός ἐστιν ἀγαθός.
However the verb ἐστι can be omitted in Greek. It is possible to
say "the man is good" as written above or the following two ways:

ὁ ἄνθρωπος ἀγαθός.
ἀγαθὸς ὁ ἄνθρωπος.

Notice that in either case ἀγαθός does not have the article
before it. This distinction between number 5 and 6 is only possible
where the article is present.

7. The adjective can stand in place of a noun as in English.
This is called the substantival use.

Example: The _just_ shall live by faith.

Because Greek adjectives have gender, when used as substantives,
the masculine usually stand for man or men, the feminine for woman
or women (singular or plural), and the neuter for thing or things.

ὁ ἀγαθός   the good man
ἡ ἀγαθή   the good woman
τὸ ἀγαθόν   the good thing
οἱ ἀγαθοί   the good men

8. Vocabulary

ἀγαθός good
ἅγιος holy
ἀλλά but, except
ἄλλος other, another
δίκαιος just
νεανίας, ὁ young man
δέ but, and (postpositive)
κατά according to (with accusative); down from, against
(with genitive)

εἶδον I saw, they saw
καλός beautiful, good
μαθητής, ὁ disciple
νεκρός dead
ὁδός, ἡ way, road
πονηρός evil
προφήτης, ὁ prophet

Exercises

A. Recognition

1. μαθητής
2. προφῆται
3. ἀγαθοί
4. καλήν
5. δίκαιαν
6. ἀγαθαί

7. προφήτῃ
8. νεανίαν
9. ἀγαθά
10. καλάς
11. νεκροῦς
12. μικρᾶς

B. Translate into English

1. κατὰ τὸν προφήτην ἀγαθὸς ὁ νόμος.
2. ἡ ἁγιὰ ὁδὸς ἄγει εἰς τὸν οὐρανόν.
3. εἶδον τὸν δίκαιον μαθητήν.
4. οἱ δὲ νεκροὶ οὐκ ἐσθίουσιν.
5. ἄλλος δὲ ἀποστέλλεται εἰς τὸν κόσμον τὸν πονηρόν.
6. τὰ καλὰ τέκνα ἄγεται ὑπὸ τοῦ πονηροῦ προφήτου πρὸς τὴν ὁδὸν αὐτοῦ.
7. ἡ καρδία πονηρά.
8. ἀλλὰ οἱ δίκαιοι ἀκούουσιν τὸν ἀγαθὸν λόγον.
9. γράφετε τῷ μαθητῇ τῷ ἀγαθῷ.
10. τίς ἔχει τὴν δόξαν ἐκ τοῦ οὐρανοῦ;

C. Translate into Greek

1. The good way leads into heaven.
2. According to the holy prophet the disciple is just.

DEPONENT VERBS. THE FUTURE INDICATIVE

1. Certain verbs do not have an active form but are translated as active verbs. These are called deponent verbs. In the
present they have the same endings as the passive. These should
be designated as deponent rather than passive for the voice. The
conjugation for γίνομαι, I become, is as follows:

	Singular			Plural	
1	γίνομαι	I become	γινόμεθα	We become
2	γίνῃ	You become	γίνεσθε	You become
3	γίνεται	He becomes	γίνονται	They become

Notice that these endings are identical with the passive.
It is very important that you can tell whether a verb is deponent
or not if you are to translate it correctly. These deponents will
be presented with the passive ending in the vocabulary, as in
γίνομαι. The regular verbs will be presented with the active ending as in λύω.

2. In the active the future tense is very simple. One needs
only add σ before the regular present active ending.

	Singular			Plural	
1	λύσω	I shall loose	λύσομεν	We shall loose
2	λύσεις	You will loose	λύσετε	You will loose
3	λύσει	He will loose	λύσουσι(ν)	They will loose

In recognizing the future the student should remember that
ψ (ps) and ξ (ks) are double consonants whose final consonant is
a σ. When π, β or φ of the verb root combines with the σ in the
future, the result is a ψ. Example: πέμπω, I send; πέμψω, I shall
send. When κ, γ, χ combine with σ in the future, the result is a
ξ. Example: ἄγω, I lead; ἄξω, I shall lead. The consonants τ, δ,
ζ, θ drop before the σ. Example: πείθω, I persuade; πείσω, I
shall persuade. The future of διδάσκω is διδάξω.

3. In the future passive, θησ is added before the present
passive endings. Since θη is always the sign of the passive and
the σ that of the future, the student should not have any trouble
recognizing this form.

1	λυθήσομαι I will be loosed	λυθησόμεθα We shall be loosed
2	λυθήσῃ You will be loosed	λυθήσεσθε You will be loosed
3	λυθήσεται He will be loosed	λυθήσονται They will be loosed

4. Compound verbs are those that have a combination of a preposition or prepositions with the main verb, such as εἰσέρχομαι, I go in, enter. When a prepositional phrase follows a compound verb, usually the preposition will be repeated. Example: εἰσέρχομαι εἰς τὸν οἶκον , I go into the house.

5. Vocabulary

ἔρχομαι I come, go	προσέρχομαι I come to, go to
ἀπέρχομαι I go away, depart	προσεύχομαι I pray
εἰσέρχομαι I go in, come in	βαπτίζω I baptize
ἐξέρχομαι I go out	διδάσκω I teach
ἀποκρίνομαι I answer	ζωή, ἡ life
γίνομαι I become, come into existence, happen	διά through (with genitive)
πορεύομαι I go	

Exercises

A. Recognition

1. ἔρχῃ
2. βαπτίσομεν
3. διδαχθήσομαι
4. βαπτισθησόμεθα
5. πορεύεσθε
6. διδάξετε
7. ἀποκρίνονται

8. πορεύομαι
9. εἰσέρχεσθε
10. ἀκουσθήσονται
11. ἀποκρίνεται
12. προσευχόμεθα
13. ἀκούσω
14. πιστεύσουσιν

B. Translate into English

1. πορεύομαι πρὸς τὸν προφήτην καὶ ἀκούσω τῶν λόγων αὐτοῦ(his).
2. πιστεύουσιν ὅτι γίνεται ὁ κόσμος διὰ τοῦ λόγου τοῦ θεοῦ.
3. προσευχόμεθα τῷ δικαίῳ θεῷ καὶ ἀποκρίνεται.
4. εἰσέρχεσθε εἰς τὸν οἶκον.
5. οἱ λόγοι τοῦ κυρίου ἀκουσθήσονται ἐν τῷ κόσμῳ.
6. ἀλλὰ οὐκ ἀκουσθήσεται ὁ λόγος τοῦ ἀνθρώπου.
7. βαπτίσουσιν οἱ μαθηταὶ τὰ τέκνα ὅτι ἐξέρχονται ἐκ τοῦ πονηροῦ κόσμου.
8. ἡ ζωὴ γίνεται ἐκ τοῦ θεοῦ τοῦ ἁγίου.
9. διδάξουσιν οἱ ἀγαθοὶ προφῆται τοῖς τέκνοις τὴν ὁδὸν τῆς ζωῆς.
10. διὰ τοῦ κυρίου ὁ νόμος λαμβάνεται.

C. Translate into Greek

1. We shall believe in the Lord
2. You (sing.) are coming into the house.

LESSON 10

CONTRACT VERBS

1. Besides the regular verbs that end in ω and the deponents which we have just studied, there are the contract verbs which end in αω, εω, or οω, the first two types being much more common. In the vocabulary and dictionary these will be presented in the uncontracted form such as ἀγαπάω or ποιέω.

2. Rules of contraction

    a. Two related vowels form the common long vowel. Thus ο and ω make ω; ε and η make η.

    b. The ο vowels, ο and ω, prevail over the other vowels. Thus ω and α, ε, or ο make ω; ο and α make ω.

    c. When α comes together with ε or η, whichever comes first overcomes the other. Thus α and ε=α and α and η=α, but ε and α=η.

    d. The most common exceptions to the above are ε and ε= ει, ε and ο=ου, and ε and ει=ει, ο and ο=ου, ο and ει and ο and η=οι.

    e. When a vowel precedes a diphthong that begins with a different type of vowel, it contracts with the first vowel. The second vowel disappears unless it is an iota in which case it becomes a subscript.

3. Accents on contractions

    If the accent on the uncontracted form occurs on the first of the two contracted syllables, it becomes a circumflex; e.g., ἀγαπάω becomes ἀγαπῶ. If the accent of the original form fell on the second of the two contracted syllables, it remains acute; e.g., λαλεέτω becomes λαλείτω. The regular verb rule holds when the accent does not fall on the contracted form.

4. You have already learned the regular verb endings of the present active indicative. The stem of the contract verbs ends in either α, ε, or ο. When these join with the ending, a contraction takes place. We present the forms of α and ε stem verbs, ἀγαπάω, I love, and ποιέω, I do or make.

1	ἀγαπά/ω	ἀγαπῶ	ποιέ/ω	ποιῶ
S 2	ἀγαπά/εις	ἀγαπᾷς	ποιέ/εις	ποιεῖς
3	ἀγαπά/ει	ἀγαπᾷ	ποιέ/ει	ποιεῖ

27

	1	ἀγαπά/ομεν	ἀγαπῶμεν	ποιέ/ομεν	ποιοῦμεν
P	2	ἀγαπά/ετε	ἀγαπᾶτε	ποιέ/ετε	ποιεῖτε
	3	ἀγαπά/ουσι(ν)	ἀγαπῶσι(ν)	ποιέ/ουσι(ν)	ποιοῦσι(ν)

Since recognition is the important thing, the student should concentrate on those parts of the endings which do not change. These are ω, ς, --, μεν, τε, σι(ν). Second, the student should observe that in the contraction, the αω verbs will generally favor the α before these endings, the εω verbs the ε, and the οω verbs the ο.

Naturally no contraction takes place if the ending begins with a consonant such as in the future. In such cases the contract vowels α and ε lengthens to η before the σ. Thus ἀγαπάω becomes ἀγαπήσω and ποιέω, ποιήσω. The student should have no trouble recognizing any of the future forms.

5. Vocabulary

ἀγαπάω I love
γεννάω I beget
ζητέω I seek
καλέω I call
λαλέω I speak
παρακαλέω I beseech, exhort, console
περιπατέω I walk

ποιέω I do
ἀγάπη, ἡ love
ἀλήθεια, ἡ truth
ἐκκλησία, ἡ church
λαός, ὁ people
φωνή, ἡ voice, sound

καλέω and παρακαλέω contrary to the above rule regarding verbs retain their ε before consonantal endings, e.g., καλέσω.

Exercises

A. Contraction and Recognition

1. ο+ο=
2. ε+ε=
3. ο+α=
4. ο+ε=
5. α+ε=
6. α+ω=
7. ε+ει=
8. ε+ω=
9. α+ει=
10. ε+α=

11. ε+ο=
12. ε+ου=
13. ἀγαπᾶτε
14. ἀγαπῶσι
15. ζητοῦμεν
16. γεννᾷ
17. ποιοῦσιν
18. ἀγαπῶμεν
19. λαλῶ
20. ἀγαπᾷς

B. Translate into English

1. ζητοῦμεν τὴν ἀγάπην καὶ τὴν ἀλήθειαν.
2. ἀγαπᾷ ὁ λαὸς τὴν ἐκκλησίαν.

28

3. λαλεῖτε τὴν ἀλήθειαν τῷ λαῷ.
4. ἀγαπᾶτε τὸν κόσμον καὶ οὐ περιπατεῖτε κατὰ τὴν ἀλήθειαν.
5. καλοῦσιν τὸν λαὸν ἐν μεγάλη (great) φωνῇ.
6. γεννήσει ὁ θεὸς τέκνα ἀγάπης.
7. παρακαλέσομεν τὴν ἐκκλησίαν ἐν λόγοις ἀληθείας.
8. ποιήσεις τὸν κόσμον διὰ τοῦ υἱοῦ.
9. λαλεῖ ὁ δοῦλος τῷ κυρίῳ τὴν ἀλήθειαν.

LESSON 11

PERSONAL PRONOUNS

1. You have already learned the personal pronouns ἐγώ (I) and σύ (you, s.). The rest of the first person forms follow:

	Singular			Plural	
Nominative	ἐγώ	I		ἡμεῖς	we
Genitive	μου	of me, my		ἡμῶν	of us, our
Dative	μοι	to or for me		ἡμῖν	to or for us
Accusative	με	me		ἡμᾶς	us

The forms ἐμοῦ, ἐμοί, ἐμέ are emphatic forms of the genitive, dative, and accusative singular but do not occur as frequently as the forms above. They are easily recognizable once the above forms have been learned. The plural forms appear frequently and should be mastered.

2. The second person of the personal pronoun.

	Singular		Plural	
Nominative	σύ	you	ὑμεῖς	you
Genitive	σου	of you, your	ὑμῶν	of you, your
Dative	σοι	to or for you	ὑμῖν	to or for you
Accusative	σε	you	ὑμᾶς	you

The forms σοῦ, σοί, σέ are emphatic forms of the genitive, dative, and accusative singular. The emphatic forms in the first and second person are generally used with prepositions and where emphasis is desired.

Notice that except for the nominative singular forms which you have already learned, the pattern of endings are identical between the above two pronouns. One way to distinguish between the plurals is to remember that when there is a υ it means you. The η must then refer to the first person plural, we.

3. The third person pronoun unlike the first two persons has gender. Therefore, there are three forms for the singular and three forms for the plural. However, the endings are not new. The masculine and neuter follow the second declension (ο) nouns and the feminine the first declension (η) nouns.

30

	Singular			Plural		
	M	N	F	M	N	F
Nom	αὐτός	αὐτό	αὐτή	αὐτοί	αὐτά	αὐταί
Gen	αὐτοῦ	αὐτοῦ	αὐτῆς	αὐτῶν	αὐτῶν	αὐτῶν
Dat	αὐτῷ	αὐτῷ	αὐτῇ	αὐτοῖς	αὐτοῖς	αὐταῖς
Acc	αὐτόν	αὐτό	αὐτήν	αὐτούς	αὐτά	αὐτάς

The student should be aware that the translation of these third person personal pronouns do not necessarily correspond with their gender. This is due to the fact that in Greek masculine and feminine gender as well as neuter are ascribed to objects and neuter gender to persons. The word for "world" is masculine. If the pronoun αὐτοῦ refers to "world," the phrase ἡ δόξα αὐτοῦ should not be translated "his glory" but "its glory." The word for "child" is neuter. If the pronoun αὐτοῦ refers to "child," the phrase ὁ πατὴρ αὐτοῦ should not be translated "its father" but "his father" or "her father." The translation should always be made according to English usage.

4. The nominative forms of these pronouns are ordinarily used as personal pronouns for emphasis. Usually they are not found since the verb ending indicates what person is involved.

5. The final vowel of prepositions is frequently dropped before words that begin with a vowel or a diphthong. This is called an elision and is indicated by an apostrophe. Thus μετὰ ἀνθρώπου becomes μετ' ἀνθρώπου. If the word following the preposition which elides has a rough breathing and the preposition now ends in a final τ or π, these consonants change to a θ and φ respectively. Thus μετὰ ἡμῶν becomes μεθ' ἡμῶν and ὑπὸ ἡμῶν becomes ὑφ' ἡμῶν.

6. Vocabulary

δύο two
ἐγείρω I raise up
ἕως until
ἤ or, than
καθώς as, even as
μετά with (with gen.); after (with acc.)
νῦν now

οὕτως thus, so
πάλιν again
περί concerning, about (with gen.); around (with acc.)
τότε then
ὑπέρ in behalf of (with gen.); above (with acc.)

Exercises

A. Recognition

1. ἡμεῖς
2. σοι
3. αὐτῷ
4. μου

5. σου
6. αὐτό
7. μοι
8. ἡμῖν

9. ὑμῶν
10. ἡμᾶς
11. σοι
12. αὐτούς

13. αὐταῖς
14. αὐτῇ
15. αὐτάς
16. αὐτή

31

B. Translate into English

1. ἐγὼ λέγω ὑμῖν· πορεύεσθε μετ' ἐμοῦ καθὼς αὐτὸς πορεύεται.
2. τότε ἀκούσει τὰ τέκνα τὴν φωνὴν τοῦ κυρίου αὐτῶν καὶ αὐτὸς ἄξει αὐτὰ εἰς τὴν βασιλείαν αὐτοῦ.
3. λαλήσουσιν περὶ τῆς ἀληθείας σοι ἢ ἡμῖν.
4. οἱ δύο εἰσέρχονται πάλιν εἰς τὸν οἶκον ἡμῶν.
5. οὕτως νῦν ἐγείρει τοὺς νεκρούς.
6. λαλεῖ οὖν ὑπὲρ ὑμῶν.
7. ἕως ὁ ἀδελφός σου ἔρχεται, λαλήσεις τὴν ἀλήθειαν.
8. πιστεύσετε ἕως τότε καθὼς πιστεύσω.
9. ἀγαπᾷ τὸν ἀδελφὸν αὐτῆς.
10. ζητοῦμεν δύο ἀνθρώπους.

LESSON 12

REVIEW 2

1. Review the vocabulary in Lessons 7-11. Place the words
on cards and then see how many you know. Then concentrate on those
you do not know. Include the words from Lessons 2-5 and do the
same for these.

2. Study and compare the first declension nouns on page 19.

a. What are the differences in the feminine singular nouns?
What is the rule back of these changes?
b. What are the differences between the masculine and
feminine singular nouns of the first declension?
c. What differences do you find in the plural endings of
all these nouns?

3. Study the present passive indicative endings and their
translation in Lesson 7. Be able to recognize these endings and
to indicate what person and voice each ending represents. What
person and voice do these endings indicate? ὁμεθα, ω, εις, εσθε,
ουσι, ομαι, εται, ει, ομεν, ονται, η, ετε. Be sure that you can do
this without going over all the forms. Translate the following:
λυόμεθα, ἀκούεται, πιστεύεσθε, λύῃ, λαμβάνεσθε, ἄγονται.

4. Study the adjectives and their declension in Lesson 8.
Notice how the masculine and neuter follow the second declension
and the feminine follows the first declension noun endings.

5. Study the use of the adjective in Lesson 8 and then
translate the following: ὁ ἀγαθὸς ἄνθρωπος, ὁ ἄνθρωπος ὁ ἀγαθός,
ἀγαθὸς ὁ ἄνθρωπος, οἱ ἀγαθοὶ πιστεύουσι, ὁ ἄνθρωπος ἀγαθός.

6. Study the future active and passive indicative of λύω on
page 25. Compare them with the corresponding present forms.

a. What is the difference between the present active and
future active indicative forms?
b. What is the difference between the present passive and
the future passive indicative forms?
c. Indicate what tense, person, and voice the following
are: θήσομαι, σω, θησόμεθα, θήσονται, σεις, σομεν, θήσῃ,
σετε, θήσεσθε, σουσι, θήσεται.

7. Study the translation of these future forms in Lesson 9

33

and then translate the following: λύσουσι, πιστεύσω, πιστεύσετε, λυθήσῃ, λύσετε, πιστεύσεις, λυθήσονται, ἀκουσθήσεσθε, πιστεύσομεν, ἀκουσθησόμεθα, λυθήσομαι, πιστεύσει.

8. What is a deponent verb? Study the present deponent endings in Lesson 9. Are they different from the passive endings of the regular verb? Translate the following: γίνομαι, ἐρχόμεθα, ἀποκρίνῃ, πορεύεται, εἰσέρχονται, προσεύχεσθε.

9. Study the contract verbs and the contractions that take place (Lesson 10). What happens when α contracts with ει? with ε? with ω, ο, or ου? What happens when ε contracts with ε or ει? with ω? with ο or ου? What happens in the future of contract verbs? Combine the following: ἀγαπά/ει, ποιέ/εις, ποιέ/ομεν, ἀγαπά/ομεν, ποιέ/ω, ἀγαπά/σω, ποιέ/σεις.

10. Review the personal pronouns in Lesson 11. Be able to recognize any of these forms by itself. Notice that the third person has the same endings as the second and first declension nouns and that the singular and plural endings of the first and second person are virtually identical, the only difference being in the nominative singular. Identify and translate the following: αὐτῶν, ἡμεῖς, ἐμοῦ, σου, ἐμοί, ὑμῖν, ἡμᾶς, σύ, αὐτῷ, αὐταῖς, ὑμεῖς, ἡμῶν, σε.

LESSON 13

READING 2

A.   Ἰωάννης[1] ἀποστέλλεται ὑπὸ θεοῦ. ἔρχεται καὶ λαλεῖ τοῖς
λαοῖς περὶ τοῦ υἱοῦ τοῦ θεοῦ. ὁ υἱὸς ἐστίν ἡ ζωὴ τῶν ἀνθρώπων.
ἀγαπῶσιν δὲ οἱ ἄνθρωποι ἁμαρτίαν μᾶλλον[2] ἢ ζωήν. οὐ λαμβάνουσι
τὴν ζωὴν καὶ τὰ τέκνα τοῦ θεοῦ οὐ γίνονται.

     βλέπουσιν τὴν δόξαν αὐτοῦ, πλήρης[3]ἀληθείας καὶ ἀγάπης, ἀλλὰ
οὐ λαμβάνουσιν αὐτόν. πονηραὶ αἱ καρδίαι αὐτῶν καὶ οὐ ζητοῦσι
τὴν ἀγαθὴν ὁδόν.

     ὁ Ἰωάννης λαλεῖ τῷ λαῷ αὐτοῦ καὶ ἐρωτῶσιν[4]αὐτόν. σὺ τίς εἶ;
καὶ ἀποκρίνεται· ἐγὼ οὐκ εἰμί ὁ χριστός. καὶ πάλιν ἐρωτῶσιν αὐτόν·
τί οὖν; ὁ προφήτης εἶ σύ; καὶ λέγει· οὔ. ἐγὼ φωνὴ ἐν τῇ ἐρήμῳ,[5]
δοῦλος θεοῦ. διδάσκω,καλῶ, παρακαλῶ, καὶ βαπτίζω ἕως ὁ Ἰησοῦς
ἔρχεται. τότε διδάξει καὶ βαπτίσει καὶ ποιήσει ὑμᾶς τέκνα θεοῦ.
λαλήσει τὴν ἀλήθειαν καὶ περιπατήσει ὡς[6] δίκαιος καὶ ἀγαθὸς ἄνθρωπος. κληθήσεται[7] ὁ ἄνθρωπος τῆς ἀγάπης. ποιήσει πονηροὺς ἀνθρώπους ἁγίους. ἐγερεῖ[8] τοὺς νεκροὺς καὶ βαλεῖ[9] ἁμαρτίαν ἀπ' ἀνθρώπων. βασιλείαν καὶ ἐκκλησίαν ποιήσει. νῦν δὲ διδάσκεσθε καὶ
βαπτίζεσθε ὑπ' ἐμοῦ. τότε διδαχθήσεσθε καὶ βαπτισθήσεσθε ὑπ' αὐτοῦ.
γενήσεσθε[10] οἱ μαθηταὶ αὐτοῦ καὶ περιπατήσετε μετ' αὐτοῦ ἐν τῇ
ἀληθείᾳ αὐτοῦ. διδάξει περὶ τῆς ὁδοῦ τῆς ἀγάπης καθὼς ὁ πατὴρ[11]
αὐτοῦ διδάσκει αὐτόν.

[1]John [2]more, rather [3]full [4]they ask [5]wilderness [6]as [7]from
καλέω [8]he will raise [9]he will cast [10]you will become [11]father

B.   ἐγὼ εἰμι ἡ ἀλήθεια καὶ ὁ λαός μου ἀκούει τὴν φωνήν μου.
ζητοῦνται ὑπὸ τοῦ θεοῦ διὰ τῆς ἀγάπης. καλοῦνται καὶ παρακαλοῦνται
ὑπὸ τῶν προφητῶν αὐτοῦ. προσεύξονται τῷ ἁγίῳ θεῷ καὶ ἀκούσει αὐτῶν.
αἱ ἁμαρτίαι αὐτῶν ἐκβάλλονται ἐκ τῶν καρδίων. οἱ νεκροὶ ἐν τῇ
ἁμαρτίᾳ ἕξουσιν[1] ζωὴν ἐν τῷ κυρίῳ. ὁ νόμος γράφεται ἐν ταῖς καρδίαις αὐτῶν καὶ γίνονται οἱ υἱοὶ τοῦ θεοῦ. εἰσέρχονται εἰς τὴν
ἐκκλησίαν μετὰ τῶν ἀδελφῶν καὶ ἀκούσουσιν τοὺς λόγους τῆς ἀληθείας
καὶ τῆς ἀγάπης. περιπατήσουσιν ἐν τῇ ὁδῷ τῆς ζωῆς.

[1]shall have

35

LESSON 14

THIRD DECLENSION NOUNS. THE USE OF αὐτός

1. You have learned the first and second declension nouns. The last group is the third declension nouns. There are different types of third declension nouns. It may appear difficult because of the variety of forms but if the student concentrates on recognition rather than on memorization he will not find these too difficult. What is important also is to learn the genitive singular with the nominative singular form since the stem is in the genitive. Thus with ὄνομα the genitive ὀνόματος has the stem which is ὀνοματ.

The most frequently occurring forms are the neuter nouns whose stem ends in τ or δ.

	Singular	Plural
Nominative	ὄνομα name	ὀνόματα
Genitive	ὀνόματος	ὀνομάτων
Dative	ὀνόματι	ὀνόμασι(ν)
Accusative	ὄνομα	ὀνόματα

Remember that in all neuter nouns the nominative and accusative singular forms are identical and the nominative and accusative plural forms are identical. Remember also that the genitive plural (ων) is the same in all declensions and all nouns. The pattern for these nouns is the following:

	Singular	Plural
Nominative	--	α
Genitive	ος	ων
Dative	ι	σι(ν)
Accusative	--	α

In the dative plural the τ of the original τσ has dropped out. This happens quite regularly when the stem ends in τ, δ, ντ, and ν.

2. The feminine nouns whose stem ends in τ or δ.

	Singular		Plural	
Nom	χάρις grace	νύξ night	χάριτες	νύκτες
Gen	χάριτος	νυκτός	χαρίτων	νυκτῶν
Dat	χάριτι	νυκτί	χάρισι(ν)	νυξί(ν)
Acc	χάριν	νύκτα	χάριτας	νύκτας

3. The masculine nouns whose stem ends in τ or δ.

	Singular		Plural
Nominative	ἄρχων	ruler	ἄρχοντες
Genitive	ἄρχοντος		ἀρχόντων
Dative	ἄρχοντι		ἄρχουσι(ν)
Accusative	ἄρχοντα		ἄρχοντας

The pattern which emerges from the feminine and masculine nouns of this type is the following:

	Singular	Plural
Nominative	--	ες
Genitive	ος	ων
Dative	ι	σι(ν)
Accusative	α	ας

This pattern should be mastered. This pattern is very much like that of the neuter noun except at the places where you expect the differences--in the accusative endings and the nominative plural. χάριν is irregular but we recognize the ν as an accusative singular from the first and second declension nouns.

4. The use of αὐτός. We have already indicated that αὐτός is the third person personal pronoun. However, it is used in two other ways:

   a. When used with a noun in the same number, gender, and case and preceded by the article, it is used intensively and is translated as "same." Thus ὁ αὐτὸς ἄνθρωπος or ὁ ἄνθρωπος ὁ αὐτός, "The same man."
   b. When not preceded by the article but in the same number, gender, and case, it should be translated as "self." Thus αὐτος ὁ ἄνθρωπος or ὁ ἄνθρωπος αὐτός, "The man himself." It is also used this way with personal pronouns. Thus αὐτοὶ ὑμεῖς is translated "you yourselves."

   5. Vocabulary

αἷμα, αἵματος, τό blood
ἄρχων, ἄρχοντος, ὁ ruler
ἐλπίς, ἐλπίδος, ἡ hope
θέλημα, θελήματος, τό will
νύξ, νυκτός, ἡ night
ὄνομα, ὀνόματος, τό name
πνεῦμα, πνεύματος, τό spirit,
  Spirit, wind

πούς, ποδός, ὁ foot
ῥῆμα, ῥήματος, τό word
στόμα, στόματος, τό mouth
σῶμα, σώματος, τό body
ὕδωρ, ὕδατος, τό water
φῶς, φωτός, τό light
ἀπόστολος, ὁ apostle
χάρις, χάριτος, ἡ grace

Exercises

   A. Recognition

   1. αἵματι   2. στόματος

37

3. θελημάτων
4. νυξί
5. ἄρχοντα
6. χάριν

7. ἄρχουσι
8. ὀνόματα
9. νύκτα
10. ἄρχοντες

1. τὸ ἅγιον πνεῦμα ἄγει τοὺς ἀνθρώπους εἰς τὸ φῶς.
2. τὸ ῥῆμα τοῦ ἄρχοντος ἐστίν καθὼς φῶς ἐν τῇ νυκτί.
3. ἐξέρχεται τὸ ὕδωρ τῆς ζωῆς ἐκ τοῦ στόματος αὐτοῦ.
4. ἐξέρχονται τὸ ὕδωρ καὶ τὸ αἷμα ἐκ τοῦ σώματος τοῦ κυρίου.
5. ὁ ἄνθρωπος ποιήσει τὸ θέλημα αὐτοῦ.
6. γράφομεν ὑμῖν περὶ τῆς αὐτῆς ἐλπίδος.
7. αὐτοὶ οἱ ἀπόστολοι πιστεύουσιν ἐν τῷ ὀνόματι αὐτοῦ.
8. οἱ πόδες αὐτοῦ περιπατοῦσιν ἐν τῷ φωτί.

LESSON 15

DEMONSTRATIVE PRONOUNS

1. There are two sets of demonstrative pronouns--οὗτος (this) and ἐκεῖνος (that). Like nouns and adjectives, they have number, gender, and case since they modify nouns.

	Singular			Plural		
	M	N	F	M	N	F
Nom	οὗτος	τοῦτο	αὕτη	οὗτοι	ταῦτα	αὗται
Gen	τούτου	τούτου	ταύτης	τούτων	τούτων	τούτων
Dat	τούτῳ	τούτῳ	ταύτῃ	τούτοις	τούτοις	ταύταις
Acc	τοῦτον	τοῦτο	ταύτην	τούτους	ταῦτα	ταύτας

Notice that the masculine and neuter forms follow the second declension and the feminine forms the first declension. Notice also that only the nominative forms of the masculine and feminine do not take the τ, that the ταυ precedes if α or η is in the ending (ταύτης, ταῦτα) rather than του. The neuter singular nominative and accusative end in ο rather than ον.

2. The forms of the demonstrative pronoun ἐκεῖνος, that.

	Singular			Plural		
	M	N	F	M	N	F
Nom	ἐκεῖνος	ἐκεῖνο	ἐκείνη	ἐκεῖνοι	ἐκεῖνα	ἐκεῖναι
Gen	ἐκείνου	ἐκείνου	ἐκείνης	ἐκείνων	ἐκείνων	ἐκείνων
Dat	ἐκείνῳ	ἐκείνῳ	ἐκείνη	ἐκείνοις	ἐκείνοις	ἐκείναις
Acc	ἐκεῖνον	ἐκεῖνο	ἐκείνην	ἐκείνους	ἐκεῖνα	ἐκείνας

These endings follow the same pattern with οὗτος above.

3. When these pronouns are used with the noun, the noun always takes the article: οὗτος ὁ ἄνθρωπος or ὁ ἄνθρωπος οὗτος, this man; ἐκείνη ἡ δόξα or ἡ δόξα ἐκείνη, that glory.

4. Like adjectives they can stand alone as substantives. The gender indicates who is being referred to. Ordinarily the masculine refers to man, the feminine to woman and the neuter to thing. οὗτος, this man; αὕτη, this woman; ἐκεῖνο, that thing; οὗτοι, these men.

5. Vocabulary

ἀποθνήσκω I die
ἐξουσία, ἡ authority

θάνατος, ὁ death
ἴδιος one's own

κρίνω I judge
μένω I remain
ὅλος,-η,-ον whole
ὁράω I see
ὅτε when
πῶς how

σύν with (with gen.)
σώζω I save
ψυχή, ἡ soul
ὥρα, ἡ hour
οὐδέ and not, not even (οὐδέ. . .
οὐδέ, neither . . . nor)

Exercises

A. Recognition and translation

1. τούτους
2. τούτοις
3. ἐκεῖνα
4. τοῦτο
5. ἐκείναις

6. ἐκείνας
7. ἐκεῖνο
8. οὗτος
9. ἐκείνη
10. τούτου

11. ταῦτα
12. ταύτης
13. τούτῳ
14. ἐκεῖναι
15. ἐκείνων

B. Translate into English

1. πῶς σώσει οὗτος ὁ ἄνθρωπος ἡμᾶς;
2. ἐκεῖναι μένουσιν ἐν ἰδίοις οἴκοις.
3. κρίνει τὸν ὅλον κόσμον.
4. ἔρχεται ὥρα καὶ νῦν ἐστιν ὅτε ταῦτα τὰ τέκνα ἀκούσει τὴν φωνὴν τοῦ θεοῦ.
5. οὐδὲ ἐξουσίαν ἔχετε οὐδὲ βασιλείαν.
6. οὗτοι ἀποθνῄσκουσιν ἀλλὰ ἐκεῖνοι οὐκ ἀποθνῄσκουσιν.
7. ἄγει τούτους εἰς θάνατον.
8. περιπατεῖ σὺν ἐμοὶ ἐν νυκτὶ καὶ ἐν ἡμέρᾳ.

LESSON 16

MORE THIRD DECLENSION NOUNS. CONTRACT VERBS IN οω

1. Third declension nouns with a ν ending: αἰών, ὁ, age.

	Singular	Plural
Nominative	αἰών	αἰῶνες
Genitive	αἰῶνος	αἰώνων
Dative	αἰῶνι	αἰῶσι(ν)
Accusative	αἰῶνα	αἰῶνας

This follows the regular pattern of third declension nouns learned earlier.

2. Third declension nouns with a ρ ending: πατήρ, ὁ, father; χείρ, ἡ, hand; σωτήρ, ὁ, savior.

	Singular			Plural		
Nom	πατήρ	χείρ	σωτήρ	πατέρες	χεῖρες	σωτῆρες
Gen	πατρός	χειρός	σωτῆρος	πατέρων	χειρῶν	σωτηρῶν
Dat	πατρί	χειρί	σωτῆρι	πατράσι(ν)	χέρσι(ν)	σωτῆρσι(ν)
Acc	πατέρα	χεῖρα	σωτῆρα	πατέρας	χεῖρας	σωτῆρας

While some changes take place in the stem of πατήρ such as πατρ and πατερ, the endings should present no difficulty since they are regular third declension endings.

3. Third declension nouns with a semi-vowel ending: πόλις, ἡ, city; βασιλεύς, ὁ, king.

	Singular		Plural	
Nom	πόλις	βασιλεύς	πόλεις	βασιλεῖς
Gen	πόλεως	βασιλέως	πόλεων	βασιλέων
Dat	πόλει	βασιλεῖ	πόλεσι(ν)	βασιλεῦσι(ν)
Acc	πόλιν	βασιλέα	πόλεις	βασιλεῖς

The basic differences here are the genitive singular which takes the ως instead of ος and the nominative and accusative plural which take εις.

4. The contract verbs in οω: πληρόω, I fill, fulfill.

	Singular		Plural	
1	πληρό/ω	=πληρῶ	πληρό/ομεν	=πληροῦμεν
2	πληρό/εις	=πληροῖς	πληρό/ετε	=πληροῦτε
3	πληρό/ει	=πληροῖ	πληρό/ουσι(ν)	=πληροῦσι(ν)

41

Notice that in οω verbs ου or οι precede the ending beginning
with a consonant which is already familiar to you. The only exception is the first person singular which always remains the same.

5. Vocabulary

αἰών, αἰῶνος, ὁ age
ἀνήρ, ἀνδρός, ὁ man, husband
βασιλεύς, βασιλέως, ὁ king
γυνή, γυναικός, ἡ woman, wife
δύναμις, δυνάμεως, ἡ power
μητήρ, μητρός, ἡ mother
παρά from (with gen.); beside,
in the presence of (with dat.);
alongside of (with acc.)

πατήρ, πατρός, ὁ father
πίστις, πίστεως, ἡ faith
πόλις, πόλεως, ἡ city
σάρξ, σαρκός, ἡ flesh
σωτήρ, σωτῆρος, ὁ Savior
πληρόω I fill, fulfill
χείρ, χειρός, ἡ hand

Exercises

A. Recognition. Give number and case.

1. ἀνδρί
2. πίστιν
3. αἰῶνες
4. χάριτι
5. βασιλεῖς

6. μητράσι
7. δυναμέων
8. σαρκάς
9. πόλεσι
10. ἄνδρα

B. Translate into English

1. οὗτος ἐστίν ὁ οἶκος τοῦ βασιλέως.
2. ἡ μήτηρ τῶν γυναικῶν εἰσέρχεται εἰς τὴν πόλιν.
3. ἐκεῖνοι οἱ ἄνδρες περιπατήσουσιν ἐν δύναμει.
4. γίνεται ὁ Ἰησοῦς ἄνθρωπος τῆς σαρκὸς καὶ τοῦ αἵματος.
5. αὕτη ἡ πόλις ἐστίν ἐν τῇ βασιλείᾳ τοῦ αἰῶνος τούτου.
6. ἔχει δύναμιν ἐν ταῖς χέρσιν αὐτοῦ.
7. λαμβάνουσιν χάριν καὶ ἀλήθειαν διὰ τοῦ Χριστοῦ.
8. ἀγαπᾷ τὸν πατέρα αὐτοῦ καὶ τὴν μητέρα αὐτοῦ.
9. ζητεῖτε σημεῖον παρ' αὐτῶν.

LESSON 17

RELATIVE PRONOUNS. FUTURE OF LIQUID VERBS

1. The relative pronouns are relatively simple to recognize.
They have the same endings as the article. The basic differences
are in the masculine nominative singular (which however looks like
the ending of the nominative ending of the noun) and the omission
of the τ. Remember also that it is accented and always takes the
rough breathing.

| | Singular | | | Plural | | |
	M	N	F	M	N	F
Nominative	ὅς	ὅ	ἥ	οἵ	ἅ	αἵ
Genitive	οὗ	οὗ	ἧς	ὧν	ὧν	ὧν
Dative	ᾧ	ᾧ	ᾗ	οἷς	οἷς	αἷς
Accusative	ὅν	ὅ	ἥν	οὕς	ἅ	ἅς

Relative pronouns when referring to people are translated
in the nominative as who, that; in the genitive, of whom; in the
dative, to or for whom; in the accusative, whom. The translation is
the same whether in the singular or the plural. When referring to
a thing, it should be translated in the nominative as that or which;
in the genitive, of which; in the dative, to or for which; in the
accusative, that or which. The translation is the same whether
it is in the plural or singular.

Relative pronouns agree with their antecedent in number and
gender. The case will be determined by use.

ὁ ἄνθρωπος ὅς διδάσκει ἡμᾶς ἔρχεται.
The man who teaches us comes.

ὁ ἄνθρωπος ὅν γινώσκομεν μένει μεθ' ἡμῶν.
The man whom we know remains with us.

Sometimes the antecedent is not expressed. In such cases
the corresponding pronoun must be added before the relative pronoun: ὅς, he who; ἥ, she who; ὅ, that which.

ὅ ἀκούσομεν διδάξομεν.
That which we shall hear we shall teach.

2. Liquid verbs are those whose stem ends in λ, μ, ν, ρ.
Liquid verbs do not take the σ to indicate the future. Instead
they become like the εω contract verbs in the present in contraction and accent. The stem sometimes is also shortened. Thus

43

βάλλω becomes βαλῶ. The future of κρίνω, I judge, is as follows:

	Singular	Plural
1	κρινῶ	κρινοῦμεν
2	κρινεῖς	κρινεῖτε
3	κρινεῖ	κρινοῦσι(ν)

Compare these with the present endings:

1	κρίνω	κρίνομεν
2	κρίνεις	κρίνετε
3	κρίνει	κρίνουσι(ν)

Notice that the accent in the future always is the ˜ instead of the ΄, and that the accent has shifted forward one syllable. Other frequently occurring future forms of the liquid verbs are:

ἀποστελῶ (ἀποστέλλω) I shall send   ἐγερῶ (ἐγείρω) I shall raise
ἀποκτενῶ (ἀποκτείνω) I shall kill   ἐρῶ (λέγω) I shall say, speak
ἀρῶ (αἴρω) I shall take away, take up   μενῶ (μένω) I shall remain
βαλῶ (βάλλω) I shall cast, throw   σπερῶ (σπείρω) I shall sow

3. Vocabulary

αἴρω I take up, take away   ἕτοιμος, ον, η ready, prepared
ἀποκτείνω I kill   θάλασσα, ἡ sea
ἄρτος, ὁ bread   οἰκία, ἡ house
ἀρχιερεύς, ἀρχιερέως, ὁ high   ὀφθαλμός, ὁ eye
  priest   σπείρω I sow
δικαιοσύνη, ἡ righteousness   τόπος, ὁ place
εἰρήνη, ἡ peace   ἐρῶ I shall say
ἐκεῖ there
ἕτερος, ον, α other, another,
  different

Exercises

A. Recognition

1. ὅς	7. ἧς	13. κρινῶ
2. ἅς	8. αἷς	14. κρίνεις
3. ᾗ	9. αἵ	15. κρινοῦμεν
4. ᾧ	10. οἷς	16. κρινεῖτε
5. ὅν	11. ἥ	17. κρίνεις
6. οὗ	12. ὧν	18. κρινεῖς

B. Translation

1. ὁ ἄρτος ὃν ἐσθίουσιν ἐν τῇ οἰκίᾳ αὐτῶν οὐ μενεῖ.
2. οὐκ ἐρῶ τῷ ἀρχιερεῖ περὶ τῆς δικαιοσύνης καὶ τῆς εἰρήνης.

44

3. σπεροῦσιν ἐν τούτῳ τῷ τόπῳ ἃ σπείρουσιν ἐν τῷ ἑτέρῳ τόπῳ.
4. ἀποκτενεῖ ὑμᾶς ἐν θαλάσσῃ.
5. ἡ εἰρήνη ἣν ἔχω μενεῖ μετ' ἐμοῦ.
6. ἐν ταῖς χέρσιν αὐτῶν ἀροῦσιν σέ.
7. ἔρχεσθε ὅτι ταῦτά ἐστιν ἕτοιμα.
8. αἴρει ἃ σπείρουσιν.

LESSON 18

THE IMPERFECT INDICATIVE

1. In Greek instead of only the simple past tense (aorist), there is also the continuous action in the past (imperfect). The sign of the past tense is the augment, i.e., the ε which precedes the stem of the verb. In compound verbs (those with a preposition before the stem) the augment always precedes the stem rather than the preposition. Thus ἐκβάλλω becomes ἐξέβαλλον in the imperfect (Notice that the κ becomes a ξ before the ε.) When the stem of a verb begins with a vowel, the augment cannot be the ε. Usually the vowel lengthens. Thus α becomes η, ε becomes η, ο becomes ω. The diphthongs ει and αι may become η and ευ and οι may become ηυ or ῳ respectively but may remain unchanged. We present the imperfect active indicative of λύω.

	Singular			Plural
1	ἔλυον	I was loosing	ἐλύομεν	We were loosing
2	ἔλυες	You were loosing	ἐλύετε	You were loosing
3	ἔλυε(ν)	He was loosing	ἔλυον	They were loosing

2. The imperfect passive indicative of λύω.

	Singular			Plural
1	ἐλυόμην	I was being loosed	ἐλυόμεθα	We were being loosed
2	ἐλύου	You were being loosed	ἐλύεσθε	You were being loosed
3	ἐλύετο	He was being loosed	ἐλύοντο	They were being loosed

Both the active and passive forms have some similarities to the present indicative forms you have learned, especially in the first and second person plural endings. The ς in the active second person singular and the dropping of the ς in the third person singular of the active are also similar. In the passive, the third person forms are also similar. In the present the third person has εται and ονται, here ετο and οντο.

The passive translation must have the past tense of the verb "to be" plus the word "being" (which makes it passive) and the past participle of the main verb.

3. Vocabulary

ἀκολουθέω I follow (takes dative)
ἀναβαίνω I go up
καταβαίνω I go down

ἕκαστος,ον,η each
ἐκβάλλω I cast out
ἐνώπιον before (with gen.)

ἔτι still, yet, even   πρῶτος, ον, η first
καιρός, ὁ time   φοβέομαι I fear, am afraid; not
ἐπί over, on (with genitive)   deponent, only pass. in NT; act.
    at, on the basis of (with dative)   = cause to fear
    on, to, upon, against (with accusative)

Exercises

A. Recognition

    1. ἐλάμβανεν   6. ἠγείρεσθε
    2. ἐπιστεύετε   7. ἀπεθνήσκομεν
    3. ἐγράφοντο   8. ἐσῴζου
    4. ἐπορεύετο   9. ἐκρινόμην
    5. ἀπέστελλες   10. ἔμενον

B. Translate into English

    1. ἀνεβαίνομεν εἰς τὴν πόλιν ἀλλὰ ἐξεβαλλόμεθα.
    2. ἐν ἐκείνῳ τῷ καιρῷ ἐπορεύετο πρὸς τὸν ἀπόστολον.
    3. ἔκαστος ἔχει ἔτι καιρόν.
    4. ἐπίστευον εἰς (in) τοὺς πρώτους προφήτας ἀλλὰ νῦν
       ἀκολουθοῦσιν τῷ κυρίῳ.
    5. φοβεῖσθε τοὺς ἀνθρώπους οὓς ἐξέβαλλον;
    6. περιπατεῖ ἐνώπιον αὐτοῦ ἐν δικαιοσύνῃ.
    7. ἔχει ἐξουσίαν ἐν οὐρανῷ καὶ ἐπὶ τῆς γῆς.
    8. ἐλαμβάνοντο οἱ ἀπόστολοι ἐν τῇ πόλει.

47

LESSON 19

REVIEW 3 (LESSONS 14-18)

1. Review the third declension nouns in Lesson 14 and 16, except the τέλος group, especially the basic endings of this declension. A few deviations from these endings take place in the πόλις group. Observe these. For recognition purposes these basic endings should suffice. Give number and case for the following: πατρός, αἰῶνες, ὀνόματι, ἐλπίδος, χάρισι, σωτῆρος, ὀνόματα, πόλεως, βασιλεῖς, χάριν, ἀρχόντων.

2. Review the uses of αὐτός in Lesson 14 and translate the following:
αὐτὸς ἐγὼ ἀκούω τὸν λόγον τοῦ κυρίου.
αὐτὸς ὁ ἄνθρωπος ἔρχεται.
ὁ αὐτὸς ἄνθρωπος οὐκ ἔρχεται.

3. Review the demonstrative pronouns in Lesson 15. Notice that the masculine and neuter are second declension while the feminine is first declension. Observe especially the neuter nominative and accusative singular endings. Remember that the article is always used with the demonstrative unless it is used substantively. Thus οὗτος ὁ ἄνθρωπος and οὗτος πιστεύει.

4. Review the contract verbs in οω in Lesson 16. What does ο + ει make? ο + ο? ο + ε? Give the contracted forms of the following: πληρό/ει, πληρό/ομεν, πληρό/ετε.

5. Review the relative pronouns in Lesson 17. Notice that basically they are the same as the articles except that the rough breathing takes the place of the τ. Identify and translate the following: οὗ, ᾗ, οὕς, οἷς, ἅς, ἅ, ὅς, ᾧ, οὕ, ἥν, αἷς, ὅν.

6. Review the future of liquid verbs in Lesson 17. What happens to liquid verbs in the future? How would you recognize them? Indicate what tense the following are and translate them: κρινῶ, κρίνω, κρινεῖς, κρινεῖ, κρίνει, κρίνομεν, κρίνετε, κρινοῦμεν.

7. Review the imperfect active and passive indicative of λύω in Lesson 18. Compare them with their corresponding present active and passive forms. Observe that the imperfect has the augment and the present stem and that the endings are very similar to the present in both the active and passive voices. Be sure you can identify the endings as active or passive, by person and number, and tense. ε--ομεν, ε--εσθε, ε--οντο, ε--ον, ε--ετε, ε--ε, ε--ετο,

ε--ες, ε--ου, ε--ομην.

Review the translation of the imperfect. Remember that the ing is always used. Translate the following:ἐλυόμην, ἐπίστευε, ἐλυόμεθα, ἐλύου, ἐλαμβάνετε, ἔλυον, ἐκρίνοντο, ἐλύετε, ἐλύετο.

8. Review the vocabulary.

A.   πάλιν ὁ 'Ιωάννης διδάσκει καὶ δύο ἐκ τῶν μαθητῶν αὐτοῦ, καὶ
βλέπουσι τὸν 'Ιησοῦν ὅς περιπατεῖ ἐν τῇ ὁδῷ. οἱ δύο ἀκολουθοῦσιν
αὐτῷ καὶ ἀκούουσιν αὐτόν. ὁ δὲ 'Ιησοῦς λέγει αὐτοῖς· τί ζητεῖτε;
εἶπον δὲ αὐτῷ· διδάσκαλε,[1] ποῦ[2] μένεις; λέγει αὐτοῖς· ἔρχεσθε.[3]
εἶδον ποῦ μένει, καὶ μετ' ἐκείνου ἔμειναν[4] τὴν ἡμέραν ἐκείνην.
ὥρα ἦν[5] ὡς δεκάτη.[6] ἦν 'Ανδρέας ὁ ἀδελφὸς Σίμωνος Πέτρου, εἷς[7]
ἐκ τῶν δύο ὅς ἤκουεν καὶ ἠκολούθει 'Ιωάννῃ. εὑρίσκει οὗτος πρῶτον
τὸν ἀδελφὸν τὸν ἴδιον Σίμωνα καὶ λέγει αὐτῷ· εὑρήκαμεν[8] τὸν
Μεσσίαν. καὶ Σίμων λέγει· πῶς γινώσκετε; ποῦ ἐστίν; ὁ 'Ανδρέας
λέγει· ὅτε ἐμείναμεν[9] μετ' αὐτοῦ ἐδίδασκεν τὴν ἀλήθειαν τῷ λαῷ ἐν
ἐξουσίᾳ καὶ τὰ ῥήματα αὐτοῦ ἐλέγετο ἐν ἀγάπῃ καὶ ἐν δικαιοσύνῃ.
καὶ ἐξέβαλλεν τὰ πνεύματα τὰ πονερὴ καὶ ἔσωζεν τὰς ψυχὰς τῶν
ἀνθρώπων. ἐστὶν τὸ πνεῦμα τοῦ θεοῦ μετ' αὐτοῦ. οὐ κρίνει, αἴρει
δὲ τὰς ἁμαρτίας ἀπὸ τῶν ἀνθρώπων. δίδωσιν[10] ἡμῖν τὸν ἄρτον καὶ τὸ
ὕδωρ τῆς ζωῆς, ἐλπίδα, καὶ εἰρήνην τῆς καρδίας. οὐ φοβούμεθα, οὐ
γὰρ ὀφόμεθα[11] τὸν θάνατον. ὁ ἄνθρωπος ὅς πιστεύει ἐν αὐτῷ στήσει[12]
ἐνώπιον αὐτοῦ ἐν δόξῃ. ἐκεῖ οὐκ ἀποθανοῦνται καὶ οὐκ ἀποκτενοῦσιν.
μενοῦσιν μετὰ θεοῦ εἰς τὸν αἰῶνα.[13]

[1]teacher (vocative) [2]where [3]come [4]they remained [5]was [6]tenth [7]one
[8]we have found [9]we remained [10]he gives [11]we shall see [12]he will
stand [13]forever

B.   ἐπορεύοντο δὲ αὐτῷ ὄχλοι καὶ λέγει πρὸς αὐτούς, εἴ τις[1]
ἔρχεται πρός με καὶ οὐ μισεῖ[2] τὸν πατέρα αὐτοῦ καὶ τὴν μητέρα καὶ
τὴν γυναῖκα καὶ τὰ τέκνα καὶ τοὺς ἀδελφοὺς καὶ τὰς ἀδελφάς, ἔτι
καὶ τὴν ψυχὴν αὐτοῦ, οὐ δύναται[3] εἶναι[4] μου μαθητής. καὶ ἐδίδασκεν αὐτοὺς περὶ τῆς βασιλέως αὐτοῦ. ἐζήτουν ἀκουλουθῆσαι[5] αὐτῷ ὅτι
ἠθέλησαν[6] ἔχειν[7] τὸ φῶς καὶ τὴν ἐλπίδα. καὶ νῦν κατὰ τὸ θέλημα
τοῦ θεοῦ καὶ τὸ πνεῦμα περιπατοῦσιν τῇ χάριτι διὰ πίστεως. ἀπο-
στελεῖ ὁ θεὸς αὐτοὺς τοῖς λαοῖς καὶ δώσει[8] αὐτοῖς ἐξουσίαν καὶ
ἐροῦσιν μετὰ δυνάμεως.

[1]anyone [2]hates [3]he is able [4]to be [5]to follow [6]they desired
[7]to have [8]he shall give

LESSON 21

SECOND AORIST. DECLENSION OF γένος. IMPERFECT OF εἰμί.

1. There are two types of simple past (aorist) endings.
These are called first and second aorists. The English verb <u>walk</u>
has the past tense <u>walked</u>, but the past tense of <u>buy</u> is <u>bought</u>.
As certain English verbs have one type of ending in the past tense
and others a different type, so it is the case also in Greek. Certain Greek verbs have the first aorist endings and other the second
aorist endings. We present first the second aorist verbs with the
use of the verb, λείπω, I leave.

	Singular			Plural	
1	ἔλιπον	I left	ἐλίπομεν		We left
2	ἔλιπες	You left	ἐλίπετε		You left
3	ἔλιπε(ν)	He left	ἔλιπον		They left

The first thing to observe is that it has an augment (the
imperfect and aorist indicative take the augment); second, it has
exactly the same endings as the imperfect; third, it has a different
stem (λιπ) from the present (λειπ). This last is to distinguish
it from the imperfect which would be:

1	ἔλειπον	I was leaving	ἐλείπομεν		We were leaving
2	ἔλειπες	You were leaving	ἐλείπετε		You were leaving
3	ἔλειπε(ν)	He was leaving	ἔλειπον		They were leaving

2. The third declension neuter nouns like γένος, τό, race
(ἔτος, τό, year; ἔθνος, τό, nation; plural, Gentiles or nations;
τέλος, τό, end) have the following endings:

	Singular	Plural
Nominative	γένος	γένη
Genitive	γένους	γενῶν
Dative	γένει	γένεσι(ν)
Accusative	γένος	γένη

Remember that neuter nouns have identical forms in the nominative and accusative singular and in the nominative and accusative
plural. The dative forms follow the regular third declension ending.
What is different is the genitive singular and the nominative and
accusative plural endings. Concentrate on these.

3. The imperfect indicative of εἰμί.

	Singular		Plural	
1	ἤμην	I was	ἦμεν, ἤμεθα	We were
2	ἦς, ἦσθα	You were	ἦτε	You were
3	ἦν	He was	ἦσαν	They were

εἰμί does not have voice. It does not have an aorist tense
either. The imperfect is the only past tense for this verb. The
endings are not difficult since they are similar to endings you
have seen before. The only one that is different is ἤμην. Concentrate on this. The alternative forms of the second person singular and first person plural are not too common.

4. Vocabulary

ἀπέθανον (ἀποθνήσκω) I died
ἔβαλον (βάλλω) I cast, threw
εἶδον (βλέπω, ὁράω) I saw
εἶπον (λέγω) I said
ἔλαβον (λαμβάνω) I took, received
ἔπεσον (πίπτω) I fell
ἔσχον (ἔχω) I had

εὗρον (εὑρίσκω) I found
ἔφαγον (ἐσθίω) I ate
ἦλθον (ἔρχομαι) I came
ἔφη (φημί) only 3rd pers. used
  in NT--He said
ἤγαγον (ἄγω) I led
ἥμαρτον (ἀμαρτάνω) I sinned
κατέβην (καταβαίνω) I went down

γένος, γένους, τό race
ἔθνος, ἔθνους, τό nation; pl.
  Gentiles

τέλος, τέλους, τό end
λείπω I leave
ἔτος, ἔτους, τό year

κατέβην is a bit irregular in that the η of the root is
maintained throughout without the thematic vowel and the third
person plural form is κατέβησαν like the first aorist instead of
the second aorist.

Exercises

A. Recognition

1. ἐλάβομεν
2. ἦλθον
3. κατέβη
4. ἀπεθάνετε
5. ἔβαλες

6. τέλους
7. γένη
8. γένει
9. ἦς
10. ἤμην

B. Translate into English

1. ἐλάμβανον τὴν ἀλήθειαν ἀπὸ τῶν ἐθνῶν.
2. ἐλάβομεν τὰ ἔθνη εἰς τὴν ἐκκλησίαν.
3. ἔσχεν ἡ γυνὴ ἄνδρα ἔτη δύο.
4. ἦλθον ἐκ τούτου τοῦ γένους πρὸς τοὺς ἀποστόλους.
5. τὸ γὰρ τέλος ἐκείνων ζωή.

6. ἔπεσες ὅτι οὐκ εἶδες.
7. κατέβημεν καὶ εὕρομεν τὴν ἀλήθειαν.
8. ἐξεβάλετε ἃ οὐκ ἐφάγετε.
9. εἴδετε τὸν ἄνθρωπον ὃς ἀπέθανεν.
10. ἔφη ὅτι ἦλθον καὶ ἤγαγον αὐτὸν εἰς τὴν ὁδὸν τῆς εἰρήνης.

LESSON 22

FIRST AORIST ACTIVE AND PASSIVE VERBS

1. Most verbs are first aorist. The first aorist active indicative of λύω follows:

	Singular			Plural	
1	ἔλυσα	I loosed	ἐλύσαμεν		We loosed
2	ἔλυσας	You loosed	ἐλύσατε		You loosed
3	ἔλυσε(ν)	He loosed	ἔλυσαν		They loosed

Notice (1) the augment and (2) the σ usually with an α in the ending. Notice also the familiar endings indicating the person and number: ς (2d sing.), ε (3d sing.), μεν (1st plur.), τε (2d plur.).

2. Contract verbs in the first aorist, as in the future, lengthen the ε and ο to η and ω respectively and the α is changed to η before the σ of the aorist endings. Thus ποιέω becomes ἐποίησα; ἀγαπάω becomes ἠγάπησα; πληρόω becomes ἐπλήρωσα. καλέω, however, keeps the ε.

3. The first aorist passive indicative of λύω is very simple to recognize since it has the augment and θη in the endings.

	Singular			Plural	
1	ἐλύθην	I was loosed	ἐλύθημεν		We were loosed
2	ἐλύθης	You were loosed	ἐλύθητε		You were loosed
3	ἐλύθη	He was loosed	ἐλύθησαν		They were loosed

The endings of the aorist passive are very much like the imperfect except for the third person plural (ν, ς, -, μεν, τε, σαν). Before the θ certain final consonants will change to φ (π, β), χ (κ, γ) or σ (τ, δ, θ) but these should not confuse you in recognizing the basic stem and the ending. E.g., πέμπω becomes ἐπέμφθην and ἄγω, ἤχθην.

4. Vocabulary

αἰτέω I ask	κεφαλή, ἡ head
ἀνοίγω I open	μᾶλλον rather, more
ἑπτά seven	μαρτυρέω I witness, testify
εὐαγγέλιον, τό gospel	ὅπου where
κάθημαι I sit	πέμπω I send

Exercises

A. Recognition

1. ἐπίστευσαν
2. ἐβαπτίσαμεν
3. περιεπάτησας
4. ἐποιήσατε
5. ἠκούσθημεν

6. ἐβαπτίσθη
7. ἐγίνωσκε
8. ἐγεννήθησαν
9. ἐδίδαξαν
10. ἐδιδάχθην

B. Translate into English

1. ἐβαπτίσατε τὰ τέκνα ἃ ἐπίστευσεν τῷ εὐαγγελίῳ.
2. οἱ ἑπτὰ δοῦλοι ἐβαπτίσθησαν ὑπὸ τοῦ ἀποστόλου.
3. ἐμαρτύρησεν κατὰ τὴν ἀλήθειαν τοῦ εὐαγγελίου.
4. ἔπεμψαν αὐτὸν ὅπου ὁ ἀρχιερεὺς ἔπεσεν.
5. οὐκ ᾐτήσατε ἐν τῷ ὀνόματι αὐτοῦ.
6. κάθημαι ἐν τῷ ἱερῷ.
7. ἤνοιξαν τοὺς ὀφθαλμοὺς αὐτῶν καὶ εἶδον τὸν βασιλέα.
8. ἡ κεφαλὴ τοῦ ἀνδρός ἐστιν ὁ Χριστὸς μᾶλλον ἢ τῆς γυναικος αὐτοῦ.
9. ἐδιδάχθη τοὺς λόγους τῆς ζωῆς.
10. ἐλύθησαν οἱ οἶκοι.

PERFECT ACTIVE AND PASSIVE INDICATIVE. FUTURE OF εἰμί

1. The perfect tense refers to action completed in the past with the results of that action continuing into the present. The first perfect active indicative of λύω follows:

	Singular		Plural	
1	λέλυκα	I have loosed	λελύκαμεν	We have loosed
2	λέλυκας	You have loosed	λελύκατε	You have loosed
3	λέλυκε(ν)	He has loosed	λέλυκαν, -κασι(ν)	
				They have loosed

The sign of the perfect is the reduplication of the beginning consonant with ε (λε) and the κ in the ending. The endings otherwise are the same as the first aorist active indicative except that the perfect drops the thematic vowel, i.e., the ο or ε which usually comes after the stem. The third person pural has two forms. The contract verbs as in the aorist change their vowels to η (α/ε) or ω (ο).

2. The first perfect passive indicative of λύω follows:

	Singular		Plural	
1	λέλυμαι	I have been loosed	λελύμεθα	We have been loosed
2	λέλυσαι	You have been loosed	λέλυσθε	You have been loosed
3	λέλυται	He has been loosed	λέλυνται	They have been loosed

Observe the reduplication with the endings of the present passive indicative except for the second person singular (this is the regular ending, the other is irregular). Notice also the absence of the thematic vowel.

Verbs beginning with a vowel cannot reduplicate; instead if the beginning vowels are α and ε they become η and the ο, ω.

3. The future indicative of εἰμί.

	Singular		Plural	
1	ἔσομαι	I shall be	ἐσόμεθα	We shall be
2	ἔσῃ	You shall be	ἔσεσθε	You shall be
3	ἔσται	He shall be	ἔσονται	They shall be

Notice that the σ signifies the future. The endings follow the present passive indicative, except that the third person singular drops the thematic vowel ε before the ται. However, this should cause no difficulty as far as recognition is concerned.

4. Vocabulary

ἀγαπητός, ον, η beloved
ἀλλήλων of one another (gen. plural); ἀλλήλοις (dat. plural); ἀλλήλους (acc. plural)
ἀπολύω I release
γραμματεύς, εως, ὁ scribe
δαιμόνιον, τό demon
αἰώνιος, ον, ος eternal

δοκέω I think, seem
ἐντολή, ἡ commandment
πίνω I drink
πῦρ, πυρός, τό fire
τηρέω I keep
ὑπάγω I depart
χαίρω I rejoice
πρόσωπον, τό face

Exercises

A. Recognition

1. πεπιστεύκαμεν
2. λελαλήκασιν
3. περιπεπάτηκας
4. τετήρημαι
5. ἔσονται

6. πεπίστευται
7. πεποίησθε
8. ἔσῃ
9. ἐσόμεθα
10. λελαλήκατε

B. Translate into English

1. τετηρήκαμεν τὰς ἐντολὰς δαιμονίων.
2. οἱ γραμματεῖς ἀπολέλυκαν τὰ τέκνα ταῖς μήτρασιν αὐτῶν.
3. χαίρει ὅτι λελάληκεν τοῖς ἀγαπητοῖς ἀδελφοῖς.
4. λελαλήκασιν πρὸς ἀλλήλους.
5. ὑπάγετε πρὸς τὸν αἰώνιον πατέρα.
6. ἔσῃ προφήτης καὶ βαπτίσεις ἐν πνεύματι ἁγίῳ καὶ πυρί.
7. δοκοῦσιν ὅτι λέλυνται ἀπὸ τῶν ἁμαρτίων.
8. πιστεύσετε εἰς τὸν κύριον καὶ πινεῖτε τὸ ὕδωρ τῆς ζωῆς.

LESSON 24

IRREGULAR PERFECTS.   SECOND AORIST PASSIVES.   LIQUID AORISTS

1. There are certain irregular but very common perfect verbs that should be learned. They all have the κ but either the stem or the augment is irregular. They should not be difficult to recognize.

> ἀκήκοα (ἀκούω) I have heard
> ἀναβέβηκα (ἀναβαίνω) I have gone up, ascended
> ἀπέσταλκα (ἀποστέλλω) I have sent
> ἔγνωκα (γινώσκω) I have known
> εἴρηκα (λέγω) I have spoken
> ἔσχηκα (ἔχω) I have had
> ἑώρακα (ὁράω) I have seen
> εὕρηκα (εὑρίσκω) I have found

The two below are regularly occurring second perfect forms (without the κ):

> γέγονα (γίνομαι) I have become
> ἐλήλυθα (ἔρχομαι) I have come, I have gone

2. The verbs of the second aorist passive are conjugated in the indicative exactly as the first aorist passive but without the θ.

	Singular			Plural
1	ἐγράφην	I was written	ἐγράφημεν	We were written
2	ἐγράφης	You were written	ἐγράφητε	You were written
3	ἐγράφη	He was written	ἐγράφησαν	They were written

3. The aorist indicative of liquid verbs (verbs whose stem ends in λ, μ, ν, or ρ) takes the first aorist forms except for the σ. The stem sometimes changes but should cause no problem as far as recognition is concerned. The following forms occur relatively frequently:

> ἀπέστειλα (ἀποστέλλω) I sent
> ἔμεινα (μένω) I remained
> ἔκρινα (κρίνω) I judged
> ἤγειρα (ἐγείρω) I raised up

θέλω, I will, wish, desire, is a liquid but is irregular in reverting to the first aorist (ἠθέλησα) and also takes η as an augment, but should be easy to recognize.

58

4. Vocabulary

διδάσκαλος, ὁ teacher
ἔξω adv. without, outside; prep. outside (with gen.)
ἱμάτιον, τό garment
καρπός, ὁ fruit
κηρύσσω I proclaim, preach
ὄρος, ὄρους, τό mountain

θρόνος, ὁ throne
οὔτε...οὔτε neither. . . nor
πιστός, ον, η faithful, believing
σάββατον, τό Sabbath
πλοῖον, τό boat

Exercises

A. Recognition

1. ἐγνώκαμεν
2. ἑωράκατε
3. ἐλήλυθας
4. εὕρηκεν
5. ἐγράφητε

6. ἐκρίναμεν
7. ἠγείρατε
8. ἔσχηκαν
9. ἀκήκοας
10. ἀναβέβηκεν

B. Translate into English

1. οὔτε ἑώρακεν οὔτε ἀκήκοεν τὸν πιστὸν διδάσκαλον.
2. ἐγράφησαν οἱ λόγοι ἐπὶ τὸ ὄρος.
3. ἔμεινεν ἐν τῷ πλοίῳ.
4. ἐλήλυθαν ἔξω καὶ ἤγειραν τοὺς νεκρούς.
5. οἱ πιστοὶ κηρύσσουσιν τὸν λόγον ἐν τοῖς σάββασιν καὶ ἔσχηκαν καρπούς.
6. ἑώρακα τὸν θρόνον τοῦ θεοῦ.
7. γέγονας πιστός.
8. ἠθέλησεν τὸ ἱμάτιον τῆς δικαιοσύνης.

LESSON 25

THE PRESENT, FUTURE, AND IMPERFECT MIDDLE INDICATIVE

1. Thus far we have learned the active and the passive
voice. In the first the subject performs the action of the verb.
In the passive the subject is being acted upon. We now come to the
middle voice. In the middle the subject performs the action but is
acting upon himself or in some way that concerns himself. Thus it
is more active than passive in meaning and with certain verbs which
imply action on oneself it is translated like an active.

Active	νύπτω τους πόδας σου.	I wash your feet.
Middle	νύπτομαι τους πόδας μου.	I wash my feet.

However, when the middle indicates that the subject is
acting in some way that concerns himself, it should be translated
like the active with "for myself, yourself, etc." or with "myself
yourself, etc." The present middle indicative of λύω follows:

	Singular		Plural
1	λύομαι I loose for myself	λυόμεθα	We loose for ourselves
2	λύῃ You loose for yourself	λύεσθε	You loose for yourselves
3	λύεται He looses for himself	λύονται	They loose for themselves

Notice that these forms are identical with the passive.
The context must determine which it is but usually it will be
passive since the middle is not too common. However since the deponents have this same ending, in order not to confuse the voice
and translate incorrectly, it is necessary to master the deponent
verbs.

2. The future middle indicative of λύω follows:

	Singular		Plural
1	λύσομαι I shall loose for myself	λυσομεθα	We shall loose for ourselves
	λύσῃ You shall loose for yourself	λύσεσθε	You shall loose for yourselves
	λύσεται He shall loose for himself	λύσονται	They shall loose for themselves

Notice that the future middle is identical to the present
middle except that it adds the future sign (σ) before the ending
of the present. What was said about the present middle holds true
for the future middle.

60

3. The imperfect middle indicative of λύω follows:

	Singular		Plural	
1	ἐλυόμην	I was loosing for myself	ἐλυόμεθα	We were loosing for ourselves
2	ἐλύου	You were loosing for yourself	ἐλύεσθε	You were loosing for yourselves
3	ἐλύετο	He was loosing for himself	ἐλύοντο	They were loosing for themselves

Notice that the imperfect middle is identical to the imperfect passive. What was said about the present middle holds true for the imperfect middle.

4. Deponent verbs take either a middle or passive form but are always translated in the active. Thus δέχεται he receives; ἀπεκρίθη, he answered.

5. Vocabulary

ἀρχή, ἡ beginning
ἀσπάζομαι I greet, salute
δέχομαι I receive
δοξάζω I glorify
ἐπερωτάω I ask, demand
ἐρωτάω I ask, request
ἤδη already, now

κράζω I cry
νίπτω I wash
συνάγω I gather together
τρεῖς, τρία three
φέρω I bear, carry
ὧδε hither, here

Exercises

A. Recognition

1. ἐρωτήσεται
2. κράζομαι
3. συνάγονται
4. ἐφερόμην
5. δέχεται

6. ἐπιστευόμεθα
7. νίψεσθε
8. δοξάσονται
9. ἐβλέπεσθε
10. ἐνίπτου

B. Translate into English (in some cases the context will indicate that the form is passive rather than middle).

1. ἐν τῇ ἀρχῇ ἐλέγετο ὁ διδάσκαλος.
2. τρεῖς ἄνθρωποι ἐφέροντο τὸ πλοῖον.
3. ἀσπάζεται τοὺς ἀδελφους καὶ συνάγει αὐτοὺς εἰς τὴν ἐκκλησίαν.
4. δεχόμεθα τὸ τέκνον ὃ νίπτεται.
5. δοξάζεται ὁ θεὸς ἤδη ὑπὸ τῶν ἀνθρώπων.
6. ἐκράζοντο ὅτι οὐκ ἐλαμβάνοντο.
7. ἠρώτησεν ἡμᾶς· τίς ἐνίπτετο;
8. ἐδέχοντο τὴν χάριν τοῦ θεοῦ.

61

LESSON 26

REVIEW 4 (LESSONS 21-25)

1. Review the second aorist active and passive indicative in Lesson 21 and 24. Compare the endings with the imperfect in the active. The passive endings are exactly the same as the first aorist passive except that it has no ϑ. Remember that the second aorist does not take the present stem usually. Identify and translate: ἔλυον, ἔλιπεν, ἐγράφημεν, ἐλύπομεν, ἐγράφησαν, ἐλύπετε, ἐλύομεν, ἔλιπον.

2. Review the imperfect and the future forms of εἰμί and their translation in Lessons 21 and 23. Remember that it is deponent in the future and the imperfect always begins with an η with endings like the second aorist passive indicative. Identify and translate the following: ἦτε, ἔσται, ἤμην, ἔσῃ, ἔσομαι, ἦν, ἦς, ἔσονται, ἦσαν, ἐσόμεθα, ἦμεν, ἔσεσθε.

3. Review the first aorist active and passive indicative in Lesson 22. Remember that the sign of the first aorist active is the augment with the σ and the passive, the augment with the ϑη. Learn these endings well. Review also their translation. Identify and translate: ἐλύθη, ἔλυσεν, ἐλύσαμεν, ἐλύθητε, ἐλύσατε, ἐλύθην, ἐλύσατε, ἐλύθης, ἔλυσας, ἐλύθημεν, ἔλυσαν, ἐλύθησαν, ἔλυσα.

4. Review the third declension neuter noun, γένος, τό. In what way does this differ from the basic endings of third declension nouns? Identify the following: τέλος, τέλους, γένη, γένεσι, τέλει, τελῶν.

5. Review the first perfect active and passive indicative in Lesson 23. Compare the perfect with the aorist in Lesson 24. Compare the passive with the present passive. In what way do they differ? Remember that the reduplication is the sign of the perfect. Identify and translate: λέλυμαι, λέλυκεν, λελύμεθα, λελύκαμεν, λέλυνται, λέλυσθε, λελύκατε, λέλυκας, λελύκασι, λέλυσαι.

6. Review the irregular perfects in Lesson 24 and translate the following: ἀκηκόαμεν, γέγονας, ἀπεστάλκατε, ἀναβέβηκεν, ἔγνωκαν, εὕρηκεν, ἑωράκαμεν, ἔσχηκεν, ἐλήλυθας.

7. Review the liquid aorist indicative verbs in Lesson 24. What is a liquid verb? What happens in the aorist to liquid verbs? Translate the following: ἤγειραν, ἐκρίναμεν, ἀπέστειλεν, ἔμεινα, ἠθέλησεν.

8. Review the forms of the middle voice in Lesson 25 and their translation. Compare the forms of the middle with the passive in the present, future and imperfect in Lessons 7, 9, and 17. Translate the following: λυσόμεθα, λύεσθε, ἐλύετο, λύσομαι, ἐλύου, λύεται, λύσεται, ἐλυόμεθα, ἐλυόμην, λύσεσθε, λύονται.

9. Review the vocabulary.

LESSON 27

READING 4

A.   ἦν δὲ ἄνθρωπος ἐκ τῶν Φαρισαίων, ὄνομα αὐτοῦ Νικόδημος ἦν,
ἄρχων τῶν Ἰουδαίων. οὗτος ἦλθεν πρὸς αὐτὸν ἐν τῇ νυκτὶ καὶ εἶπεν
αὐτῷ· σὺ εἶ ὁ διδάσκαλος ἐκ τοῦ οὐρανοῦ. ποιεῖς σημεῖα ἃ δείκνυ-
σίν[1] μοι ὅτι ὁ θεὸς μετὰ σοῦ ἐστίν. πῶς εἰσέρχεται ἄνθρωπος εἰς
τὴν βασιλείαν τοῦ θεοῦ; ἀπεκρίθη[2] ὁ Ἰησοῦς καὶ εἶπεν αὐτῷ· λέγω
σοι· εἰσέρχεται εἰς τὴν βασιλείαν ἄνθρωπος ὅτε γεγέννηται ἐξ ὕδατος
καὶ πνεύματος ἁγίου. σάρξ ἐστιν νῦν ὅτι γεγέννηται ἐκ τῆς σαρκός.
Νικόδημος εἶπεν αὐτῷ· πῶς δύναμαι[3] γεννηθῆναι[4] ἐκ πνεύματος;
Ἰησοῦς ἀπεκρίθη αὐτῷ· σὺ εἶ ὁ διδάσκαλος τοῦ Ἰσραὴλ καὶ ταῦτα
οὐ γινώσκεις; ἀμὴν ἀμὴν λέγω σοι ὅτι ὃ οἴδαμεν[5] καὶ ὃ ἑωράκαμεν
λαλοῦμεν, καὶ τοὺς λόγους ἡμῶν οὐ λαμβάνεις. εἰ τὰ[6] τῆς γῆς εἶπον
σοι καὶ οὐ πιστεύεις, πιστεύσεις εἰ λέγω σοι τὰ τοῦ οὐρανοῦ;
οὐδεὶς[7] ἀναβέβηκεν εἰς τὸν οὐρανὸν εἰ μὴ[8] ὁ υἱὸς τοῦ ἀνθρώπου ὃς
καὶ καταβέβηκεν. ὁ υἱὸς ἀποθανεῖται[9] ὥστε[10] ὁ πιστεύων[11] δύναται[12]
ἔχειν[13] ζωὴν αἰώνιον. οὕτως γὰρ ἠγάπησεν ὁ θεὸς τὸν κόσμον ὥστε[14]
τὸν υἱὸν τὸν μονογενῆ[15] ἔδωκεν[16] ἵνα ὁ πιστεύων εἰς αὐτὸν ἔχῃ[17]
ζωὴν αἰώνιον. οὐ γὰρ ἀπέστειλεν ὁ θεὸς τὸν υἱὸν εἰς τὸν κόσμον
ἵνα κρίνῃ[18] τὸν κόσμον, ἀλλ' ἵνα σωθῇ[19] ὁ κόσμος δι' αὐτοῦ. ὁ
πιστεύων εἰς αὐτὸν οὐ κρίνεται. αὕτη δὲ ἐστιν ἡ κρίσις ὅτι τὸ φῶς
ἐλήλυθεν εἰς τὸν κόσμον καὶ ἠγάπησαν οἱ ἄνθρωποι μᾶλλον τὸ σκότος[20]
ἢ τὸ φῶς· ἦν γὰρ αὐτῶν πονηρὰ τὰ ἔργα.

[1]show [2]answered [3]am I able [4]to be born [5]we know [6]the things
[7]no one [8]except [9]shall die [10]so that [11]the one who believes
[12]is able [13]to have [14]so that [15]only [16]he gave [17]he might have
[18]he might judge [19]might be saved [20]darkness

B.   Ἀγαπητοί, οὐκ ἐντολὴν[1] καινὴν γράφω ἀλλ' ἐντολὴν ἣν ἐλάβετε
ἐν τῇ ἀρχῇ ὅτι ἀγαπᾶτε ἀλλήλους. ἦτε ἐν τῇ σκοτίᾳ καὶ ἡμάρτετε,
ἀλλὰ νῦν ἐστὲ ἐν τῷ φωτὶ καὶ εὑρήκατε εἰρήνην. ὁ ἄρχων[2] τοῦ κόσμου
ἤγαγεν ὑμᾶς ἀλλὰ νῦν ἀπεθάνετε τῇ ἁμαρτίᾳ καὶ ἐλάβετε τὸν κύριον.
πεπιστεύκατε καὶ τετηρήκατε τὰς ἐντολὰς καὶ νῦν χαίρετε ἐν τῷ πνεύματι. ἀκηκόατε τὴν ἀλήθειαν καὶ ἐληλύθατε πρὸς τὸν πατέρα. πιστὸς
ὁ θεός. τηρήσει ὑμᾶς εἰς τὸ τέλος καὶ δώσει[3] ὑμῖν ζωὴν αἰώνιον.

[1]new [2]ruler [3]he shall give

LESSON 28

AORIST MIDDLE INDICATIVE. PERFECT MIDDLE INDICATIVE

1. The first aorist middle indicative

	Singular		Plural	
1	ἐλυσάμην	I loosed for myself	ἐλυσάμεθα	We loosed for ourselves
2	ἐλύσω	You loosed for yourself	ἐλύσασθε	You loosed for yourselves
3	ἐλύσατο	He loosed for himself	ἐλύσαντο	They loosed for themselves

The sign of the aorist active and middle indicative is the augment (ε) and the σα. The endings that follow the σ are the same as the imperfect middle except for the second singular. This may be translated also as "I loosed myself," etc.

2. The second aorist middle indicative

	Singular		Plural	
1	ἐλιπόμην	I left for myself	ἐλιπόμεθα	We left for ourselves
2	ἐλίπου	You left for yourself	ἐλίπεσθε	You left for yourselves
3	ἐλίπετο	He left for himself	ἐλίποντο	They left for themselves

The sign of the second aorist indicative is the augment (ε) with the change of stem (the present is λείπω). Notice that the endings are identical with the imperfect middle.

3. The perfect middle indicative

	Singular		Plural	
1	λέλυμαι	I have loosed for myself	λελύμεθα	We have loosed for ourselves
2	λέλυσαι	You have loosed for yourself	λέλυσθε	You have loosed for yourselves
3	λέλυται	He has loosed for himself	λέλυνται	They have loosed for themselves

This form is identical with the perfect passive indicative. Remember that in the present, imperfect, and perfect, the middle and passive forms are identical.

4. The adverb

The characteristic ending of an adverb is ὡς which is usually added to the stem of the adjective. Thus ἀληθής, true, becomes ἀληθῶς, truly; καλός, good, becomes καλῶς, well.

5. Vocabulary

ἀληθῶς truly
ἁμαρτάνω I sin
γλῶσσα, ἡ tongue, language
δεξιός, ον, α right
διό wherefore
λοιπός, ον, η remaining; subst. the rest; adv. henceforth
μεσός, ον, η in the middle

οὐχί not (strengthened form of οὐ)
χαρά, ἡ joy
πλείων, πλείονος larger, more
προσκυνέω I worship
συναγωγή, ἡ synagogue
τοιοῦτος, ουτον, αυτη such
ὑπάρχω I am, exist
φημί I say

Exercises

A. Recognition

1. προσεκυνήσαντο
2. λέλυνται
3. ἐβάλετο
4. ἐλαβόμεθα
5. ἐδοξάσασθε

6. πεπίστευμαι
7. λέλυσαι
8. ἐλύποντο
9. ἐλυσάμην
10. ἐλιπόμεθα

B. Translate into English

1. ἐν τῇ γλώσσῃ φημὶ τῷ τοιούτῳ· ἀληθῶς οὐχὶ ἁμαρτάνεις.
2. συνήγαγον τοὺς λαοὺς ἐν τῇ συναγωγῇ καὶ προσεκύνησαν τῷ κυρίῳ.
3. διὸ ἡ γραφὴ λέγει· λαμβάνουσιν αὐτὸν μετὰ χαρᾶς.
4. ποιήσει πλείονα σημεῖα ἐν ἐκείνῃ τῇ ἡμέρᾳ.
5. ἐλάβεσθε τὸν κύριον.
6. ἐποιήσαντο τὰ ἀγαθά.
7. τοιαύτῃ ἐξουσίᾳ ἐλάλει αὐτοῖς τὸν λόγον.
8. τότε ἐρεῖ ὁ βασιλευς τοῖς ἀνθρώποις ἐκ δεξιᾶς (hand, understood) αὐτοῦ.
9. ἐκεῖ εἰμὶ ἐν μέσῳ αὐτῷ.
10. ἡμῶν ὁ οἶκος ἐν οὐρανοῖς ὑπάρχει.

LESSON 29

FUTURE DEPONENTS.   CONTRACT VERBS IN THE IMPERFECT

1. There are certain verbs which are not deponent in the
present but are deponent in the future. These should be thorough-
ly learned.

ἀποθανοῦμαι (ἀποθνῄσκω) I shall   λήμψομαι (λαμβάνω) I shall
 die   receive
βήσομαι (βαίνω) I shall go   ὄψομαι (βλέπω or ὁράω) I shall
γνώσομαι (γινώσκω) I shall know   see
ἔσομαι (εἰμί) I shall be   πίομαι (πίνω) I shall drink
εὑρήσομαι (εὑρίσκω) I shall find φάγομαι (ἐσθίω) I shall eat

It is important to recognize these as deponents in order to
translate them correctly.

The following are somewhat irregular in the future although
they are deponents in the present as well:

γενήσομαι (γίνομαι) I shall   ἐλεύσομαι (ἔρχομαι) I shall
 become   come, go

2. The contract verbs in the imperfect active indicative.
Remember that the imperfect endings are ον, ες, ε, ομεν, ετε, ον.

The εω verbs. The contractions are only between ε + ο = ου
and ε + ε =ει. The passive (the middle is identical) has basically
the same types of contractions.

	Singular		Plural	
1	ἐποίε/ον	ἐποίουν	ἐποιέ/ομεν	ἐποιοῦμεν
2	ἐποίε/ες	ἐποίεις	ἐποιέ/ετε	ἐποιεῖτε
3	ἐποίε/ε(ν)	ἐποίει	ἐποίε/ον	εποίουν

The αω verbs. The contractions here are only between α + ο
= ω and α + ε = α.

	Singular		Plural	
1	ἠγάπα/ον	ἠγάπων	ἠγαπά/ομεν	ἠγαπῶμεν
2	ἠγάπα/ες	ἠγάπας	ἠγαπά/ετε	ἠγαπᾶτε
3	ἠγάπα/ε	ἠγάπα	ἠγάπα/ον	ἠγάπων

67

The οω verbs. The contractions are only between o + o = ου and o + ε = ου.

	Singular		Plural	
1	ἐπλήρο/ον	ἐπλήρουν	ἐπληρό/ομεν	ἐπληροῦμεν
2	ἐπλήρο/ες	ἐπλήρους	ἐπληρό/ετε	ἐπληροῦτε
3	ἐπλήρο/ε	ἐπλήρου	ἐπλήρο/ον	ἐπλήρουν

For recognition purposes, what needs to be kept in mind are the two signs of the imperfect--the augment and the present stem. These can be readily recognized in all of these forms, so recognition should cause no problem. If it were a first aorist, it would have a σ and if it were a second aorist, it would have a change of stem from the present.

3. Vocabulary

ἐπαγγελία, ἡ promise
ἔσχατος, ον, η last
εὐαγγελίζω I preach good
  tidings; usually deponent

παραβολή, ἡ parable
σοφία, ἡ wisdom
χρόνος, ὁ time

Exercises

A. Recognition

1. φάγεται
2. λημψόμεθα
3. γνώση
4. καταβήσεσθε
5. ὄψονται

6. ἐπλήρουν
7. ἠγάπων
8. ἐποίει
9. ἐποιοῦμεν
10. ἐπληροῦτε

B. Translate into English

1. λήμψονται τὴν σοφίαν ἐν τῇ ἐσχάτῃ ἡμέρᾳ.
2. ἐποίει τὰς ἐπαγγελίας τοῖς ἔθνεσιν.
3. ἐν τούτῳ τῷ χρόνῳ ἐλεύσεται ἡ βασιλεία;
4. ἠγάπων τὰς παραβολὰς ἃς εἶπεν ὁ Ιησοῦς.
5. φάγονται τοὺς καρποὺς οὓς ἔσπειραν.
6. γνώσονται οἱ δοῦλοι τὸν κύριον αὐτῶν.
7. εὐαγγελίζομεν ἐν παραβολαῖς.
8. ὄψεσθε τὸν καρπὸν τῶν ἔργων ὑμῶν.

LESSON 30

THE SUBJUNCTIVE MOOD

1. The subjunctive mood. Up to this point we have studied
only the indicative mood which simply makes a statement or asks
a question. The subjunctive mood expresses a thought or wish
rather than an actual fact. It is the mood which has an element
of uncertainty since the action is not yet fulfilled. Thus: I
am coming in order that I may see him. This expresses a purpose
which is not yet fulfilled. The next example expresses a future
condition which still remains unfulfilled. If we should go to
church, we would meet the Lord.

The forms of the subjunctive are very simple. First, there
are only two tenses--the present and the aorist. Remember that the
aorist is a past tense only in the indicative and the augment indicates this. In the subjunctive there is never an augment in the
aorist and the aorist indicates simple or punctiliar action, not
past action, in contrast to continuous or linear action of the
present. The distinctive sign of the subjunctive is the long
vowel in the ending.

2. The present active subjunctive.

Singular
1 λύω   that I might loose   λύωμεν   that we might loose
        if I should loose/loose   if we should loose/loose
2 λύῃς that you might loose   λύητε   that you might loose
        if you should loose/loose   if you should loose/loose
3 λύῃ   that he might loose   λύωσι(ν)   that they might loose
        if he should loose/loose   if they should loose/
                                             loose

The subjunctive in most cases is used after ἵνα and ἐάν.
The translation given above is that following ἵνα and ἐάν respectively. Notice that these endings are the same as the present
active indicative except that they all take the corresponding long
vowels unless those vowels were already long.

69

3. The present middle subjunctive

	Singular		Plural
1	λύωμαι	that I might loose for myself	λυώμεθα that we might loose for ourselves
2	λύῃ	that you might loose for yourself / if you should loose/ loose for yourself	λύησθε that you might loose for yourselves / if you should loose/ loose for yourselves
3	λύηται	that he might loose for himself / if he should loose/ loose for himself	λύωνται that they might loose/ loose for themselves / if they should loose/ loose for themselves

4. The present passive subjunctive

	Singular		Plural
1	λύωμαι	that I might be loosed / if I should be loosed/ be loosed	λυώμεθα that we might be loosed / if we should be loosed/ be loosed
2	λύῃ	that you might be loosed / if you should be loosed/ be loosed	λύησθε that you might be loosed / if you should be loosed/ be loosed
3	λύηται	that he might be loosed / if he should be loosed/ be loosed	λύωνται that they might be loosed / if they should be loosed/ be loosed

Notice that the present middle and passive subjunctive are identical in form and, except for the long thematic vowels, have the same endings as their corresponding voices in the indicative.

5. The first aorist active subjunctive

	Singular	Plural
1	λύσω	λύσωμεν
2	λύσῃς	λύσητε
3	λύσῃ	λύσωσι(ν)

The translation of the aorist subjunctive, both first and second aorist, is the same as in the present. The distinction is in the kind of action rather than the time. The present emphasizes continuous action and if one wanted to indicate this he could add the word "continue," e.g., "that I might continue to loose." The aorist indicates simple or punctiliar action and should be translated the same as the present above. Remember, however, that the present indicates continuous action.

Notice that the only difference between this and the present active subjunctive is the addition of the σ before the long vowels in the ending. The subjunctives do not take the augment in the aorist.

70

6. The first aorist middle subjunctive

	Singular	Plural
1	λύσωμαι	λυσώμεθα
2	λύσῃ	λύσησθε
3	λύσηται	λύσωνται

The addition of the σ is the only difference between this and the present middle subjunctive.

7. The first aorist passive subjunctive

	Singular	Plural
1	λυθῶ	λυθῶμεν
2	λυθῇς	λυθῆτε
3	λυθῇ	λυθῶσι(ν)

There are three things to observe in the aorist passive subjunctive: (1) the presence of the θ which is a sure sign of the passive; (2) the endings are the same as the active forms; (3) the irregular accenting, falling always on the long vowel.

8. The second aorist active subjunctive

	Singular	Plural
1	λίπω	λίπωμεν
2	λίπῃς	λίπητε
3	λίπῃ	λίπωσι(ν)

9. The second aorist middle subjunctive

	Singular	Plural
1	λίπωμαι	λιπώμεθα
2	λίπῃ	λίπησθε
3	λίπηται	λίπωνται

10. The second aorist passive subjunctive

	Singular	Plural
1	λιπῶ	λιπῶμεν
2	λιπῇς	λιπῆτε
3	λιπῇ	λιπῶσι(ν)

The only difference between this and the active above is the shifting of the accent.

71

11. Vocabulary

ἀδελφή, ἡ sister
ἀληθής, ες, ης true
ἀληθινός, ον, η true, genuine
ἄρτι now
ἀσθενέω I am sick, weak
ἄχρι, ἄχρις as far as, up to (with gen.); as conjunction, until
γονεύς, γονέως, ὁ begetter; pl. parents
διψάω I thirst
ἐγγύς near
ἵνα in order that
μή not, ordinarily used with the subjunctive and imperative
   moods, the infinitive, and the participle. Also with
   questions to indicate a negative answer.

Exercises

A. Recognition

1. λυθῇ
2. λύσωμαι
3. λυσώμεθα
4. βαπτύσωμεν
5. λύσηται

6. λύῃ
7. ἀκούητε
8. λύῃς
9. πιστεύσωσιν
10. λυθῶμεν

B. Translate into English

1. εἶπεν αὐτοῖς ἵνα μένωσιν ἐν τῷ φωτὶ ἄχρι θανάτου.
2. αἱ ἀδελφαὶ καὶ οἱ γονεῖς αὐτοῦ ἦλθον ἵνα βαπτίσῃ ὁ ἄρχων
   αὐτούς.
3. ἡ μαρτυρία σου οὐκ ἔστιν ἀληθής.
4. δίκαιαι καὶ ἀληθιναὶ αἱ ὁδοί σου.
5. οὗτός ἐστιν ἀληθῶς ὁ σωτὴρ τοῦ κόσμου.
6. ἔρχεται ἄρτι πρὸς τὸ φῶς ἵνα βλέπωσιν αὐτοῦ τὰ ἔργα ὅτι
   ἐστὶν ἀληθής.
7. ἤκουσεν ὅτι ἠσθένει.
8. τὸ ὕδωρ τῆς ζωῆς ἐστιν ἐγγὺς ἵνα μὴ διψῶμεν.

LESSON 31

THE USES OF THE SUBJUNCTIVE

1. The most common use of the subjunctive is to indicate an unfulfilled purpose following ἵνα and ὅπως (in order that).

ἦλθεν ἵνα μαρτυρήσῃ. He came in order that he might testify.
ἦλθον ὅπως προσκυνήσω αὐτόν. I came in order that I might worship him.

2. The next common use of the subjunctive is to indicate a future condition with ἐάν.

μακάριοί ἐστε ἐαν ποιῆτε αὐτά. Blessed are you if you should do them.

3. The hortatory subjunctive. The first person plural form (without ἵνα or ἐάν) is used for exhortation.

ἀγαπῶμεν ἀλλήλους. Let us love one another.

4. Other uses of the subjunctive are not as common. If the student wishes to pursue these at the present time, he can check the footnote at the end of the chapter.[1]

5. The present subjunctive of εἰμί.

1	ὦ	that I might be	ὦμεν	that we might be
		if I should be		if we should be
2	ᾖς	that you might be	ἦτε	that you might be
		if you should be		if you should be
3	ᾖ	that he might be	ὦσι(ν)	that they might be
		if he should be		if they should be

The present subjunctive of εἰμί is very simple since it has only one form and is simply the endings of the regular verb form.

6. Vocabulary

ἐμαυτοῦ myself
ἐορτή, ἡ feast, festival
ἐργάζομαι I work, labor
θαυμάζω I marvel, wonder

θεάομαι I behold, see
θύρα, ἡ door
μαρτυρία, ἡ testimony, witness
νικάω I overcome, gain victory

73

ὁμολογέω I confess
σκοτία, ἡ darkness

τεκνίον, τό little child
φανερόω I reveal, make known, manifest

Exercises

A. Recognition

1. πιστεύητε
2. δοξασθῇ
3. περιπατῇ
4. μαρτυρήσῃ
5. πιστεύσωσιν

6. λύσω
7. φανερωθῇ
8. λέγῃ
9. γεννηθῇς
10. γένηται

B. Translate into English

1. ἦλθον πρὸς τὴν ἑορτὴν ἵνα ὁμολογήσω αὐτὸν καὶ φανερώσω ἐμαυτὸν τῷ μαθητῇ αὐτοῦ.
2. ἐργάζεται ἐν τῇ σκοτίᾳ ἵνα νικήσῃ τὰ τεκνία τοῦ φωτός.
3. ἐθεασάμεθα τὴν δόξαν αὐτοῦ καὶ τὸ τέκνον ἐθαύμασεν.
4. ἦλθεν ἵνα ᾖ ἡ θύρα εἰς τὴν ζωήν.
5. ἐργαζώμεθα τὰ ἔργα τοῦ θεοῦ.
6. ἐὰν τις αὐτὸν ὁμολογήσῃ, σωθήσεται.
7. ὡμολόγησεν αὐτόν.
8. νενίκηκα τὸν κόσμον ἵνα νικήσητε τὸν κόσμον.

---

[1]Other uses of the subjunctive.

1. Prohibitory subjunctive. The aorist subjunctive is used for negative commands and is translated as an imperative.

μὴ θαυμάσῃς. Do not marvel (John 3:7).

2. Deliberative subjunctive. This is placed in a form of a question in which consideration is being made as to the best possible action to take. This is best translated in the form of the English future since it deals with future action. The Greek also expresses this in the future indicative.

δῶμεν ἢ μὴ δῶμεν; Shall we give or shall we not give? (Mark 12:14).

3. Subjunctive of emphatic negation. To express this strong negation the subjunctive frequently is used with a double negative. This should be translated with the English future.

κἀγὼ δίδωμι αὐτοῖς ζωὴν αἰώνιον, καὶ οὐ μὴ ἀπόλωνται εἰς τὸν αἰῶνα. And I give to them life eternal, and they shall never perish (John 10:28).

74

4. Whoever clauses.

ὃς δ' ἂν πίῃ ἐκ τοῦ ὕδατος οὗ ἐγὼ δώσω αὐτῷ οὐ μὴ διψήσει εἰς τὸν αἰῶνα. Whoever should drink of the water which I shall give him shall never thirst (John 4:14).

The ἄν, translated <u>ever</u>, adds vagueness and uncertainty and is appropriate with the subjunctive.

LESSON 32

REVIEW 5 (Lessons 26-31)

1. Review the first aorist, second aorist, and perfect middle indicatives in Lesson 28 and their translations. Remember that the second aorist middle has the same endings as the imperfect, the perfect middle is the same as the perfect passive, and the first aorist middle is very similar to the imperfect. Translate the following: ἐλύσατο, ἐλύπου, λέλυσαι, ἐλύσασθε, ἐλύποντο, λελύμεθα, ἐλυσάμεθα, ἐλύπεσθε.

2. Review the future deponents. Translate the following: λήμφομαι, ἔσομαι, γενήσομαι, εὑρήσομαι, βήσομαι, ὄψομαι, φάγομαι, ἐλεύσομαι.

3. Review the contracts in the imperfect. Remember the rules of contractions. Give the contracted form of the following: ἐποίε + ον, ἐποίε + ε, ἐπλήρο + ον, ἐποιέ + ομεν, ἠγάπα + ον, ἠγάπα + ε, ἠγαπά + ομεν, ἠγαπά + ετε, ἐπληρό + ετε.

4. Review the forms of the subjunctive mood and their translation on Lesson 30. How many tenses are there? What does the aorist represent? What is the difference between the present and the aorist forms? What is <u>the</u> sign of the subjunctive? Translate the following: λυθῶμεν, λύσῃ, λύωμαι, λυώμεθα, λύσητε, λύωμεν, λύηται, λυθῇς, λύσωμεν, ὦσιν, ᾖς, ὦ, ὦμεν.

5. Review the uses of the subjunctive in Lesson 31. Translate the following: ποιῶμεν τὰ ἀγαθά. ἦλθεν ἵνα ἄνθρωποι ἀκολουθήθωσιν αὐτῷ.

LESSON 33

READING 5

A.   Ὃν ἦν ἀπ' ἀρχῆς, ὃ ἀκηκόαμεν, ὃ ἑωράκαμεν ἐν¹ τοῖς ὀφθαλμοῖς ἡμῶν, ὃ ἐθεασάμεθα μαρτυροῦμεν ὑμῖν. ἐστὶν ὁ λόγος καὶ ἡ
ζωή. ἦν πρὸς τὸν πατέρα καὶ ἐφανερώθη ἡμῖν. μαρτυροῦμεν ταῦτα
ὑμῖν ἵνα ὑμεῖς κοινωνίαν² ἔχητε μεθ' ἡμῶν. καὶ ἡ κοινωνία ἡμῶν
μετὰ τοῦ πατρὸς καὶ μετὰ τοῦ υἱοῦ 'Ιησοῦ Χριστοῦ. καὶ ταῦτα
γράφομεν ἵνα ἡ χαρὰ ἡμῶν πληρωθῇ.

       καὶ ἔστιν οὗτος ὁ λόγος ὃν ἀκηκόαμεν ἀπ' αὐτοῦ καὶ μαρτυ-
ροῦμεν ὑμῖν, ὅτι ὁ θεὸς φῶς ἐστὶν καὶ σκοτία ἐν αὐτῷ οὐκ ἔστιν.
ἐὰν εἴπωμεν ὅτι κοινωνίαν ἔχομεν μετ' αὐτοῦ καὶ ἐν τῷ σκότει περιπατῶμεν, οὐ ποιοῦμεν τὴν ἀλήθειαν. ἐὰν δὲ ἐν τῷ φωτὶ περιπατῶμεν
ὡς³ αὐτός ἐστιν ἐν τῷ φωτί, κοινωνίαν ἔχομεν μετ' ἀλλήλων καὶ τὸ
αἷμα 'Ιησοῦ τοῦ υἱοῦ αὐτοῦ καθαρίσει⁴ ἡμᾶς ἀφ' ἁμαρτίας ἡμῶν. ἐὰν
εἴπωμεν ὅτι ἁμαρτίαν οὐκ ἔχομεν, ἑαυτοὺς⁵ πλανῶμεν⁶ καὶ ἡ ἀλήθεια
οὐκ ἔστιν ἐν ἡμῖν. ἐὰν ὁμολογῶμεν τὰς ἁμαρτίας ἡμῶν, πιστός ἐστιν
καὶ δίκαιος, ἵνα καθαρίσῃ⁷ ἡμᾶς ἀφ' ἁμαρτίας ἡμῶν. ἐὰν εἴπωμεν
ὅτι οὐχ ἡμαρτήκαμεν, ψεύστην⁸ ποιοῦμεν αὐτὸν καὶ ὁ λόγος αὐτοῦ
οὐκ ἔστιν ἐν ἡμῖν. ταῦτα γράφω ὑμῖν ἵνα μὴ ἁμάρτητε, καὶ ἐάν τις
ἁμάρτῃ, ἀδελφὸν ἔχομεν πρὸς τὸν πατέρα, 'Ιησοῦν Χριστὸν δίκαιον.
καὶ ἐν τούτῳ γινώσκομεν ὅτι ἐγνώκαμεν αὐτόν, ἐὰν τὰς ἐντολὰς αὐτοῦ
τηρῶμεν.

¹with ²fellowship ³as ⁴shall cleanse ⁵ourselves ⁶we deceive
⁷he should cleanse ⁸liar

B.   'Αγαπητοί, ἀγαπῶμεν ἀλλήλους ὅτι ἡ ἀγάπη ἐκ τοῦ θεοῦ ἐστίν.
ἀληθῶς τοιοῦτος γεγέννηται ἐκ τοῦ θεοῦ καὶ γινώσκει αὐτόν. ἐν
τούτῳ ἐφανερώθη ἡ ἀγάπη τοῦ θεοῦ ἐν ἡμῖν, ὅτι τὸν υἱὸν αὐτοῦ
ἀπέσταλκεν εἰς τὸν κόσμον ἵνα ζήσωμεν¹ δι' αὐτοῦ. οὐκ ἠγαπήκαμεν
τὸν θεόν, ἀλλ' ἠγάπησεν ἡμᾶς καὶ ἀπέστειλεν τὸν υἱὸν αὐτοῦ περὶ
τῶν ἁμαρτίων. ἐὰν ἀγαπῶμεν ἀλλήλους, ὁ θεὸς ἐν ἡμῖν μένει. καὶ
ἐὰν περιπατῶμεν ἐν τῇ ὁδῷ αὐτοῦ, δώσει² ἡμῖν ζωῆν. καὶ ἐγνώκαμεν
καὶ πεπιστεύκαμεν τὴν ἀγάπην ἣν³ ἔχει ὁ θεὸς ἐν ἡμῖν. ἐάν τις εἴπῃ
ὅτι ἀγαπῶ τὸν θεόν, καὶ τὸν ἀδελφὸν αὐτοῦ μισῇ⁴, ψεύστης⁵ ἐστίν.

¹we might live ²he will give ³which ⁴he should hate ⁵liar

77

LESSON 34

THE PRESENT IMPERATIVE

1. The imperative mood expresses a command. There are only two tenses in this mood--the present (linear or continuous action) and the aorist (punctiliar or simple action). The learning of the imperative forms should begin with the second person plural since it is the same as the indicative form (but without the augment in the aorist). Since the present forms of the second person plural are identical the context only will determine whether it is indicative or imperative. Once the second person plural form is known, replace the final ε with an ω and you have the third person singular form and with ωσαν you have the third person plural form. This holds true for the present and aorist and in the active, middle, and passive voices. The second person singular form is the only one that has to be memorized. There are no first person forms.

Since it is a bit awkward to indicate continuous action for the present, the translation given for the present will be the same as the aorist. The student should keep in mind, however, that the present emphasizes continuous action while the aorist indicates simple or punctiliar action. If he whould desire to make this distinction in the translation, he can translate the present by adding the word "continue." Thus for the second person singular, "Continue to loose," and for the third person singular, "Let him continue to loose."

2. The present active imperative

	Singular			Plural
2	λῦε	Loose	λύετε	Loose
3	λυέτω	Let him loose	λυέτωσαν	Let them loose

3. The present middle imperative

	Singular			Plural
2	λύου	Loose for yourself	λύεσθε	Loose for yourselves
3	λυέσθω	Let him loose for himself	λυεσθωσαν	Let them loose for themselves

4. The present passive imperative

	Singular			Plural
2	λύου	Be loosed	λύεσθε	Be loosed
3	λυέσθω	Let him be loosed	λυέσθωσαν	Let them be loosed

As always in the present the middle and passive forms are identical.

5. The present imperative of εἰμί. This verb has only the present tense.

	Singular			Plural
2	ἴσθι	Be	ἐστέ	Be
3	ἔστω	Let him be	ἔστωσαν	Let them be

6. After a comparative such as μείζων (greater), the thing or person compared is in the genitive case (the genitive of comparison) if ἤ (than) is not used. The genitive of comparison is translated "than . . . ." Thus ἐστιν μείζων μου, "He is greater than I." If "than" is used the second thing compared is in the same case as the first thing to which it is compared. The regular comparative ending is -τερος, -ον, -α, and the superlative -τατος, -ον, -η.

7. μή is used in an interrogative sentence to indicate that a negative response is expected.

μὴ σὺ μείζων εἶ τοῦ πατρὸς ἡμῶν Ἰακώβ, ...;

To bring out the force of this negative, this sentence may be translated "You are not greater than our father Jacob, are you?"

8. Vocabulary

κακός, ον α evil, bad
κεῖμαι I lie, recline
κλαίω I weep
κραυγάζω I cry out, shout
κρίσις, ἡ judgment
μείζων greater; comparative of μέγας, μεγάλου great (3rd decl.)

μισέω I hate
μνημεῖον, τό tomb, grave
μόνος, ον, η alone; used as adverb it means only
οἶνος, ὁ wine
ὀπίσω after, behind
οὐκέτι, μηκέτι no longer

Exercises

A. Recognition

1. λύου
2. πίστευε
3. λυέτωσαν

4. μενέτω
5. λυέσθω
6. λυέσθωσαν

79

7. νίπτου   9. ἐχέτωσαν
8. ἀκούετε   10. λῦε

B. Translate into English

1. μὴ κλαῖε διὰ τὴν κρίσιν.
2. φωνῇ μεγάλη ἐκραύγασεν ὡς εἶδεν αὐτὸν ἐν τῷ μνημείῳ.
3. μὴ πίνετε οἶνον.
4. μισείτω κακά.
5. μὴ ἔστιν δοῦλος μείζων τοῦ κυρίου αὐτοῦ;
6. ἔρχου ὀπίσω μου.
7. ἐμίσησάν με.
8. μὴ φοβοῦ, μόνον πίστευε.

LESSON 35

THE AORIST IMPERATIVE

1. The student should keep in mind that the aorist in the
imperative does not indicate past action (therefore it has no
augment) but only simple or punctiliar action.

The first aorist active imperative

	Singular		Plural	
2	λῦσον	Loose	λύσατε	Loose
3	λυσάτω	Let him loose	λυσάτωσαν	Let them loose

Remember that the key to learning these forms is the second
person plural. Notice that in the form above and below it is the
indicative except that it drops the augment. The third person
forms have the ω and ωσαν endings. This is true throughout the
different voices.

2. The first aorist middle imperative

	Singular		Plural	
2	λῦσαι	Loose for yourself	λύσασθε	Loose for yourselves
3	λυσάσθω	Let him loose for himself	λυσάσθωσαν	Let them loose for themselves

3. The first aorist passive imperative

	Singular		Plural	
2	λύθητι	Be loosed	λύθητε	Be loosed
3	λυθήτω	Let him be loosed	λυθήτωσαν	Let them be loosed

4. The second aorist active imperative of λείπω.

	Singular		Plural	
2	λίπε	Leave	λίπετε	Leave
3	λιπέτω	Let him leave	λιπέτωσαν	Let them leave

Notice that the second aorist endings are the same as the
present endings in the active and middle voices. The passive as
usual follows the first aorist except that it drops the ϑ.

81

5. The second aorist middle imperative

	Singular			Plural	
2	λύπου	Leave for yourself		λύπεσθε	Leave for yourselves
3	λιπέσθω	Let him leave for himself		λιπέσθωσαν	Let them leave for themselves

6. The second aorist passive imperative

	Singular			Plural	
2	λύπητι	Be left		λύπητε	Be left
3	λιπήτω	Let him be left		λιπήτωσαν -έντων	Let them be left

7. Vocabulary

οὔπω not yet
πάντοτε always
παρρησία, ἡ openness, confidence
πάσχα, τό Passover
πέραν beyond
πιάζω I lay hold, arrest

πόθεν whence
ποιμήν, ποιμένος, ὁ shepherd
ποῦ where
πρό before
πρόβατον, τό sheep

Exercises

A. Recognition and translation

1. λύσατε
2. πίστευσον
3. λύθητι
4. πιασάτωσαν
5. λῦσαι

6. θαυμασάσθω
7. λύσασθε
8. ζητησάτω
9. λυθήτω
10. ποίησον

B. Translate into English

1. δοξάσατε πάντοτε τὸν ἀληθινὸν ποιμένα.
2. πιασάσθω τὰ πρόβατα.
3. ζητησάτωσαν τὴν βασιλείαν καὶ τὴν δικαιοσύνην αὐτῆς.
4. οὔπω πιστεύει εἰς αὐτόν.
5. πόθεν ἔρχεται τὰ πρόβατα καὶ ποῦ πορεύεται;
6. εἰπὲ τὸν λόγον παρρησίᾳ.
7. φάγετε τὸ πάσχα πέραν τοῦ Ἰορδάνου πρὸ ἐμοῦ.
8. λύσατε τοῦτο τὸ ἱερόν.

THE PRESENT AND AORIST INFINITIVE

1. The infinitive in Greek is used very much as it is used in English. It has neither person nor number. The tense indicates kind of action, not time as in the subjunctive and imperative. Thus the aorist does not take the augment. The present indicates continuous action and the aorist simple action.

		Present		First Aorist
Present	λύειν	to loose	λῦσαι	to loose
Middle	λύεσθαι	to loose for one's self	λύσασθαι	to loose for one's self
Passive	λύεσθαι	to be loosed	λυθῆναι	to be loosed

As in the imperative and subjunctive, no distinction is made in the translation above between the present and the aorist. Again, if the distinction is desired, the student can add "continue." Thus "to continue to loose" or "to continue to be loosed."

2. The second aorist infinitive forms take the present endings in the active and middle but the first aorist ending without the ϑ in the passive.

The second aorist infinitive

Active	λιπεῖν	to leave
Middle	λιπέσθαι	to leave for one's self
Passive	λιπῆναι	to be left

3. Vocabulary

δεῖ it is necessary (for)
δύναμαι I am able, can
ἔξεστι it is lawful
μέλλω I am about to
ῥαββί rabbi, master
σεαυτοῦ yourself (2nd sing.)
σός, σόν, σή your (2nd sing.)
σταυρόω I crucify

στρατιώτης, ὁ soldier
ταράσσω I disturb, trouble
τιμάω I honor
ὑγιής sound, well, healthy
ὑπηρέτης, ὁ servant, officer
φιλέω I love
φίλος, ὁ friend
φωνέω I call, invite

Exercises

A. Recognition and translation

1. λύσασθαι
2. πιστεύειν
3. λαλῆσαι
4. ἔρχεσθαι
5. εἰπεῖν

6. λυθῆναι
7. ἐκβάλεσθαι
8. εἰσελθεῖν
9. ἐγερθῆναι
10. λυπῆναι

B. Translate into English

1. ῥαββί, ἔξεστι σταυρῶσαι τοῦτον τὸν ἄνθρωπον;
2. δεῖ τιμῆσαι καὶ φιλῆσαι τὸν σὸν φίλον.
3. οἱ στρατιῶται καὶ οἱ ὑπηρέται δύνανται[1] ταράσσειν τοὺς ὄχλους.
4. δεῖ φανερῶσαι σεαυτὸν καὶ φωνῆσαι τοὺς στρατιώτας.
5. ὁ ὑπηρέτης ἐστὶν ὑγιὴς καὶ δύναται εἰπεῖν.
6. δεῖ λυθῆναι τοῦτο τὸ ἱερόν.
7. δύναμαι ἐλθεῖν πρὸς τὸν σὸν φίλον.
8. μέλλω λαλεῖν μετ᾽ αὐτοῦ.

---

[1]δύναμαι is a deponent verb and takes the regular endings of deponent verbs but has certain irregularities. In the present and imperfect it takes the α throughout instead of the thematic vowels ε or ο. It also takes two forms for the present second singular form. In the present the forms are:

	Singular		Plural	
1	δύναμαι	I am able, can	δυνάμεθα	We are able, can
2	δύνασαι or δύνῃ	You are able, can	δύνασθε	You are able, can
3	δύναται	He is able, can	δύνανται	They are able, can

The imperfect may also take the ε or the η as augment, ἠδυνάμην or ἐδυνάμην. The aorist also takes the η as augment, ἠδυνήθην. The future is δυνήσομαι. Notice that in the aorist and future the α lengthens to an η as in contract verbs.

THE PERFECT INFINITIVE.   INFINITIVE OF εἰμί.   USES OF INFINITIVE

     1. The perfect infinitive takes the reduplication but no thematic vowel. As always the middle and passive are identical in the perfect.

Active	λελυκέναι	to have loosed
Middle	λελύσθαι	to have loosed for one's self
Passive	λελύσθαι	to have been loosed

     2. The infinitive of the verb "to be" has only one form--εἶναι, to be.

     Notice that all the infinitive forms except for the present and second aorist active forms have an αι as the last letters in the ending. While this is not conclusive, nevertheless, when one sees this in a verb form one should suspect an infinitive unless some strong signs point against it.

     3. The uses of the infinitive. Greek infinitives function in most cases in the same way as English infinitives. Its most frequent use is to indicate purpose, e.g., Matt. 2:2, ἤλθομεν προσκυνῆσαι, "we came to worship." This usage should cause no problem. However, the infinitive used with a preposition may be more difficult. These are usually found with an article, in the case that the preposition takes, with a noun or two nouns in the accusative case. These should be translated as though they were adverbial clauses (the preposition serving as the adverbial conjunction). The noun in the accusative case becomes the subject of the clause. If there are two nouns, both in the accusative case, one will become the subject and the other the object of the infinitive. The context will determine the subject. We present some examples of this type of use.

    ἀλλὰ μετὰ τὸ ἐγερθῆναί με προάξω ὑμᾶς εἰς τὴν Γαλιλαίαν.
But after I have been raised up, I shall go before you into Galilee (Mark 14:28).

    οἶδεν γὰρ ὁ πατὴρ ὑμῶν ὧν χρείαν ἔχετε πρὸ τοῦ ὑμᾶς αἰτῆσαι αὐτόν.
For your Father knows of what things you have need before you ask him (Matt. 6:8).

    ἐν τῷ ὑποστρέφειν αὐτοὺς ὑπέμεινεν Ἰησοῦς. . . .
While they were returning, Jesus remained. . . . (Lk 2:43).

ἐν is usually translated <u>while</u> with the infinitive. The time of the infinitive is the same as the main verb.

καὶ δύναμις κυρίου ἦν εἰς τὸ ἰᾶσθαι αὐτόν.
And the power of the Lord was (present) in order that he might heal (them) (Luke 5:17).

The infinitive with εἰς indicates purpose or result.

The infinitive is also used in indirect discourse. But this use is not too common. The same is true for its use as an imperative.

4. In a few instances when καί precedes a word beginning with a vowel, crasis (mixing) takes place, making what appears to be one word. When crasis takes place the ι of the καί drops out, the vowels coming together then contract and take an '. The following are common examples of crasis in the NT: καὶ ἐγώ, and I, κἀγώ; καὶ ἐμοί, and to me, κἀμοί; καὶ ἐκεῖ, and there, κἀκεῖ; καὶ ἐκεῖθεν, and thence, κἀκεῖθεν; καὶ ἐκεῖνος, and that one, κἀκεῖνος; καὶ ἐάν or ἄν, and if, κἄν.

5. Vocabulary

ἄρχομαι I begin
ἔμπροσθεν before, in front of (with genitive)
εὐθύς immediately
θεωρέω I look at, behold
παιδίον, τό infant, child
πείθω I persuade

λίθος, ὁ stone
μακάριος, ον, α blessed, happy
μηδέ but not, nor, not even (used with moods other than indicative)
ὅπως in order that, that
πρεσβύτερος, ον, α elder (adj.); also as substantive

Exercises

A. Recognition and translation

1. λελύσθαι
2. εἶναι
3. βληθῆναι
4. λαβεῖν
5. λελυκέναι

6. πιστεύειν
7. ἀποθανεῖν
8. λυθῆναι
9. δοξάζεσθαι
10. σωθῆναι

B. Translate into English

1. εὐθὺς ἄρχεται ἐκβαλεῖν τὰ παιδία ἐκ τοῦ οἴκου.
2. μετὰ τὸ λελύσθαι τοὺς λίθους ἐκ τοῦ ἱεροῦ, εἶδεν τοὺς ἀρχιερεῖς.
3. κἀγὼ κάθημαι ἔμπροσθεν τοῦ μακαρίου ἀποστόλου καὶ τοῦ πρεσβυτέρου ἀδελφοῦ.

4. πείθει τὸ παιδίον εἰσελθεῖν εἰς τὸν οἶκον.
5. ἐν δὲ τῷ λέγειν αὐτόν, ὁ ἀπόστολος εἰσῆλθεν.
6. μετὰ τὸ λαβεῖν αὐτὸν τὴν μαρτυρίαν, ἐδίδαξεν τὸ παιδίον.
7. ἦλθεν ὅπως σώσῃ ἡμᾶς.
8. ἀπέθανεν εἰς τὸ σωθῆναι αὐτούς.

LESSON 38

REVIEW 6 (LESSONS 34-37)

1. Review the forms of the imperative and their translation in Lessons 34 and 35. Remember the second plural is the key
to the endings. Remember that the aorist does not indicate past
time but simple or punctiliar action. Identify and translate the
following: λυσάτωσαν, λυέσθω, λῦου, λυσάσθω, λῦπε, λυσάτω, λιπέσθω,
ἔστω, λιπέτω, ἴσθι, λυέτωσαν.

2. Review the forms of the infinitive and their translation in Lessons 36 and 37. Remember that the aorist does not
indicate past time but simple action and that αι at the end of a
verb is usually a sign of the infinitive. Identify and translate
the following: λύεσθαι, λιπῆναι, λελυκέναι, λυθῆναι, λῦσαι, λύειν,
εἶναι, λύσασθαι, λιπεῖν, λελύσθαι.

3. Review the uses of the infinitive in Lesson 37 and translate the following:

μετὰ τὸ ἐλθεῖν αὐτόν, ὁ διδάσκαλος εἶπεν τῷ λαῷ.

ἐν τῷ περιπατεῖν αὐτόν, εἶδεν τὸν ἀπόστολον.

LESSON 39

READING 6

A.　'Ο μένων¹ ἐν ἐμοὶ κἀγὼ ἐν αὐτῷ, οὗτος φέρει² καρπὸν πολὺν³
ὅτι χωρὶς⁴ ἐμοῦ οὐ δύνασθε ποιεῖν οὐδέν.⁵ ἐὰν μείνητε ἐν ἐμοὶ καὶ
τὰ ῥήματά μου ἐν ὑμῖν μείνῃ, ὃ ἐὰν⁶ θέλητε⁷ αἰτήσασθε, καὶ γενήσεται. προσεύξασθε, καὶ ἀκούσει ὑμᾶς. ἐν τούτῳ ἐδοξάσθη ὁ πατήρ
μου, ἵνα καρπὸν πολὺν⁸ φέρητε⁹ καὶ γενήσεσθε μαθηταί μου. καθὼς
ἠγάπησέν με ὁ πατήρ, κἀγὼ ὑμᾶς ἠγάπησα. μείνατε ἐν τῇ ἀγάπῃ μου,
περιπατήσατε κατὰ τὸ θέλημά μου. ἐὰν τὰς ἐντολάς μου τηρήσητε,
μενεῖτε ἐν τῇ ἀγάπῃ μου, καθὼς ἐγὼ τοῦ πατρός μου τὰς ἐντολὰς
τετήρηκα καὶ μένω αὐτοῦ ἐν τῇ ἀγάπῃ. ταῦτα λελάληκα ὑμῖν ἵνα ἡ
χαρά μου ἐν ὑμῖν ᾖ καὶ ἡ χαρὰ ὑμῶν πληρωθῇ. αὕτη ἐστὶν ἡ ἐντολή
μου ἵνα ἀγαπᾶτε ἀλλήλους καθὼς ἠγάπησα ὑμᾶς. μείζονα ταύτης ἀγάπην
οὐδεὶς¹⁰ ἔχει. καὶ ταῦτα ἐντέλλομαι¹¹ ὑμῖν· ἀγαπᾶτε ἀλλήλους,
μισεῖτε τὸ πονηρόν, τηρήσατε τὰς ἐντολάς μου, περιπατήσατε ἐν
εἰρήνῃ, καὶ διδάξατε τοὺς ἀδελφούς. ποιησάτωσαν τὰ ἀγαθά, πληρω-
σάτωσαν τὸ θέλημα τοῦ πατρός, πορευέσθωσαν εἰς τὸν κόσμον δου-
λεύειν¹² τὸν λαὸν καὶ ποιεῖν τὰ καλά. διδάξατε δὲ καὶ τὸν πρεσ-
βύτερον τῆς ἐκκλησίας. ἔστω δίκαιος καὶ ἅγιος, λαλείτω τὴν ἀλήθειαν ἐν ἀγάπῃ, πληρωσάτω τὸ ἔργον τοῦ θεοῦ, προσευχέσθω πάντοτε.
οὗτος δύναται ποιῆσαι πόλλα¹³ ἀγαθὰ καὶ δουλεύειν¹⁴ τὸν κυρίον.
ἀλλὰ αὐτὸν δεῖ εἶναι ταπεινός.¹⁵ πρὶν¹⁶ θεῖναι¹⁷ ὑμᾶς αὐτόν,
δοκιμάσατε¹⁸ αὐτόν. μετὰ τὸ θεῖναι ὑμᾶς αὐτὸν παρακαλεῖτε αὐτόν.

¹the one who abides ²bears ³much ⁴apart from, without ⁵anything,
nothing ⁶whatever ⁷you should wish ⁸much ⁹you should bear ¹⁰no one
¹¹I command ¹²to serve ¹³much, many ¹⁴to serve ¹⁵humble ¹⁶before
¹⁷to appoint ¹⁸test, prove

B.　μετὰ τὸ βαπτισθῆναι αὐτὸν ἦλθεν ὁ 'Ιησοῦς εἰς τὴν Γαλιλαίαν κηρύσσειν τὸ εὐαγγέλιον. εἶπεν ὅτι πεπλήρωται ὁ καιρὸς καὶ
ἤγγικεν¹ ἡ βασιλεία· μετανοήσατε καὶ πιστεύσατε ἐν τῷ εὐαγγελίῳ.
δύνασθε γενέσθαι τὰ τέκνα τοῦ θεοῦ ἐὰν πιστεύσητε. εἶδεν οὖν
Σίμωνα καὶ τὸν ἀδελφὸν αὐτοῦ καὶ εἶπεν. ἔλθετε καὶ ἀκολουθήσατέ
μοι καὶ ποιήσω ὑμᾶς γενέσθαι ἁλεεῖς² ἀνθρώπων. καὶ εὐθὺς ἠκολούθησαν αὐτῷ. εὗρεν καὶ 'Ιωάννην καὶ τὸν ἀδελφὸν αὐτοῦ ἐν τῷ πλοίῳ.
ἐκάλεσεν αὐτοὺς καὶ ἀφῆκαν³ τὸν πατέρα αὐτῶν καὶ ἀπῆλθον ὀπίσω
αὐτοῦ.

¹has drawn near ²fishers ³they left

89

LESSON 40

THE PRESENT PARTICIPLE

1. The participle is a verbal adjective and has character-istics of a verb and an adjective. Thus it has tense and voice like the verb and number, gender, and case like the adjective. The participle is at the same time the most important and most difficult aspect of the Greek language from the standpoint of translation. The forms, however, are not difficult: the feminine participles follow the first declension throughout; the masculine and neuter follow the third declension in the active voice through-out and in the aorist passive, and the second declension in the middle voice throughout and the present and perfect passive. You have already learned all the forms of the endings. It is important to learn the nominative singular forms of all the declensions since they give you clues to the rest of the forms. The translation of the participles will not be provided at this time but will follow in Lesson 42 since the translation depends on its use in a sentence.

2. The present active participle

	Singular			Plural		
	M	N	F	M	N	F
N	λύων	λῦον	λύουσα	λύοντες	λύοντα	λύουσαι
G	λύοντος	λύοντος	λυούσης	λυόντων	λυόντων	λυουσῶν
D	λύοντι	λύοντι	λυούσῃ	λύουσι(ν)	λύουσι(ν)	λυούσαις
A	λύοντα	λῦον	λύουσαν	λύοντας	λύοντα	λυούσας

Observe the similarities between the masculine and neuter and the identical forms (nominative and accusative) in the neuter. In most cases the οντ and ουσ should help you to identify the form as active participle in the present.

3. The present middle and passive participle

	Singular			Plural		
	M	N	F	M	N	F
N	λυόμενος	λυόμενον	λυομένη	λυόμενοι	λυόμενα	λυόμεναι
G	λυομένου	λυομένου	λυομένης	λυομένων	λυομένων	λυομένων
D	λυομένῳ	λυομένῳ	λυομένῃ	λυομένοις	λυομένοις	λυομέναις
A	λυόμενον	λυόμενον	λυομένην	λυομένους	λυόμενα	λυομένας

Observe again the similarities between the masculine and neuter and the identical forms in the neuter. The ομεν in the ending with the present stem should help you identify the form as a present middle and passive participle.

4. The present participle of εἰμί

	Singular			Plural		
	M	N	F	M	N	F
N	ὤν	ὄν	οὖσα	ὄντες	ὄντα	οὖσαι
G	ὄντος	ὄντος	οὔσης	ὄντων	ὄντων	οὐσῶν
D	ὄντι	ὄντι	οὔσῃ	οὖσι(ν)	οὖσι(ν)	οὔσαις
A	ὄντα	ὄν	οὖσαν	ὄντας	ὄντα	οὔσας

εἰμί has only the present tense and only one form corresponding to the active voice endings. If you know the participle forms of the regular verb, you should have no trouble learning and recognizing these since they are the endings without the stem. Remember that εἰμί has no voice.

5. Vocabulary

ἁμαρτωλός, ον, ος sinful; as a noun, a sinner
φόβος, ὁ fear

διώκω I pursue, persecute
θεραπεύω I heal

Exercises

A. Recognition

1. λῦον
2. διωκόμενοι
3. λυόμενα
4. λαμβάνοντας
5. ὄντι
6. πιστεύουσα
7. λυούσαις
8. σωζόμενοι
9. λύουσι
10. δεχόμενος

11. ὄν
12. πιστευοντες
13. λυομένη
14. διδασκόμενοι.
15. λυομένους
16. βαπτίζοντα
17. λύοντος
18. σῶζον
19. ὄντες
20. ἀναβαινούσῃ

91

THE AORIST PARTICIPLE

1. The second aorist active participle

	Singular			Plural		
	M	N	F	M	N	F
N	λιπών	λιπόν	λιποῦσα	λιπόντες	λιπόντα	λιποῦσαι
G	λιπόντος	λιπόντος	λιπούσης	λιπόντων	λιπόντων	λιπουσῶν
D	λιπόντι	λιπόντι	λιπούσῃ	λιποῦσι(ν)	λιποῦσι(ν)	λιπούσαις
A	λιπόντα	λιπόν	λιποῦσαν	λιπόντας	λιπόντα	λιπούσας

2. The second aorist middle participle

	Singular			Plural		
	M	N	F	M	N	F
N	λιπόμενος	λιπόμενον	λιπομένη	λιπόμενοι	λιπόμενα	λιπόμεναι
G	λιπομένου	λιπομένου	λιπομένης	λιπομένων	λιπομένων	λιπομένων
D	λιπομένῳ	λιπομένῳ	λιπομένῃ	λιπομένοις	λιπομένοις	λιπομέναις
A	λιπόμενον	λιπόμενον	λιπομένην	λιπομένους	λιπόμενα	λιπομένας

Keep in mind that the aorist participles do not take the augment. The second aorist always has a different stem from the present. Otherwise the forms of the second aorist participle in the active and middle are identical with those of the present participle. The second aorist passive participle is different from the present but follows the pattern of following the third declension endings in the masculine and neuter and the first declension in the feminine.

3. The second aorist passive particple

	Singular			Plural		
	M	N	F	M	N	F
N	λιπείς	λιπέν	λιπεῖσα	λιπέντες	λιπέντα	λιπεῖσαι
G	λιπέντος	λιπέντος	λιπείσης	λιπέντων	λιπέντων	λιπεισῶν
D	λιπέντι	λιπέντι	λιπείσῃ	λιπεῖσι(ν)	λιπεῖσι(ν)	λιπείσαις
A	λιπέντα	λιπέν	λιπεῖσαν	λιπέντας	λιπέντα	λιπείσας

The characteristic sign of the second aorist passive participle is the ε before the ντ in the masculine and neuter third declension endings and the ει before the σ of the feminine first declension endings.

4. The first aorist active particple

	Singular			Plural	
M	**N**	**F**	**M**	**N**	**F**
N λύσας	λῦσαν	λύσασα	λύσαντες	λύσαντα	λύσασαι
G λύσαντος	λύσαντος	λυσάσης	λυσάντων	λυσάντων	λυσασῶν
D λύσαντι	λύσαντι	λυσάσῃ	λύσασι(ν)	λῦσασι(ν)	λυσάσαις
A λύσαντα	λῦσαν	λύσασαν	λύσαντας	λύσαντα	λυσάσας

The aorist participle does not take an augment but the σαντ should be the sign that tells you that it is an aorist active participle in the masculine or neuter and the σασ that it is aorist active participle in the feminine.

5. The first aorist middle participle

	Singular			Plural	
M	**N**	**F**	**M**	**N**	**F**
N λυσάμενος	λυσάμενον	λυσαμένη	λυσάμενοι	λυσάμενα	λυσάμεναι
G λυσαμένου	λυσαμένου	λυσαμένης	λυσαμένων	λυσαμένων	λυσαμένων
D λυσαμένῳ	λυσαμένῳ	λυσαμένῃ	λυσαμένοις	λυσαμένοις	λυσαμέναις
A λυσάμενον	λυσάμενον	λυσαμένην	λυσαμένους	λυσάμενα	λυσαμένας

Notice the second declension endings in the masculine and neuter forms and the first declension endings in the feminine forms. The σαμεν should tell you that the form is an aorist middle participle.

6. The first aorist passive participle

	Singular			Plural	
M	**N**	**F**	**M**	**N**	**F**
N λυθείς	λυθέν	λυθεῖσα	λυθέντες	λυθέντα	λυθεῖσαι
G λυθέντος	λυθέντος	λυθείσης	λυθέντων	λυθέντων	λυθεισῶν
D λυθέντι	λυθέντι	λυθείσῃ	λυθεῖσι(ν)	λυθεῖσι(ν)	λυθείσαις
A λυθέντα	λυθέν	λυθεῖσαν	λυθέντας	λυθέντα	λυθείσας

The endings are the same as those of the second aorist passive participle except that this adds the ϑ. The sign of the first aorist passive participle is the ϑεντ in the masculine and neuter and the ϑεισ in the feminine. It is important to learn the nominative singluar forms for all of the participles.

7. Vocabulary

βλασφημέω I blaspheme, revile
διάβολος, ὁ devil
διδαχή, ἡ teaching
ἐλπίζω I hope
μυστήριον, τό mystery

93

Exercises

A. Recognition

1. λύσαντος
2. πιστεύσαντες
3. λύσασαι
4. κηρύξαντα
5. λυσάμενοι
6. λυθέντι
7. ἀκουσάντων
8. λαβόντα
9. σώσαντα
10. θεασάμενος

11. ἐγερθέντος
12. λυθέν
13. διωχθέντας
14. λαβών
15. πορευσαμένου
16. εἰσελθόντος
17. δεξάμενοι
18. ποιήσαντι
19. ἀκούσας
20. βληθέντες

LESSON 42

TRANSLATING PARTICIPLES

1. The attributive use of the participle. There are two basic types of participles, adjectival and adverbial. The adjectival participle almost always has the article preceding it while the adverbial never has the article. There are two kinds of adjectival participles corresponding to the adjectives, the attributive and the substantival. In the attributive, the participle is always accompanied by a noun or pronoun antecedent. Tense in the participles basically indicates kind of action but when used adjectivally time is usually also indicated. The noun or pronoun and participle may be in any case.

Present participle   ὁ ἄνθρωπος ὁ γράφων or ὁ γράφων ἄνθρωπος
                     The man who writes (or is writing).

Aorist participle   ὁ ἄνθρωπος ὁ γράψας or ὁ γράψας ἄνθρωπος
                     The man who wrote.

Observe how the attributive participle is translated as "who writes" and "who wrote."

2. The substantival use of the participle. This is similar to the substantival use of the adjective, where the adjective stands in place of the noun--ὁ ἀγαθός = the good man.

                                                he
Present participle   ὁ γράφων   the one who writes (is writing)
                               the man

                                                he
Aorist participle   ὁ γράψας   the one who wrote
                               the man

3. The adverbial use of the present participle. When the present participle is used adverbially, the time of the participle is the same as that of the main verb. This means that if the main verb is in the present tense, the present participle will be translated in the present tense. If the main verb is in any past tense (imperfect, aorist, perfect), the present participle will be translated as an imperfect since it must agree in time (in this case, past) and since it is linear and continuous action being a present participle.

λέγων ταῦτα, βλέπει τὸν κύριον. While he is saying these things,
he sees the Lord.

Since the main verb βλέπει is in the present tense, the
present participle is translated in the present.

λέγων ταῦτα, εἶδεν τὸν κύριον.
While he was saying these things, he saw the Lord.

λέγων ταῦτα, ἔβλεπεν τὸν κύριον.
While he was saying these things, he was seeing the Lord.

Since the main verb in each of the sentences is a past
tense (an aorist and an imperfect), the present participle must
be translated as an imperfect.

4. The adverbial use of the aorist participle. The time
of the aorist participle is prior to that of the main verb. This
means that if the action of the main verb is in the present, the
aorist participle will be translated as a present participle. And
since most participles are temporal, the aorist participle will be
usually translated by "after" introducing a temporal clause.

εἰπὼν ταῦτα, βλέπει τὸν κύριον.
After he has said these things, he sees the Lord.

If the action of the main verb is in the past, the aorist
participle will be translated as a past perfect.

εἰπὼν ταῦτα, εἶδεν τὸν κύριον.
After he had said these things, he saw the Lord.

It should be remembered that since participles do not have
persons, the person of the participle is determined by the person
of the main verb. A singular participle can stand for "I, you, he,
she," or "it," and the plural for "we, you" or "they." Notice the
examples below based on the sentences above.

λέγων ταῦτα, βλέπω τὸν κύριον.
While I am saying these things, I see the Lord.

λέγων ταῦτα, βλέπεις τὸν κύριον.
While you are saying these things, you see the Lord.

εἰπόντες ταῦτα, βλέπομεν τὸν κύριον.
After we have said these things, we see the Lord.

εἰπόντες ταῦτα, βλέπουσιν τὸν κύριον.
After they have said these things, they see the Lord.

5. Vocabulary

βασιλεύω I reign, rule
ἐπιστολή, ἡ letter

σταυρός, ὁ cross
οἶδα I know; perfect form with present meaning

Exercises

A. Translate into English

1. ὁ ἁμαρτωλὸς ὁ ὁμολογῶν τὰς ἁμαρτίας αὐτοῦ οὐκ ἔστιν κακός.
2. πιστεύει εἰς τὸν κύριον τὸν θεραπεύοντα ἀνθρώπους.
3. ὁ πιστεύων οὐκ ἔχει φόβον.
4. ὁ βλασφήμησας οὐκ οἶδεν τὸ μυστήριον ἀλλ' ἔρχεται ἐκ τοῦ διαβόλου.
5. ὁ ἄνθρωπος ὁ λαβὼν τὸν κύριον λαμβάνει τὴν διδαχὴν αὐτοῦ.
6. ἐλπίζων ἐργάζεται.
7. διδάσκων τὰ τέκνα, ὁ ἀπόστολος εἶδεν τὸν δοῦλον.
8. λαβόντες τὰς ἐπιστολάς, ἤλθομεν εἰς τὴν πόλιν.
9. οἱ μαθηται οἱ λαβόντες τὸν κύριον ἐξῆλθον ἐκ τῆς ἐκκλησίας.
10. προσεκύνησαν τῷ κυρίῳ εἰσελθόντι εἰς τὸ ἱερόν.
11. φιλεῖ τὸν διάβολον καὶ βλασφημεῖ τὸν θεόν.
12. ἐδίωξαν τὸν ποιήσαντα τὸν κόσμον.
13. εἰσελθόντες εἰς τὸν οἶκον, ὄψεσθε τὸν ἄρχοντα.
14. εἰπόντες ταῦτα πρὸς τὸν κύριον, εἰσήλθετε εἰς τὴν ἐκκλησίαν.

Because of the difficulty of translating participles and the need for more practice, a few more examples are provided.

1. ὁ ἐκ τοῦ οὐρανοῦ ἐρχόμενος λέγει τοῖς ὄχλοις.
2. ἀγαπᾷ τὸν πατέρα τὸν πέμψαντα αὐτόν.
3. πιστεύσαντες εἰς τὸν κύριον, εἰσήλθομεν εἰς τὴν ζωήν.
4. περιπατεῖ ἐν τῇ ὁδῷ τοῦ κυρίου ἀκούσας τοῦ λόγου.
5. ὁ ἄρτος τοῦ θεοῦ ἐστὶν ὁ καταβαίνων ἐκ τοῦ οὐρανοῦ.
6. διδάσκων τὰ τέκνα, βλέπω τὸν δοῦλον.
7. ὁ ζητῶν τὴν δόξαν τοῦ πέμψαντος αὐτόν τηρήσει τὰς ἐντολὰς αὐτοῦ.
8. δίδαξας τὸν ἀπόστολον, εἰσῆλθεν εἰς τὴν πόλιν.
9. ἐλθὼν πρὸς τοὺς δούλους ἐδίδαξεν αὐτοῖς τὸν νόμον.
10. εἰπὼν τῷ πατρί, ἀπέστειλας τοὺς ἀποστόλους τοῖς ἔθνεσιν.

THE PERFECT PARTICIPLE.   THE GENITIVE ABSOLUTE

1. The first perfect active participle

| | Singular | | | Plural | |
M	N	F	M	N	F
N λελυκώς	λελυκός	λελυκυῖα	λελυκότες	λελυκότα	λελυκυῖαι
G λελυκότος	λελυκότος	λελυκυίας	λελυκότων	λελυκότων	λελυκυιῶν
D λελυκότι	λελυκότι	λελυκυίᾳ	λελυκόσι(ν)	λελυκόσι(ν)	λελυκυίαις
A λελυκότα	λελυκός	λελυκυῖαν	λελυκότας	λελυκότα	λελυκυίας

The sign of the first perfect active masculine and neuter participle is the combination of the reduplication, λε, and κοτ in the ending and for the feminine the reduplication and the κυ in the ending. As in the present and aorist, the masculine and neuter follow the third declension and the feminine the first declension. The translation of the perfect participle generally follows that of the indicative. ὁ λελυκώς, the one who has destroyed; γεγεννημένος, after he has been born.

2. The first perfect middle and passive participle

| | Singular | | | Plural | |
M	N	F	M	N	F
N λελυμένος	λελυμένον	λελυμένη	λελυμένοι	λελυμένα	λελυμέναι
G λελυμένου	λελυμένου	λελυμένης	λελυμένων	λελυμένων	λελυμένων
D λελυμένῳ	λελυμένῳ	λελυμένη	λελυμένοις	λελυμένοις	λελυμέναις
A λελυμένον	λελυμένον	λελυμένην	λελυμένους	λελυμένα	λελυμένας

The reduplication with μεν is a sure sign of the perfect middle and passive participle. Notice the lack of the thematic vowel ο before the μεν. The context will help determine whether the form is middle or passive. Notice also that the masculine and neuter follow the second declension and the feminine the first declension.

3. The genitive absolute is an adverbial participle which has no grammatical connection with the main clause. With the regular adverbial participle there is always agreement in number, gender, and case with some word in the main clause. Thus in εἰσελθὼν εἰς τὸν οἶκον, βλέπει τὸ τέκνον, εἰσελθών agrees in number, gender, and case with βλέπει, i.e., it is a singular masculine nominative participle agreeing with the subject in the verb, "he." This is not the case with the genitive absolute. Two other characteristics

in the genitive absolute are (a) the participle is always in the
genitive case and (b) the subject of the participle (a noun or a
pronoun) is always present and is also in the genitive case. This
means that the subject of the participle is not derived from the
main clause as is the case with the regular adverbial participle.
It is usually translated as a temporal adverbial clause, "while"
being used with the present participle and "after" with the aorist
participle.

λέγοντος τοῦ δούλου ταῦτα, οἱ μαθηταὶ διδάσκουσιν.
While the slave is saying these things, the disciples are
teaching.

ἀκούσαντος τοῦ υἱοῦ τοὺς λόγους, ὁ πατὴρ ἀπῆλθεν.
After the son heard the words, the father went away.

    4. We have discussed only one type of adverbial participle
--the temporal--with the use of "while" and "after." Other types
of adverbial participles are introduced by the adverbial conjunctions "because (causal), "if" (conditional), and "though" (concessive). In some cases, it would be much better to translate the
participle simply as a participle, that is, in the "ing" form.
Thus ἦλθεν κηρύσσων is best translated, "he came preaching." This
is true also for what are called periphrastic participles. This
should cause no problem since it is the same construction as in
English. Thus ὁ Ἰωάννης ἦν βαπτίζων, "John was baptizing." For
the present the student should not be too concerned with these
other types of adverbial participles. Until he has more expertise
in the language, he should translate the adverbial participle as
a temporal clause unless it is obviously inappropriate and does
not make sense.

    5. Verbs beginning with the letters θ, φ, χ reduplicate
in the perfect with τ, π, and κ respectively. Thus θεραπεύω becomes τεθεράπευκα and φιλέω, πεφίληκα.

    6. Vocabulary

διαθήκη, ἡ covenant, will   καινός, ον, η new
ἐκπορεύομαι I go out   σπέρμα, τό seed
εὐχαριστέω I give thanks

Exercises

    A. Recognition

    1. λελυκότος   6. γεγραμμένου (from γράφω)
    2. γεγεννημένον   7. τεθεραπευμένῳ
    3. λελυμένος   8. λελυκυῖαι
    4. λελυκυία   9. λελυμένους
    5. λελυκότι   10. ἀπεσταλμένος

B. Translate into English

1. ὁ λελυμένος ἐκ τῆς ἁμαρτίας οὐκέτι ἁμαρτάνει.
2. ἐποίησεν ὁ θεὸς καινὴν διαθήκην τὴν γεγραμμένην ἐν τῇ γραφῇ.
3. ὁ κύριος τῷ τεθεραπευμένῳ εἶπεν· πορεύου τὴν ὁδόν σου.
4. ἐκπορεύομαι ἐκ τοῦ οἴκου τοῦ λελυμένου καὶ εὐχαριστῶ τῷ θεῷ.
5. γεγεννημένος ἐκ τοῦ σπέρματος Δαυίδ, ὁ Ἰησοῦς βασιλεύσει ἐπὶ τῆς γῆς.
6. ταῦτα εἰπόντος τούτου, ἐπίστευσαν.
7. σώσαντος τοῦ θεοῦ τοῦτον, οἱ ὄχλοι οὐ βλασφημοῦσιν.
8. ποιοῦντος τοῦ πατρὸς ταῦτα, λέγει ὁ υἱὸς τῷ λαῷ.

LESSON 44

REFLEXIVE AND RECIPROCAL PRONOUNS

1. Reflexive pronouns refer back to the person mentioned. It has no special nominative form and no neuter gender in the first and second person. The personal pronoun αὐτός fulfills the reflexive function in the nominative case.

2. The first and second person singular reflexive pronoun: myself, yourself.

	M	F	M	F
G	ἐμαυτοῦ	ἐμαυτῆς	σεαυτοῦ	σεαυτῆς
D	ἐμαυτῷ	ἐμαυτῇ	σεαυτῷ	σεαυτῇ
A	ἐμαυτόν	ἐμαυτήν	σεαυτόν	σεαυτήν

Notice that the masculine forms in both the first and second person are second declension and the feminine first declension. You are already familiar with these endings. The ἐμ is the clue to the first person and the σε is the clue to the second person singular reflexive pronouns.

3. The third person singular reflexive pronoun has three genders: himself, itself, herself.

	M	N	F
G	ἑαυτοῦ	ἑαυτοῦ	ἑαυτῆς
D	ἑαυτῷ	ἑαυτῷ	ἑαυτῇ
A	ἑαυτόν	ἑαυτό	ἑαυτήν

Notice that the masculine and neuter follow the second declension forms and the feminine the first declension. The ἑ with the singular ending is the sign of the third person singular reflexive pronoun.

4. There is only one set of plural endings which serve for all three persons: ourselves, yourselves, themselves.

	M	N	F
G	ἑαυτῶν	ἑαυτῶν	ἑαυτῶν
D	ἑαυτοῖς	ἑαυτοῖς	ἑαυταῖς
A	ἑαυτούς	ἑαυτά	ἑαυτάς

The plural endings distinguish these from the third person singular. Again the masculine and neuter take second declension

101

endings and the feminine first declension endings.

5. The reciprocal pronoun is ἀλλήλων, of one another. Only three forms occur in the New Testament: ἀλλήλων, of one another, ἀλλήλοις, to or for one another, and ἀλλήλους, one another. These are all plural forms.

6. The declension of πολύς, πολλή, πολύ, much, many, has a few irregularities that one needs to observe: (1) All forms except the nominative and accusative singular of the masculine and neuter take the double λ (λλ); (2) The masculine nominative singular is πολύς and the accusative is πολύν; (3) The neuter nominative and accusative singular is πολύ. All the rest of the masculine and neuter forms are regular second declension and the feminine forms are regular first declension endings.

	Singular			Plural		
	M	N	F	M	N	F
N	πολύς	πολύ	πολλή	πολλοί	πολλά	πολλαί
G	πολλοῦ	πολλοῦ	πολλῆς	πολλῶν	πολλῶν	πολλῶν
D	πολλῷ	πολλῷ	πολλῇ	πολλοῖς	πολλοῖς	πολλαῖς
A	πολύν	πολύ	πολλήν	πολλούς	πολλά	πολλάς

7. The declension of μέγας, μεγάλη, μέγα, great, is very much like πολύς except that instead of a double λ, all forms except the nominative and accusative singular of the masculine and neuter take the long μεγαλ stem.

	Singular			Plural		
	M	N	F	M	N	F
N	μέγας	μέγα	μεγάλη	μεγάλοι	μεγάλα	μεγάλαι
G	μεγάλου	μεγάλου	μεγάλης	μεγάλων	μεγάλων	μεγάλων
D	μεγάλῳ	μεγάλῳ	μεγάλῃ	μεγάλοις	μεγάλοις	μεγάλαις
A	μέγαν	μέγα	μεγάλην	μεγάλους	μεγάλα	μεγάλας

8. Vocabulary

ἀνάστασις, ἡ resurrection
δεύτερος, ον, α second
εὐλογέω I bless

μικρός, ον, α small, little
ναός, ὁ temple

Exercises

A. Recognition

1. σεαυτόν
2. ἑαυτῶν
3. ἐμαυτῷ
4. ἑαυτοῦ
5. ἑαυτά

6. πολύν
7. πολλή
8. μεγάλου
9. μέγαν
10. πολλά

B. Translate into English

1. οὐ δύναμαι ἐγὼ ποιεῖν ἀπ' ἐμαυτοῦ οὐδέν, οὐδὲ μικρόν.
2. πολλοὶ οὖν ἀκούσαντες ἐκ τῶν μαθητῶν αὐτοῦ εἶπον· ἀληθής ἐστιν ὁ λόγος οὗτος.
3. πολλὰ οὖν καὶ ἄλλα σημεῖα ἐποίησεν ὁ Ἰησοῦς.
4. ἐν δὲ τῇ ἐσχάτῃ ἡμέρᾳ τῇ μεγάλῃ τῆς ἑορτῆς ὁ Ἰησοῦς ἔκραξεν· ἐάν τις διψᾷ ἐρχέσθω πρός με καὶ πινέτω.
5. ἀγαπήσεις τὸν ἀδλεφόν σου ὡς σεαυτόν.
6. φανέρωσον σεαυτὸν τῷ κόσμῳ.
7. μισήσουσιν ἀλλήλους καὶ οὐκ εὐλογήσουσι τὸν θεόν.
8. σπείρουσιν σπέρματα εἰς τὴν γῆν.
9. ἐγερθήσεται ἐν τῇ δευτέρᾳ ἀναστάσει καὶ ὁ θεός οὐκ ἔσται ὁ ναὸς αὐτοῦ.

LESSON 45

REVIEW 7 (LESSONS 40-44)

1. Review the forms of the present, aorist, and perfect participles in Lessons 40, 41, and 43. Remember what forms take the first declension, the second declension, and the third declension. Identify the following: λύοντος, λυομένους, λυσάσῃ, λυθέντι, λιπόντι, λυθείσῃ, λελυκυίας, λελυμένου, λύουσαν, λυούσαις, λιπούσης, ὄντα, λελυκόσι, λυσάμενον, λελυκός, λιπόντας.

2. Review the translation of the participles in Lesson 42 and then translate the following:

ὁ ἀγαπῶν τὸν ἀδελφὸν αὐτοῦ ἐξέρχεται ἐκ τοῦ θεοῦ.
εἶδον αὐτὸν διδάσκοντα τὸν λαόν.
εἶπεν τοῖς ἐλθοῦσιν.
πιστεύσας ὁ ἀπόστολος εἰσῆλθεν εἰς τὸ ἱερόν.
ἐλθόντος τοῦ διδασκάλου, ὁ ἀπόστολος ἐζήτησεν αὐτόν.

3. Review the reflexive and reciprocal pronouns in Lesson 44. Identify and translate the following: σεαυτῷ, ἑαυτό, ἑαυτούς, ἐμαυτῆς, ἑαυτόν, σεαυτήν.

4. Review the declensions of πολύς and μέγας. Identify the following: πολλοῖς, μεγάλην, πολλοῦ, πολύ, μέγαν, μεγάλου, πολλῷ, πολύν, πολλή, μεγάλους.

A.　　᾽Ησαν δὲ ῞Ελληνές[1] τινες ἐκ τῶν ἀναβαινόντων ἵνα προσκυνή-
σωσιν ἐν τῇ ἑορτῇ. οὗτοι οὖν προσῆλθον Φιλίππῳ τῷ ἀπὸ Βηθσαϊδᾶ[2]
τῆς Γαλιλαίας,[3] καὶ ἠρώτων αὐτὸν λέγοντες· θέλομεν τὸν ᾽Ιησοῦν
ἰδεῖν.[4] Φίλιππος ἔρχεται καὶ λέγει τῷ ᾽Ιησοῦ. ὁ δὲ ᾽Ιησοῦς
ἀποκρίνεται αὐτῷ λέγων· ἐλήλυθεν ἡ ὥρα ἵνα δοξασθῇ ὁ υἱὸς τοῦ
ἀνθρώπου. ἐὰν μὴ ὁ κόκκος[5] πέσων εἰς τὴν γῆν ἀποθάνῃ, αὐτὸς
μόνος μένει· ἐὰν δὲ ἀποθάνῃ, πολὺν καρπὸν φέρει. ὁ φιλῶν τὴν
ψυχὴν αὐτοῦ ἐν τῷ κόσμῳ τούτῳ εἰς τὴν ζωὴν οὐ φυλάξει[6] αὐτήν. ἐὰν
ἐμοί τις διακονῇ[7] ἐμοὶ ἀκολουθείτω καὶ ὅπου εἰμὶ ἐγώ, ἐκεῖ καὶ ὁ
διάκονος[8] ὁ ἐμὸς ἔσται. καὶ τιμήσει αὐτὸν ὁ πατήρ. νῦν ἡ ψυχή
μου τετάρακται,[9] καὶ τι εἴπω; πάτερ, σῶσόν με ἐκ τῆς ὥρας ταύτης.
ἀλλὰ διὰ τοῦτο ἦλθον εἰς τὴν ὥραν. πάτερ, δόξασόν σου τὸ ὄνομα.
ἦλθεν οὖν φωνὴ ἐκ τοῦ οὐρανοῦ. ὁ οὖν ὄχλος ὁ ἀκούσας εἶπεν·
ἄγγελος αὐτῷ λελάληκεν. εἶπεν ὁ ᾽Ιησοῦς· οὐ δι' ἐμὲ ἡ φωνὴ αὕτη
γέγονεν ἀλλὰ δι' ὑμᾶς. νῦν κρίσις ἐστὶν τοῦ κόσμου τούτου. νῦν
ὁ ἄρχων τοῦ κόσμου τούτου ἐκβληθήσεται ἔξω.

　　　　ταῦτα ἐλάλησεν ὁ ᾽Ιησοῦς καὶ ἀπελθὼν ἐκρύβη[10] ἀπ' αὐτῶν.
πεποιηκότος αὐτοῦ σημεῖα ἔμπροσθεν αὐτῶν, οὐκ ἐπίστευον εἰς αὐτόν,
ἵνα ὁ λόγος ῾Ησαΐου[11] τοῦ ποοφήτου πληρωθῇ. καὶ ὁ ᾽Ιησοῦς εἶπεν·
ὁ πιστεύων εἰς ἐμέ οὐ πιστεύει εἰς ἐμὲ ἀλλ' εἰς τὸν πέμψαντά με,
καὶ ὁ θεωρῶν ἐμὲ θεωρεῖ τὸν πέμψαντά με. ὁ ἀθετῶν[12] ἐμὲ καὶ μὴ
λαμβάνων τὰ ῥήματα μοῦ ἔχει τὸν κρίνοντα αὐτόν.

[1]Greeks [2]Bethsaida [3]Galilee [4]to see [5]grain [6]will keep [7]should
serve [8]servant [9]is troubled [10]he hid himself [11]of Isaiah
[12]rejects

B.　　καὶ εἰσπορεύονται εἰς Καφαρναούμ·[1] καὶ εὐθὺς ἐν τῷ σαββάτῳ
εἰσελθὼν εἰς τὴν συναγωγὴν ἐδίδασκεν. ἦν δὲ διδάσκων αὐτοὺς ὡς
ἐξουσίαν ὁ ἔχων, καὶ οὐχ ὡς οἱ γραμματεῖς. καὶ ἄνθρωπος ἐν πνεύματι ἀκαθάρτῳ[2] ἔκραξεν λέγων αὐτῷ· ἦλθες ἀποκτεῖναι ἡμᾶς. οἶδα σε
τίς εἶ ὁ ἅγιος τοῦ θεοῦ. εἶπεν αὐτῷ ὁ ᾽Ιησοῦς· ἐξελθὲ ἐξ αὐτοῦ
καὶ φωνῆσαν φωνῇ μεγάλῃ ἐξῆλθεν ἐξ αὐτοῦ τὸ πνεῦμα τὸ ἀκάθαρτον.
καὶ εὐθὺς ἐκ τῆς συναγωγῆς ἐξελθόντες ἦλθον εἰς τὸν οἶκον τῶν
μαθητῶν.

[1]Capernaum [2]unclean

LESSON 47

THE INDICATIVE OF THE VERB δίδωμι

1. Thus far all the verbs we have studied with the exception of εἰμί have been ω verbs. The only other type of verb conjugation is that of the μι verbs. The first of these verbs that
we take up is the verb δίδωμι, to give. One characteristic of
this verb is the reduplication in the present and imperfect with
the ι. Thus δι precedes the stem. The stem of δίδωμι is δο-,
though sometimes it will appear as δω-.

2. The present active indicative

	Singular	Plural
1	δίδωμι	δίδομεν
2	δίδως	δίδοτε
3	δίδωσι(ν)	διδόασι(ν)

3. The present middle and passive indicative

	Singular	Plural
1	δίδομαι	διδόμεθα
2	δίδοσαι	δίδοσθε
3	δίδοται	δίδονται

The endings are entirely regular. The σαι ending of the
second person singular is the regular ending that we have seen in
the perfect middle and passive indicative while the usual η is the
irregular contracted form. Also the thematic vowels have been
dropped. For all the forms of this verb see pp. 220-222.

4. The future forms δώσω, δώσομαι, δοθήσομαι are entirely
regular.

5. The imperfect active indicative

	Singular	Plural
1	ἐδίδουν	ἐδίδομεν
2	ἐδίδους	ἐδίδοτε
3	ἐδίδου	ἐδίδοσαν

Notice (1) that the presence of the reduplication with δι;
(2) ου in the singular and ο in the plural; (3) that it is entirely regular except for the third person plural which has σαν instead
of ν as in the first person singular.

106

6. The aorist forms ἔδωκα, ἐδόμην, ἐδόθην are regular except that the κ replaces the σ in the active, and the middle is second aorist.

7. The first perfect forms δέδωκα and δέδομαι are regular. Be sure to notice the difference between the aorist and perfect active forms. The aorist active is ἔδωκα and the perfect active is δέδωκα.

8. If some forms have not been given, do not be concerned since they can easily be recognized or are not frequently used.

In summary, in recognizing these forms which in general follow the regular pattern, watch for the reduplication δι which indicates a present or imperfect (with the augment preceding, it would be an imperfect), the reduplication δε which indicates a perfect, and the stem δω with augment which indicates aorist. The future also has the short stem but should cause no problems since the endings are regular.

9. Vocabulary

ἄρα then
ἔρημος, ον, ἡ solitary, deserted; as a noun, desert, wilderness (fem.)

σωτηρία, ἡ salvation
τρίτος, ον, η third
τυφλός, ον, η blind; as substantive, blind man

Exercises

A. Recognition

1. ἐδίδομεν
2. δίδοτε
3. ἔδωκε
4. δέδωκε
5. δώσετε

6. δίδοται
7. διδόασι
8. δίδωσι
9. ἐδόθη
10. δέδοται

B. Translate into English

1. ἔδωκεν τῷ τυφλῷ σωτηρίαν.
2. ἄρα ἐδίδοσαν αὐτὸ τῷ τρίτῳ ἀγγέλῳ τῷ ὄντι ἐν τῇ ἐρήμῳ.
3. θεωροῦσιν τὴν δόξαν μου ἣν δέδωκάς μοι.
4. αἰτεῖτε καὶ δοθήσεται ὑμῖν.
5. δώσουσιν αὐτοῖς ἐξουσίαν ἐπὶ πνευμάτων ἀκαθάρτων.
6. ὑμῖν δέδοται τὰ μυστήρια τῆς βασιλείας τῶν οὐρανῶν.
7. ἐδόθη ἡ κεφαλὴ αὐτῇ.
8. ἔδωκεν αὐτὸ αὐτοῖς.

107

LESSON 48

THE OTHER MOODS OF THE VERB δίδωμι

1. The present active subjunctive of δίδωμι is regular.
The second aorist active subjunctive is identical with the present except that it drops the reduplication δι. For all the forms
of this verb see pp. 220-222.

	Singular	Plural
1	διδῶ	διδῶμεν
2	διδῷς	διδῶτε
3	διδῷ	διδῶσι(ν)

2. The present active imperative of δίδωμι is regular
except for the second person singular.

	Singular	Plural
2	δίδου	δίδοτε
3	διδότω	διδότωσαν, διδόντων

The second aorist active is identical to the above except
that it drops the reduplication and its second person singular
form is δός.

3. The infinitive of the verb δίδωμι.

Present active infinitive   διδόναι
Aorist active infinitive   δοῦναι

Notice the typical αι of the infinitive.

4. The present active participle in the nominative forms
are διδούς, διδόν, διδοῦσα. The second aorist is the same without
the reduplication. The genitives are διδόντος, διδόντος, διδούσης
and the rest of the forms are regular. The present middle and
passive forms in the nominative are διδόμενος, διδόμενον, διδομένη.

5. Vocabulary

δέω I bind
ἐγγίζω I draw near
θλῖψις, θλίψεως, ἡ affliction,
    tribulation

κατοικέω I inhabit, dwell
ὅμοιος, ον, α like
ἐπί on, upon (gen.); on, in,
    above (dat.)

108

Exercises

A. Recognition

1. διδῶτε
2. δοῦναι
3. δόντι
4. δούσης
5. δῷ

6. δῷς
7. διδόντα
8. διδῶ
9. διδόναι
10. δόν

B. Translate into English

1. ἐδέξατο λόγους δοῦναι ὑμῖν.
2. δοὺς δὲ αὐτῇ χεῖρα ἤγειρεν αὐτήν.
3. καὶ οὐκ ἔστιν ἐν ἄλλῳ ἡ σωτηρία, οὐδὲ γὰρ ὄνομά ἐστιν ἕτερον ὑπὸ τὸν οὐρανὸν τὸ δεδομένον ἐν ἀνθρώποις ἐν ᾧ δεῖ σωθῆναι ἡμᾶς.
4. πάντοτε δὸς ἡμῖν τὸν ἄρτον τοῦτον.
5. ὁ γὰρ ἄρτος τοῦ θεοῦ ἐστιν ὁ διδοὺς ζωὴν τῷ κόσμῳ.
6. δότε τῷ ἔχοντι.
7. διδάσκει ἡμᾶς διδόναι ἀγαθὰ τοῖς τέκνοις ἡμῶν.
8. αἰτεῖτε ἵνα δῷ σημεῖον.
9. ἐδόξασαν τὸν θεὸν τὸν δόντα ἐξουσίαν τοῖς ἀνθρώποις.

THE VERB τίθημι

1. The present active indicative of τίθημι, I put, place, lay down. The stem is θε, although θη or θει replaces it sometimes. For all the forms of this verb see pp. 220-222.

	Singular	Plural
1	τίθημι	τίθεμεν
2	τίθης	τίθετε
3	τίθησι(ν)	τιθέασι(ν)

Notice that (1) the reduplication τι is always found in the present and imperfect; (2) like δίδωμι it has the long vowel (η) in the singular and the short vowel (ε) in the plural; (3) it is very similar to δίδωμι.

2. The present middle and passive indicative will have the reduplication with τι and the regular endings of those forms.

	Singular	Plural
1	τίθεμαι	τιθέμεθα
2	τίθεσαι	τίθεσθε
3	τίθεται	τίθενται

3. The imperfect active indicative will have the reduplication with the augment and the same endings as δίδωμι.

	Singular	Plural
1	ἐτίθην	ἐτίθεμεν
2	ἐτίθεις	ἐτίθετε
3	ἐτίθει	ἐτίθεσαν

4. The imperfect middle and passive indicative can easily be recognized since it will have the augment with the reduplication and the regular middle and passive endings of the imperfect. The first person singular form is ἐτιθέμην.

5. The first aorist active indicative drops the reduplication and takes the stem θη. Like δίδωμι it has κ in place of σ. Otherwise it is regular.

	Singular	Plural
1	ἔθηκα	ἐθήκαμεν
2	ἔθηκας	ἐθήκατε
3	ἔθηκε(ν)	ἔθηκαν

6. The aorist middle indicative is second aorist with the stem θε. It has the regular endings of the second aorist middle. It drops the reduplication. The first person singular is ἐθέμην.

7. The future forms θήσω, θήσομαι, τεθήσομαι are regular but notice the future passive. Since the stem already is θη and the passive has the θη in the ending, the stem has changed to τε.

8. The present active subjunctive has the reduplication with the long endings.

	Singular	Plural
1	τιθῶ	τιθῶμεν
2	τιθῇς	τιθῆτε
3	τιθῇ	τιθῶσι(ν)

The second aorist active subjunctive is identical with the above but without the reduplication.

9. The present active imperative has the reduplication with the stem θε.

	Singular	Plural
2	τίθει	τίθετε
3	τιθέτω	τιθέτωσαν

The second aorist active imperative is exactly the same (but without the reduplication) except for the second person singular which is θές. As usual the second person singular needs to be learned but the other forms follow the regular pattern.

10. The present active infinitive is τιθέναι; the present middle and passive infinitive, τίθεσθαι; the aorist active infinitive, θεῖναι, and the aorist middle infinitive, θέσθαι. Notice the familiar sign (αι) of the infinitive.

11. The participial forms in the present nominative are τιθείς, τιθέν, τιθεῖσα for the active and τιθέμενος, τιθέμενον, τιθεμένη for the middle and passive; for the second aorist nominanative θείς, θέν, θεῖσα in the active and θέμενος, θέμενον, θεμένη in the middle.

12. The perfect indicative reduplicates with τε and takes the stem θει with the regular endings. The first person singular in the active is τέθεικα.

13. If some forms have not been provided, do not be concerned since they can easily be recognized or are not used frequently.

Summary: It may seem that you have been given too much to learn. Remember that (1) the endings are generally regular; (2) the present, imperfect, and aorist can easily be distinguished since the present and the imperfect always have the reduplication with τι while the aorist has no reduplication; (3) the perfect reduplicates with τε; (4) it is not necessary to memorize these forms but only to recognize them.

Exercises

A. Recognition

1. τιθέασιν
2. θήσω
3. θῶ
4. ἔθηκεν
5. θῶμεν
6. τιθείς

7. ἐτίθεσαν
8. τιθέντες
9. ἔθεντο
10. τίθησιν
11. θέτε
12. τέθεικα

B. Translate into English

1. θήσω τὸ πνεῦμά μου ἐπ' αὐτόν.
2. ἔθηκεν τὸ σῶμα ἐν τῷ καινῷ αὐτοῦ μνημείῳ.
3. τιθεὶς τὰς χεῖρας ἐπ' αὐτήν, εὐλογεῖ αὐτήν.
4. ἐθεώρουν ποῦ τέθειται.
5. ἔρχεται ἵνα τὴν ψυχὴν αὐτοῦ θῇ ὑπὲρ ἡμῶν.
6. ποῦ τεθείκατε αὐτόν;
7. ἐτίθην αὐτοὺς παρὰ τὰς πόδας τῶν ἀποστόλων.
8. θεμέλιον (foundation) γὰρ ἄλλον ὁ ἄνθρωπος δύναται θεῖναι.

LESSON 50

THE VERB ἵστημι

1. The present active indicative of ἵστημι, I stand, place, has ι as reduplication. The stem is στα but also lengthens to στη. For all the forms of this verb see pp. 220-222.

	Singular	Plural
1	ἵστημι	ἵσταμεν
2	ἵστης	ἵστατε
3	ἵστησι(ν)	ἱστᾶσι(ν)

Notice (1) the ι which takes the place of the reduplication (take note of the rough breathing); (2) the lengthened stem στη in the singular and the regular stem στα in the plural; (3) the identical endings as δίδωμι and τίθημι.

2. The present middle and passive indicative are regular with the stem στα.

	Singular	Plural
1	ἵσταμαι	ἱστάμεθα
2	ἵστασαι	ἵστασθε
3	ἵσταται	ἵστανται

3. The future of ἵστημι is στήσω and is regular.

4. The imperfect active indicative

	Singular	Plural
1	ἵστην	ἵσταμεν
2	ἵστης	ἵστατε
3	ἵστη	ἵστασαν

Notice that (1) it does not take the augment but has the ι; (2) it follows the present in having the lengthened stem στη in the singular and στα in the plural; (3) since it does not take the augment three forms are identical with the present. The context will help determine what tense it is.

5. The imperfect middle and passive indicative present no difficulty except that because there is no augment two forms are identical with the present middle indicative--the first and second person plural.

113

6. The aorist indicative has two forms: the first aorist ἔστησα translated "I placed, or caused to stand," and the second aorist ἔστην translated "I stood." The first is transitive taking an object, and the second is intransitive. They follow the regular first aorist and second aorist endings respectively.

7. The first person singular of the perfect active indicative is ἔστηκα. The endings are regular. It is easy to confuse this with the first aorist corresponding to ἔδωκα and ἔθηκα but it must be remembered that ἵστημι has the first aorist with the σ--ἔστησα. The perfect, however, is always translated as a present. The pluperfect εἱστήκειν is translated as an imperfect.

8. Another peculiarity of ἵστημι is that the passive forms are translated as active.

9. The present subjunctive is regular with the ι and the aorist subjunctive is regular without the ι. The first person singular of the present active subjunctive is ἱστῶ and of the aorist active subjunctive, στῶ.

10. The present active imperative has the ι and the stem with στα and is regular except for the second person singular which is ἵστη. The aorist imperative drops the ι, takes the stem στη and the second person singular is στῆθι. It has the regular endings.

11. The present active infinitive is ἱστάναι and the middle and passive infinitive is ἵστασθαι. The aorist active infinitive is στῆναι.

12. The present nominative participles are ἱστάς, ἱστάν, ἱστᾶσα in the active and ἱστάμενος, ἱστάμενον, ἱσταμένη in the middle and passive. The aorist is identical except that it drops the ι.

13. There are two sets of perfect participle forms: the first perfect ἑστηκώς, ἑστηκός, ἑστηκυῖα and the second perfect ἑστώς, ἑστός, ἑστῶσα. Both sets of forms, though perfect, are usually translated as present.

Exercises

A. Recognition

1. ἔστησεν
2. στάς
3. ἔστη
4. στῆναι
5. στήσει

6. στάντος
7. σταθήσεται
8. ἵστην
9. ἐστήσαμεν
10. ἵσταμαι

B. Translate into English

1. ἔστησεν αὐτὸν ἐπὶ τὸ ἱερόν.
2. πῶς οὖν σταθήσεται ἡ βασιλεία αὐτοῦ;
3. ἡ μήτηρ σοῦ καὶ οἱ ἀδελφοί σου ἔξω ἑστήκασιν.
4. ὁ δὲ Ἰησοῦς ἐστάθη ἔμπροσθεν τοῦ ἄρχοντος.
5. οὐ δύναται ἡ βασιλεία στῆναι ἀλλὰ τέλος ἔχει.
6. τινὲς τῶν ἑστηκότων ἤκουσαν τὸν λόγον.
7. ἔγειρε καὶ στῆθι.
8. εἶδον τοὺς νεκροὺς ἑστῶτας ἐνώπιον τοῦ θρόνου.

LESSON 51

OTHER μι VERBS

1. The principal parts of ἀφίημι, I leave, permit, forgive, are present active indicative, ἀφίημι; future active indicative, ἀφήσω; aorist active indicative, ἀφῆκα; perfect passive indicative, ἀφέωνται; aorist passive indicative, ἀφέθην. The third person plural form is given instead of the first person singular for the perfect passive since that is the only form that is found in the New Testament. With few exceptions, its forms follow τίθημι exactly. ἀφίημι is a compound word from ἀπό (ἀφ before the rough breathing and vowel) and ἵημι. The present stem will be ιε while the ε will be the second aorist. Thus ἀφίετε is present and ἄφετε is second aorist, ἀφιέναι is present infinitive and ἀφεῖναι is second aorist. The most frequently occurring forms are the aorist active ἀφῆκα, the future active ἀφήσω, the future passive ἀφεθή-σομαι, and the aorist participle expecially in the nominative masculine plural form, ἀφέντες.

2. συνίημι, I understand, has the same verb stem as ἀφίημι and thus follows ἀφίημι exactly. It does not, however, occur as frequently as ἀφίημι.

3. δείκνυμι, I show, has a few forms in the μι system but is conjugated like verbs in the ω system. The future form is δείξω, the aorist ἔδειξα, the aorist imperative δεῖξον, the aorist infinitive δεῖξαι. More than ninety per cent of the forms found in the New Testament come from the forms given above.

4. ἀπόλλυμι is translated in the active voice as "I destroy, ruin, lose," and in the middle as "I die, perish, am lost." The future active is ἀπολέσω (the Attic future ἀπολῶ), the future middle ἀπολοῦμαι, the first aorist active ἀπώλεσα, the aorist infinitive ἀπολέσαι. The second perfect active participle ἀπο-λωλώς in the perfect middle participle usually has the meaning "lost." The present and imperfect will always have the double λλ and the future and aorist the single λ. A very few times the endings follow the ω verbs.

5. φημί, I say, appears in the great majority of the cases in the form ἔφη which can be an imperfect or second aorist indi-cative third person singular, but it is probably always the latter. The only other forms in which it appears are φημί, I say; φησί(ν) he says, and φασί(ν), they say.

116

Exercises

A. Recognition

1. ἀφῆκαν
2. ἀφίενται
3. ἀφήσει
4. ἀφέντες
5. συνίετε
6. συνιέναι
7. δείξω
8. ἔδειξεν

9. ἀπόλλυται
10. δεῖξον
11. ἀπόληται
12. ἀπώλεσεν
13. ἀπολέσει
14. ἀπολέσαι
15. ἀπολωλότα

B. Translate into English

1. τότε ἀφίησιν αὐτὸν ὁ διάβολος.
2. ἀφήκαμεν τὰς ἁμαρτίας αὐτοῖς.
3. ἀφήσει ὑμῖν ὁ πατὴρ ὑμῶν.
4. ἀφέντες αὐτὸν ἀπῆλθον πάντες.
5. τότε συνῆκαν οἱ μαθηταί.
6. ὁ συνίων συνιέτω.
7. καὶ σοὶ δείξω ἐκ τῶν ἔργων μου τὴν πίστιν.
8. ἔδειξέν μοι τὴν πόλιν τὴν ἁγίαν Ἰερουσαλήμ.
9. ἀπελθὼν δεῖξον σεαυτὸν τῷ ἱερεῖ.
10. αὐτὸν ἔβαλεν εἰς ὕδατα ἵνα ἀπολέσῃ αὐτόν.
11. εὗρον τὸ πρόβατόν μου τὸ ἀπολωλός.
12. ἦλθες ἀπολέσαι ἡμᾶς;

117

LESSON 52

REVIEW 8 (LESSONS 47-51)

Review the forms of the μι verbs (Lessons 47-51). Study
the characteristics of these verbs and identify and translate the
following:

δίδομεν	διδῶ
ἔθηκα	δούς
δεδώκαμεν	διδομένου
ἐδίδομεν	δοθήτω
ἔδωκαν	ἐδιδόμην
ἔστηκα	ἱστῶμεν
δίδοται	τιθεῖσα
δοθῆναι	τίθετε
διδότω	ἵσταμεν
ἀφῆκαν	ἀπολέσει
δεῖξον	δείξω
ἀπόληται	ἀφέντες
ἀφήσω	συνίετε

A.   Ταῦτα ἐλάλησεν ὁ 'Ιησοῦς, καὶ ἐπάρας[1] τοὺς ὀφθαλμοὺς αὐτοῦ
εἰς τὸν οὐρανὸν εἶπεν· πάτερ, ἐλήλυθεν ἡ ὥρα· δόξασόν σου τὸν
υἱόν, ἵνα ὁ υἱὸς δοξάσῃ σε, καθὼς ἔδωκας αὐτῷ ἐξουσίαν πάσης
σαρκός, ἵνα δώσῃ αὐτοῖς ζωὴν αἰώνιον. αὕτη δέ ἐστιν ἡ αἰώνιος
ζωή, ἵνα γινώσκωσίν σε τὸν μόνον ἀληθινὸν θεὸν καὶ ὃν ἀπέστειλας
'Ιησοῦν Χριστόν. ἐγώ σε ἐδόξασα ἐπὶ τῆς γῆς, τὸ ἔργον τελειώσας[2]
ὃ δέδωκάς μοι ἵνα ποιήσω· καὶ νῦν δόξασόν με σύ, πάτερ, παρὰ σεαυτῷ τῇ δόξῃ ἣν εἶχον πρὸ τοῦ τὸν κόσμον εἶναι παρὰ σοί. ἐφανέρωσά
σου τὸ ὄνομα τοῖς ἀνθρώποις οὓς ἔδωκάς μοι ἐκ τοῦ κόσμου. σοὶ
ἦσαν κάμοὶ αὐτοὺς ἔδωκας, καὶ τὸν λόγον σου τετήρηκαν. νῦν ἔγνωκαν ὅτι ταῦτα ὅσα[3] δέδωκάς μοι παρὰ σοῦ εἰσίν· ὅτι τὰ ῥήματα ἃ
ἔδωκάς μοι δέδωκα αὐτοῖς, καὶ αὐτοὶ ἔλαβον καὶ ἔγνωσαν ἀληθῶς
ὅτι παρά σου ἐξῆλθον, καὶ ἐπίστευσαν ὅτι σὺ με ἀπέστειλας.

       ταῦτα εἰπὼν 'Ιησοῦς ἐξῆλθεν σὺν τοῖς μαθηταῖς αὐτοῦ.
ἀφῆκεν αὐτοὺς καὶ τις ἦλθεν πρὸς αὐτόν· λέγει τῷ 'Ιησοῦ· τὶ τὴν
ψυχήν σου ὑπὲρ ἐμοῦ θήσεις; λέγει αὐτῷ ὁ 'Ιησοῦς· ἵνα ὁ πατὴρ
σοῦ ἄφῃ σοι τὰς ἀμαρτίας. ὁ ἀμαρτωλὸς οὐ δύναται στῆσαι ἔμπροσθεν
τοῦ θεοῦ, ἐὰν μὴ ἀφεθῇ ἡ ἀμαρτία αὐτοῦ. ἀλλὰ καὶ νῦν ἐξουσίαν
ἔχει ὁ υἱὸς τῷ ἀνθρώπῳ ἀφιέναι ἀμαρτίας ἐπὶ τῆς γῆς. λέγω οὖν σοι·
ὅτι πιστεύεις. ἀφέωνται αἱ ἀμαρτίαι σου. καὶ ἔθηκεν τὰς χεῖρας
ἐπὶ τὴν κεφαλὴν τοῦ ἀνθρώπου. μετὰ ταῦτα εὑρίσκει τὸν ἀδελφὸν
αὐτοῦ καὶ ἀφέντες πάντα ἠκολούθησαν τῷ 'Ιησοῦ.

[1]when he lifted up [2]having completed   [3]as much as

B.   καὶ τὴν ψυχήν μου τίθημι ὑπὲρ τῶν προβάτων. καὶ ἄλλα πρόβατα ἔχω ἃ οὐκ ἔστιν ὧδε. διὰ τοῦτο με ὁ πατὴρ ἀγαπᾷ ὅτι ἐγὼ
τίθημι τὴν ψυχήν μου, ἵνα πάλιν λάβω αὐτήν. οὐδεὶς αἴρει αὐτὴν
ἀπ' ἐμοῦ, ἀλλὰ θήσω αὐτὴν ἀπ' ἐμαυτοῦ. ἐξουσίαν ἔχω θεῖναι
αὐτήν, καὶ ἐξουσίαν ἔχω πάλιν λαβεῖν αὐτήν. διὰ τοῦτο οἱ
ἀπόστολοι ἔθηκαν αὐτὸν ὡς θεμέλιον[1] τῆς ἐκκλησίας καὶ ὁ θεὸς
ἔθηκεν αὐτὸν τὴν δεξιὰν[2] αὐτοῦ.

[1]foundation [2]at the right hand

LESSON 54

1 JOHN 1:1-3

1. Beginning with this lesson, a reading from the Greek
New Testament will alternate with a review of Greek grammar. We
present in this lesson a reading from 1 John. The grammar and
vocabulary will be geared to the passage to be read. There will
be some repetition for review purposes. The student should be
introduced at this point to Sakae Kubo's Reader's Greek-English
Lexicon of the New Testament since in it the vocabulary is con-
veniently set forth for each reading lesson. The student should
be made aware of the arrangement of that book. Since words
occurring more than fifty times are not repeated under chapter and
verse of the book, these should be reviewed. If the student has
learned the vocabulary presented in previous lessons, he should
already know all the words in this list. However, the student
can always refer to Appendix I, pp. 274-277, of the Lexicon if
he needs to. Words found in the Special Vocabulary should be
learned since these are also not repeated under chapter and verse.

2. Read 1 John 1:1-3 noting the helps below. The student
should read the passage orally with the helps given below. After
he has gone through once and worked out the difficult areas, then
he should write out his translation. This procedure should be
followed for each reading lesson.

3. Reading helps

1:1 ὅ. This neuter relative pronoun used several times here is
better translated "that which" instead of "that" or "which"
since it does not have an antecedent.

ἀκηκόαμεν is an irregular perfect form of ἀκούω.

ἑωράκαμεν is irregular in the sense that it has a double
augment, the ε and ω. Since its initial letter is a vowel
(ὁράω, to see), the lengthened vowel alone would ordinarily
replace the reduplication of a consonant for a perfect, but
it has also added an additional augment, the ε.

τοῖς ὀφθαλμοῖς. The dative is frequently translated with
"to" or "for" but it would not work here. The dative has
several functions besides that of an indirect object or a
dative of advantage or disadvantage. Here it functions as
an instrument and should be translated as "with."

ἐθεασάμεθα. Remember that this word is deponent which means that the middle voice should be translated as an active.

1:2 ἥτις. This is the feminine nominative form of the indefinite relative pronoun ὅστις which is a combination of the relative pronoun ὅς and the indefinite pronoun τις. Both parts are declined. The only forms used in the New Testament are the nominatives which are

	Masculine	Neuter	Feminine
S	ὅστις	ὅτι (or ὅ τι)	ἥτις
P	οὕτινες	ἅτινα	αὕτινες

Though sometimes it emphasizes quality, it has come to be used as an ordinary relative.

1:3 καί before ὑμῖν. Here and in the next two instances it must be translated as "also" instead of as "and."

μεθ' from μετά. Since the next word begins with a vowel it drops the α and since the vowel has a rough breathing, the τ becomes a θ.

ἡμετέρα, our, is a possessive adjective and is declined as any other adjective. Possessive adjectives are found only in the first and second person. They are used when emphasis is desired. The nominative forms are given below:

	First Person, my and our			Second Person, your		
S	ἐμός	ἐμόν	ἐμή	σός	σόν	σή
P	ἡμέτερος	ἡμέτερον	ἡμετέρα	ὑμέτερος	ὑμέτερον	ὑμετέρα

Frequently in Greek the verb "to be" is omitted but needs to be added in English. The last sentence is such a case.

4. Vocabulary

All words occurring more than twenty times in the New Testament should be learned and those which we list under this heading although they may be used less than twenty times. For this passage the additional following two words should be learned:

κοινωνία, ἡ
ἡμέτερος

5. Prepare a written translation of 1 John 1:1-3.

LESSON 55

GENERAL REVIEW 1

1. The key to translating Greek is a mastery of the verb.
The student must be able to recognize each individual verb form.
Each form has some identifying mark or marks. Be sure that you
are well acquainted with these. (See Reader's Lexicon, pp. 313-
315). More importantly the student should be able to translate
each form correctly. It is not enough to know the forms; the forms
must be translated correctly.

Up to this point you have learned the forms but in piece-
meal fashion. It is now time to bring everything together. In
this way, it is easier to see how one form relates to another and
thus make it easier to learn, recognize, and remember the forms.
At the present time this will serve as a review of all the verb
forms.

2. Review the present and future indicative ω verb forms
and translation in Reader's Lexicon, p. 288. For the forms only
turn to p. 318 and compare the present and future forms in the
indicative and see how they are alike and how they differ. Notice
especially the difference in the passive. (The only difference is
that the future passive adds θη before the σ). Notice that in
the present the middle and passive have identical forms.

3. Concentrate on the translation of these forms. If you
learn the translation of the present, all you need to do is to
change the translation to the future for the future tense. Remember that the middle should always be thought of as active first.
In other words begin by translating it the same way as the active
and then add "for ---self/selves." Especially concentrate on the
passive in both present and future since the future is slightly
different from the present: "I am being loosed" and "I shall be
loosed."

Exercises: Recognition and translation

1. πιστεύεις   9. ποιησόμεθα
2. ὀφθήσῃ   10. λέγω
3. ἀκούονται   11. ζητήσεσθε
4. ἀκούει   12. διδάσκομεν
5. διδαχθησόμεθα   13. ποιήσῃ
6. θέλουσι   14. κηρυχθήσομαι
7. πιστεύσω   15. πιστεύεται
8. βλέπετε   16. ἀκουσθήσεται

122

LESSON 56

1 JOHN 1:4-7

1. Read 1 John 1:4-7.

2. Reading helps

1:4 ταῦτα. This is a demonstrative pronoun. Remember that the nominative forms of this in the masculine, neuter, and feminine are οὗτος, τοῦτο and αὕτη in the singular and οὗτοι, ταῦτα, αὗται in the plural. See Lesson 15 for other forms.

ᾖ πεπληρωμένη. In Greek no auxiliary verbs are ordinarily required in the imperfect, perfect, or pluperfect tenses. However, in some cases they are used as here. When the verb "to be" is used with the present participle it emphasizes continuing action and with the perfect or pluperfect participle, continuing results. This is called a periphrastic tense.

1:5 οὐδεμία is the feminine nominative of the combination οὐδέ, not even, and εἷς, one, forming οὐδείς, no one or nothing in the neuter. οὐδέ is not declined but εἷς is. As an adjective, which it is here, it is simply translated as "no." The declension for it is as follows:

	M	N	F
N	εἷς	ἕν	μία
G	ἐνός	ἐνός	μιᾶς
D	ἐνί	ἐνί	μιᾷ
A	ἕνα	ἕν	μίαν

Naturally there is no plural form.

1:7 πάσης is the feminine singular genitive form of the pronominal adjective, πᾶς, every, all, whole, whose declension is as follows:

	Singular			Plural		
	M	N	F	M	N	F
N	πᾶς	πᾶν	πᾶσα	πάντες	πάντα	πᾶσαι
G	παντός	παντός	πάσης	πάντων	πάντων	πασῶν
D	παντί	παντί	πάσῃ	πᾶσι(ν)	πᾶσι(ν)	πάσαις
A	πάντα	πᾶν	πᾶσαν	πάντας	πάντα	πάσας

123

3. Vocabulary

   ψεύδομαι

4. Prepare a written translation of 1 John 1:4-7.

GENERAL REVIEW 2

1. Study the consonants which combine with σ and the resulting double consonant and those that drop before the σ in
Lesson 9. The verb stem of κηρύσσω is κηρυκ, not κηρυσσ, and the
future of ἔχω takes the rough breathing, ἕξω. Tell what is the
basic verb and what has happened to the verb stem to form the
following future verbs and translate them.

ἄξω   δοξάσεις
σώσω   διώξει
ἕξουσι   πέμψω
κηρύξετε   δέξομαι
διδάξει

2. Study the future of liquid verbs in Lesson 17. Notice
that these future forms are the same as those of the contract
verbs in the present. Learn well the list of common liquid verbs
that take this type of future. Translate the following:

κρίνει   ἀποστελῶ
κρινεῖ   ἀποστέλλει
ἀποκτενῶ   ἐρῶ
ἀποκτείνω   βαλῶ
ἐγερεῖς   βάλλω
ἀροῦμεν   μενῶ
αἴρετε   μενεῖς

LESSON 58

1 JOHN 1:8-2:2

1. Read 1 John 1:8-2:2

2. Reading helps

1:8 ἑαυτούς can be first, second, or third person (See Lesson 44). One form serves for all three persons in the plural. However, since it is connected with πλανῶμεν it can only be first person here, "ourselves."

πλανῶμεν could be indicative (α + ο = ω) or subjunctive (α + ω= ω) but is an indicative here since it is not in a subjunctive construction. Usually a subjunctive will have an ἐάν or ἵνα preceding it.

1:9 ὁμολογῶμεν can only be subjunctive since the present (ε + ο = ου) would be ὁμολογοῦμεν while the contraction in the subjunctive (ε + ω= ω) would give us ὁμολογῶμεν. Also the ἐάν before it signals a subjunctive.

ἀφῇ can only be an aorist subjunctive of ἀφίημι, I forgive, without the ι preceding the η. Review Lesson 51.

1:10 οὐχ. οὐκ is used instead of οὐ when the next word begins with a vowel. However, if it also has the rough breathing as in this case, it becomes οὐχ.

2:1 μή is used instead of οὐ usually with verbs outside of the indicative mood including infinitives and participles.

ἁμάρτητε comes from ἁμαρτάνω. One look at the stem indicates that it is a second aorist.

3. Vocabulary

ψεύστης, ὁ
ἱλασμός, ὁ

4. Prepare a written translation of 1 John 1:8-2:2.

LESSON 59

GENERAL REVIEW 3

1. Review the imperfect and second aorist forms in the
Reader's Lexicon, pp. 289-290. Turn to p. 318 to compare the two
forms side by side. Notice that the active and middle endings
are identical. The passive endings are quite different so concentrate on these. However the imperfect middle and passive are the
same so that you need to concentrate only on the second aorist
passive forms. Actually they are more like the active endings
except for the preceding η.

2. Turn to pp. 289-290 in the Reader's Lexicon and learn
the translation of these forms. Remember that the imperfect is
linear action in past time and therefore the ing form of the main
verb is always used in translating the active and middle. In the
passive the ing is found in the word "being." Since it is past
time the verb "was" is used with all the forms. Remember that
every verb does not have a second aorist ending. Only certain
verbs follow this pattern. The majority follow the first aorist
pattern. The second aorist is simple past action and is translated with the English past tense. Notice how the passive is translated. The auxiliary verbs "was/were" are necessary to make the
verb passive.

Recognition and translation

1. ἐλυόμην	14. ἔλυε
2. ἔλυον	15. ἐλύπεσθε
3. ἔλιπον	16. ἐλύομεν
4. ἐλύετε	17. ἐλιπόμεθα
5. ἐλυόμεθα	18. ἐστράφημεν
6. ἐλίπετε	19. ἔλυες
7. ἐστράφης	20. ἐλίπετο
8. ἐδεχόμην	21. ἐσωζόμεθα
9. ἔφαγε	22. ἐπίστευε
10. ἠσθίετε	23. ἐβάλετε
11. ἤγειρεν	24. ἐλάβομεν
12. ἐδιδασκόμην	25. ἐβάλλομεν
13. ἐδοξάζετο	

LESSON 60

I JOHN 2:3-8

1. Read I John 2:3-8.

2. Reading helps

2:3 ἐγνώκαμεν is a somewhat irregular perfect of γινώσκω
since it does not have a reduplication and has a shortened
stem. The second aorist form of it is ἔγνων   so that
there should be no confusion in recognizing this perfect
form.

2:4 ὅτι is used at times like a quotation mark before a direct
address. In such cases it is not translated.

2:5 ἄν after the relative pronoun is translated "ever." It
adds an element of indefiniteness to a clause.

2:6 μένειν is an infinitive which is used in indirect discourse.
Instead of "to remain in him," it would be smoother to
translate "that he remains in him."

2:7 εἴχετε is the imperfect of ἔχω. The second aorist form is
ἔσχον and the perfect is ἔσχηκα. Its future is irregular
in that it takes a rough breathing, ἕξω. The endings are
all regular.

2:8 ἀληθές is the neuter nominative singular form of the adjective ἀληθής. Its other forms are:

	Singular		Plural	
	MF	N	MF	N
N	ἀληθής	ἀληθές	ἀληθεῖς	ἀληθῆ
G	ἀληθοῦς	ἀληθοῦς	ἀληθῶν	ἀληθῶν
D	ἀληθεῖ	ἀληθεῖ	ἀληθέσι(ν)	ἀληθέσι(ν)
A	ἀληθῆ	ἀληθές	ἀληθεῖς	ἀληθῆ

Notice that (1) this is a third declension adjective and
(2) the masculine and feminine have the same forms.

3. Vocabulary

    παλαιός

128

LESSON 61

GENERAL REVIEW 4

1. Learn well the list of second aorist verbs and their present forms on pp. 290-291 of the Reader's Lexicon.

Recognition and translation

1. ἔβαλλε	13. ἔσχομεν
2. ἀπέθανεν	14. ἔφη
3. ἐφάγομεν	15. ἥμαρτες
4. ἔπιε	16. κατέβην
5. ἐβάλετε	17. ἦλθεν
6. εὕρετε	18. ἥμαρτον
7. ἐγενόμην	19. ἠγάγομεν
8. ἔγνω	20. ἐφάγετε
9. εἴδετε	21. ἔγνωμεν
10. ἔπεσεν	22. ἐλάβετε
11. εἶπον	23. ἐπίομεν
12. ἔβαλεν	24. ἐβάλομεν

LESSON 62

I JOHN 2:9-14

1. Read I John 2:9-14.

2. Reading helps

2:9 εἶναι, to be, is an infinitive used in indirect discourse. Translate as in 2:6.

2:11 οἶδεν is in a perfect tense but is always translated as a present. The endings follow the first perfect but without the κ.

2:12 διά with the accusative is "on account of" or "because of," with the genitive, "through."

2:13 τόν does not have a noun or other substantive following.
   14 In such cases, it should be translated "the one" or "that one." It has demonstrative force.

3. Vocabulary

σκάνδαλον, τό

4. Prepare a written translation of I John 2:9-14.

LESSON 63

GENERAL REVIEW 5

1. Review the endings for the first aorist and the first perfect indicative on pp. 291-292 in the <u>Reader's Lexicon</u>. Compare the forms side by side on p. 318. Notice that in the active the endings are identical except that the perfect has the ϰ instead of the σ. The aorist has the augment and the perfect the reduplication. In the middle and passive, it is better to compare the first aorist with the second aorist. The endings are virtually identical except that the first aorist has the σα before the endings. The second person singular forms are different. In the passive it is identical with the exception that the first aorist has the ϑη before the endings which are like the active endings of the imperfect. The perfect, like the present and imperfect, has the same forms for the middle and passive. It has endings similar to the present without the thematic vowel. It also has the reduplication. One should have very little difficulty in recognizing these forms. Verbs beginning with a vowel take an augment rather than reduplication.

2. Turn to pp. 291 and 292 in the <u>Reader's Lexicon</u> and learn the translation of these forms. Notice that the first aorist is translated as a simple past in the same way as the second aorist. The perfect has "has/have" in all its forms.

3. Notice that the second perfect forms are the same as the first perfect except that they have second perfect stems and no ϰ.

Recognition and translation

1. πεπιστεύϰαμεν		9. ἐθεράπευσεν	
2. ἐλύσατε		10. ἐποιησάμην	
3. ἐποίησεν		11. ἤλπιϰα	
4. γεγέννημαι		12. λέλυσαι	
5. ἐδίδαξας		13. γέγραπται	
6. ἐπιστεύσαμεν		14. λελάληϰα	
7. ἐδέξασθε		15. λελύμεθα	
8. ἤϰουσαν		16. μεμαρτύρημαι	

1. Read I John 2:15-21.

2. Reading helps

2:15 μὴ ἀγαπᾶτε. ἀγαπᾶτε (α + ε = α) can be either a present active indicative or imperative. However, since μή cannot be used with an indicative, this must be an imperative. Since this is a present tense, continuous action is emphasized. It should be translated "Do not continue to love" or "Stop loving."

μηδέ, not, not even, is used because it is connected with the imperative.

τά is used in the same way as τόν in vss. 13 and 14 except that it is a neuter plural and therefore should be translated, "the things."

2:16 πᾶν τό "everything which is." The "is" is understood.

2:17 εἰς τὸν αἰῶνα is an idiom meaning "forever." Sometimes it is in the plural, εἰς τοὺς αἰῶνας. Other times a genitive is added: εἰς τοὺς αἰῶνας τῶν αἰώνων, forever and ever. Ordinarily αἰῶν, ὁ means "age."

2:18 γεγόνασιν is the second perfect of γίνομαι. The first person singular is γέγονα and it has the regular perfect endings but without the κ.

2:19 ἐξ ἡμῶν. ἐκ becomes ἐξ before a word beginning with a vowel.

ἐξῆλθαν is a case of a second aorist verb taking a first aorist ending but without the σ. One would ordinarily expect ἐξῆλθον but this transition is noticed frequently in the New Testament. The student should have not trouble recognizing this and the translation is not affected.

ἦσαν, they were, is the imperfect third person plural of εἰμί.

μεμενήκεισαν is in the pluperfect tense. Pluperfects are rare but the signs are the reduplication and the ει in the ending.

	Singular		Plural	
1	(ε)λελύκειν	I had loosed	(ε)λελύκειμεν	We had loosed
2	(ε)λελύκεις	You had loosed	(ε)λελύκειτε	You had loosed
3	(ε)λελύκει	He had loosed	(ε)λελύκεισαν	They had loosed

There are basically three types of conditional sentences. The first kind is the true to fact condition (first class) in which the εἰ and the indicative are found in the protasis (the if clause).

εἰ ὁ θεὸς ὑπὲρ ἡμῶν, τίς καθ᾽ ἡμῶν;
If God is for us, who is against us?

This states a true fact--God is for us. There is no problem regarding translation. The second type which we have encountered several times already is the true future condition (third class). In these ἐάν and the verb in the subjunctive will be found in the protasis. There is no problem regarding translation. The third type is the contrary to fact condition (second class) in which εἰ and the verb in the indicative is found in the protasis but the apodosis has an ἄν as well. This is what we have in vs. 19.

εἰ γὰρ ἐξ ἡμῶν ἦσαν, μεμενήκεισαν ἄν μεθ᾽ ἡμῶν.
For if they were from us (they were not), they <u>would have</u> remained with us (which they did not).

It states the opposite of the facts. Notice how the apodosis is translated. Since the verb in the protasis is in a past tense, you translate with "would have" and the past participle "remained." If the verb in the protasis is in the present tense, you translate with "would" rather than "would have."

εἰ ἔχετε πίστιν. . . , ἐλέγετε ἄν . . . .
If you have faith, you would say. . . .

2:20 πάντες is nominative plural and the subject of the verb which is the second person plural. This should be translated "All you" or "You all."

3. Vocabulary

ψεῦδος, τό

4. Prepare a written translation of 1 John 2:15-21.

133

LESSON 65

GENERAL REVIEW 6

1. Notice what happens when certain consonants precede ϑ
on p. 291 of the Reader's Lexicon. Most of the time you can
identify these forms without any trouble even when these changes
take place. But in a few instances it is important to know what
took place before you can identify the form.

2. Learn the liquid aorist verbs (p. 291, Reader's Lexicon)
that are commonly used and be able to identify them.

3. Learn the commonly used irregular perfect verbs listed
on p. 292, Reader's Lexicon. It is imperative that you learn
these.

Recognition and translation

1. ἤχϑην
2. ἐπέμφϑημεν
3. ἀπέστειλεν
4. ἠθελήσατε
5. ἐκρίνατε
6. ἔμειναν
7. ἤγειρεν
8. ἔμεινα
9. ἀκηκόαμεν
10. ἑώρακεν

11. ἀπέσταλκας
12. εἰρήκατε
13. ἀναβεβήκαμεν
14. ἐγνώκατε
15. ἐλήλυθας
16. γέγονεν
17. ἔσχηκα
18. οἴδαμεν
19. ἀκηκόατε

134

I JOHN 2:22-29

1. Read I John 2:22-29.

2. Reading helps

2:22 τίς, who, what, why, in contrast to the indefinite pronoun τις (someone, anyone) is an interrogative pronoun. The difference is that the interrogative pronoun has the accent. It is declined exactly as τις.

εἰ μή "if not" literally but better "except."

The οὐκ is redundant and should not be translated.

2:24 μείνῃ has to be an aorist subjunctive since the present would have the present stem and would be μένῃ.

2:25 ἐπηγγείλατο from ἐπαγγέλλομαι is deponent but it is also a liquid verb, that is, a verb whose stem ends in λ, μ, ν, or ρ. Liquid verbs are first aorists without the σ. Thus this form is first aorist deponent.

2:27 ἐδίδαξεν is the aorist of διδάσκω.

2:28 σχῶμεν. Since ἔσχον is the second aorist indicative of ἔχω, σχ- represents the second aorist stem and this form is subjunctive.

2:29 εἰδῆτε is related to οἶδα, and I know, rather than εἶδον, I saw. It is the second aorist subjunctive form. The aorist subjunctive form of εἶδον would be ἴδητε. The second aorist stem of εἶδον in moods other than indicative is ἰδ. These should not be confused.

3. Prepare a written translation of I John 2:22-29.

LESSON 67

GENERAL REVIEW 7

1. The pluperfect (p. 293, <u>Reader's Lexicon</u>) is not too common but it is well to learn the main identifying marks especially of the active form, i.e., the reduplication and the ει in the ending. Some verbs do not have the augment. See Lesson 64.

2. Learn the common irregular pluperfect verbs on p. 293.

3. Learn the indicative forms of the verb "to be" on p. 293.

Recognition and translation

1. ἐλελύκειν		9. ἤμην	
2. ἐληλύθει		10. ἦσαν	
3. εἰρήκει		11. ἔσεσθε	
4. ᾔδειν		12. ἐστί	
5. ἐλελύκειμεν		13. ἦν	
6. εἶ		14. ἔσται	
7. ἐστέ		15. ἐσόμεθα	
8. ἔσῃ			

LESSON 68

I JOHN 3:1-10

1. Read I John 3:1-10.

2. Reading helps

3:1 ἴδετε is second aorist imperative of εἶδον, I saw, beheld.

κληθῶμεν comes from καλέω, I call. The α drops out in some of its forms.

ἔγνω is the second aorist of γινώσκω. The second aorist active forms follow:

	Singular	Plural
1	ἔγνων	ἔγνωμεν
2	ἔγνως	ἔγνωτε
3	ἔγνω	ἔγνωσαν

Notice that the third person plural form does not follow the regular ending of the second aorist.

3:2 ὅμοιοι. This word always takes the dative; thus αὐτῷ.

ὀφόμεθα is the future of ὁράω, to see, and is deponent in the future.

3:5 ἄρῃ is the aorist subjunctive of αἴρω, I remove. It is a liquid verb which has shortened its stem but is a first aorist without the σ.

3:6 πᾶς ὁ ἐν αὐτῷ μένων. Notice that ὁ μένων goes together but ἐν αὐτῷ has been placed between them. This type of structure is typical of Greek. This means that one should glance through the sentence to find words that agree and go with one another.

3:7 μηδείς is the same as οὐδείς except that it is used with verbs which are not in the indicative mood.

3:10 Notice that ἐστίν is the verb of the subject τὰ τέκνα. With neuter plural subjects, a singular verb is usually used.

137

LESSON 69

GENERAL REVIEW 8

1. Review what deponent verbs are (p. 294, Reader's Lexicon).

2. Learn the common deponent forms in the present (p. 294).

3. Learn the common future deponent forms (p. 295).

Recognition and translation

1. ἀπεκρίθη
2. ἔρχῃ
3. ἔρχεσθε
4. ἤρχοντο
5. ἀποκρίνεται
6. ἐγενόμην
7. ἐργάζονται
8. δέξεσθε
9. γεύεσθε
10. δύναται
11. πορεύεται
12. προσεύχεσθε
13. βησόμεθα

14. βουλόμεθα
15. ἅπτῃ
16. ἀσπάζεσθε
17. ἀρνούμεθα
18. ἀρχόμεθα
19. παραγίνεται
20. ἔσεσθε
21. λήμψεται
22. γνώσεσθε
23. ἐλεύσομαι
24. γενήσεται
25. φάγῃ
26. ὄψεσθε

LESSON 70

I JOHN 3:11-20

1. Read I John 3:11-20.

2. Reading helps

3:12 Κάϊν is Cain.

3:14 μεταβεβήκαμεν is the perfect of μεταβαίνω. The second aorist stem of βαίνω is βη and this is also found in the perfect.

3:15 μένουσαν is a present active feminine singular accusative participle of μένω modifying ζωήν which is also feminine accusative singular. Here it is best translated as "abiding."

3:16 ἔθηκεν is the first aorist with κ of τίθημι, I put or place, here I lay down is more appropriate. The lack of reduplication (with τι) is again a sure sign of an aorist.

3:18 ἀγαπῶμεν is a present subjunctive with μή. A first person plural subjunctive without ἐάν or ἵνα preceding is a hortatory subjunctive and should be translated with "Let us." Here "Let us not continue to love," or "Let us stop loving."

λόγῳ, γλώσσῃ, ἔργῳ and ἀληθείᾳ are instrumental datives and should be translated as "with." "With word," etc.

3:19 γνωσόμεθα is from γινώσκω. The future of γινώσκω has the root γνω and is deponent.

πείσομεν is the future of πείθω. The θ drops before the σ in the future.

3:20 καταγινώσκω takes as object the genitive case. ἡμῶν is the object connected to καταγινώσκω rather than a possessive with ἡ καρδία.

μείζων is the comparative form of μέγας, great. It is declined as follows:

	Singular		Plural	
	MF	N	MF	N
N	μείζων	μεῖζον	μείζονες/μείζους	μείζονα/μείζω
G	μείζονος	μείζονος	μειζόνων	μειζόνων
D	μείζονι	μείζονι	μείζοσι(ν)	μείζοσι(ν)
A	μείζονα/μείζω	μεῖζον	μείζονας/μείζους	μείζονα/μείζω

Notice that (1) the masculine and feminine have the same forms; (2) it follows the third declension throughout. In comparatives the thing compared (in this case τῆς καρδίας ἡμῶν) is always in the genitive case where ἤ, than, or a preposition is not used. This is the genitive of comparison and a "than" must be placed before it.

3. Prepare a written translation of I John 3:11-20.

GENERAL REVIEW 9

1. Review the present subjunctive of εἰμί and λύω on p. 297
in the Reader's Lexicon. Notice that the present subjunctive endings of εἰμί are the endings of the present subjunctive of λύω and
that the endings of λύω are simply the lengthened vowels of the
present indicative, active, middle and passive except for the third
person active plural which becomes ω from ου. Compare this on the
verb chart on p. 318.

2. Review the first and second aorist subjunctive of λύω and
λείπω. Notice that the σ coming before the long ending is the
only difference between the first aorist and present subjunctive
in the active and middle. The passive of the first aorist has the
ϑ but the same endings as the active. The second aorist has the
same endings as the first aorist but without the σ in the active
and middle and ϑ in the passive. Notice the difference between
the active and passive in the second aorist. Compare the endings
in the chart on p. 318.

3. Learn the translation of the subjunctive on p. 297.
Remember that the subjunctive has an aorist but it does not indicate past time. It stands for simple action. The only difference
between the translation of the present and the aorist is that the
former indicates linear action and the latter simple action. If
you wish to make the distinction, you could add "continue to" in
the present, e.g., "I might continue to loose." Notice that the
translation given is with the ἵνα and ἐάν clause respectively.

Recognition and translation

1. ὦμεν   9. λύσῃ
2. διδάσκωμεν   10. λύσητε
3. ἀκούσωσι   11. λύπωνται
4. πιστεύσωμεν   12. δέξωνται
5. σωθῶσιν   13. λύω
6. εἰσέλθωμεν   14. διδαχθῇς
7. ἔχωσι   15. λύπω
8. ἦς

LESSON 72

I JOHN 3:21-4:6

1. Read I John 3:21-4:6.

2. Reading helps

3:21 ἡμῶν is the object of καταγινώσκῃ. See on vs. 20 above.

3:22 ἐάν preceded by a relative pronoun is the same as ἄν and should be translated "ever."

τὰ ἀρεστά is an adjective used as a substantive.

3:23 πιστεύω frequently takes dative of thing believed in.

ἔδωκεν is aorist of δίδωμι. Without the reduplication with δι it cannot be imperfect and without the reduplication with δε it cannot be perfect.

3:24 οὗ is a relative pronoun in the genitive. Ordinarily one should expect ὅ since it functions as an object. Its antecedent is πνεῦμα but since it is in the genitive case (πνεύματος), the relative has been attracted to that same case. Such occurrences are not rare.

4:1 ἐξεληλύθασιν is the perfect of ἐξέρχομαι. The verb ἔρχομαι is extremely irregular as you no doubt have already found. The present is ἔρχομαι, future ἐλεύσομαι, second aorist ἦλθον, and perfect ἐλήλυθα. The last two forms are not deponent.

4:3 τὸ τοῦ ἀντιχρίστου. πνεῦμα is understood after τό.

4:2 ἐληλυθότα is the perfect participle of ἔρχομαι. The nominative forms are ἐληλυθώς, ἐληλυθός, ἐληλυθυῖα.

Ἰησοῦν Χριστὸν ἐν σαρκὶ ἐληλυθότα is indirect discourse and it would be better to translate this clause by adding a "that" before it and making the participial clause into a regular verb clause. Thus: "that Jesus Christ has come in flesh."

4:4 ἤ is always used with a comparative (μείζων) with the meaning "than." In such cases the word compared is not in the genitive but is in the same case as the other word to

142

which it is compared.

3. Vocabulary

    ψευδοπροφήτης, ὁ

4. Prepare a written translation of 1 John 3:21-4:6.

LESSON 73

GENERAL REVIEW 10

1. Read carefully pp. 296-297 in the <u>Reader's Lexicon</u> which explains the eight uses of the subjunctive.

Recognition (of underlined words) and translation

1. ἐὰν <u>ἔλθῃ</u>, λάβετε αὐτόν.
2. ἦλθεν <u>ἵνα</u> σωθῆτε.
3. <u>ἀκούωμεν</u> τῶν λόγων τοῦ κυρίου.
4. <u>μὴ εἴπῃς</u>.
5. <u>ἔλθω ἢ μὴ ἔλθω</u>;
6. ἐὰν <u>μὴ ἀκούσητε</u> τὸν κύριον, οὐ <u>μὴ πιστεύσητε</u>.
7. ὃς δι' <u>ἂν πιστεύσῃ</u>, ὄψεται τὸν θεόν.
8. ἐποίησεν ἄνθρωπον ὅπως <u>ἀγαπήσῃ</u> αὐτόν.

LESSON 74

I JOHN 4:7-16

1. Read I John 4:7-16.

2. Reading helps

4:7 ἀγαπῶμεν is another hortatory subjunctive.

4:8 ἔγνω is a gnomic aorist (an aorist expressing axioms which avail for all time) and is translated as a present.

4:9 ἀπέσταλκεν is the perfect of ἀποστέλλω.

4:10 ἀπέστειλεν is the first aorist of ἀποστέλλω. It is a liquid verb and therefore takes first aorist without the σ. Liquid verbs sometimes change their stem but this does not make them second aorist.

4:11 ἀγαπᾶν is the infinitive of ἀγαπάω. It is somewhat irregular since α + ει ordinarily contract to ᾳ. However the infinitive in contract verbs does not take the subscript.

4:12 τετελειωμένη. . .ἐστιν is a periphrastic perfect and should be translated together as "is perfected."

3. Vocabulary

μονογενής
ἱλασμός, ὁ

4. Prepare a written translation of I John 4:7-16.

145

GENERAL REVIEW 11

1. Review the imperative forms on pp. 299-300 of the
Reader's Lexicon. Remember that (1) there are no first person
forms; (2) there are only present and aorist tenses. The key to
learning the imperative forms is the second person plural since
the third person singular and plural are built upon it. The
second person plural is identical with its indicative counterpart
except that the aorist forms drop the augment. Once the second
person plural form is obtained, the third person forms drop the
ε and add ω and ωσαν respectively for the singular and the plural.
Observe each of the forms on pp. 299-300 and see how regularly
this follows. The only form one has to learn is the second person
singular in each tense and voice. Compare the forms on p. 319.

2. Learn the translation for these forms. Remember that
the aorist is not a past tense in the imperative. It only indicates simple action. The translation of the present and aorist
are basically identical except that the present implies linear
action. Here again one can add "continue to" for the present,
e.g., "Continue to loose." Notice that the third person forms
always begin with "Let" and the third person pronoun or noun subject.

Recognition and translation

1. λυσάσθωσαν	10. ἴσθι
2. λύου	11. λῦσαι
3. λιπέτω	12. λυέτωσαν
4. λυέτω	13. λύεσθε
5. λυθήτω	14. λύθητε
6. λιπέτωσαν	15. λίπητε
7. λῦσον	16. λυθήτωσαν
8. ἔστω	17. λύθητι
9. λῦε	

I JOHN 4:17-5:5

1. Read I John 4:17-5:5.

2. Reading helps

4:18 φόβος οὐκ ἔστιν. To translate a sentence smoothly, it is
sometimes necessary to add a "there" at the beginning.
This is the case where the verb is a form of the verb "to
be" or "to become," the subject is a noun, and there is no
predicate nominative or adjective. This is the situation
in this verse.

4:20 ὅτι is another example of its use as a signal for a direct
quotation and should not be translated.

5:1 γεννήσαντα is the aorist active participle of γεννάω.

5:2 ὅταν is a combination of ὅτε and ἄν, whenever.

5:4 πᾶν τὸ γεγεννημένον is neuter. The neuter is used instead
of the masculine when the thought is generalized or uni-
versalized.

νικήσασα is an aorist participle. In this context it should
be translated as a present though as a simple action
(punctiliar) rather than linear.

5:5 εἰ μή should be translated "except."

3. Prepare a written translation of I John 4:17-5:5.

GENERAL REVIEW 12

1. Review the infinitive forms on p. 301 of the <u>Reader's</u> <u>Lexicon</u>. Remember that (1) there is only one form for each tense and voice; (2) while infinitives are sometimes found in the perfect tense, they will be predominatly found in only two tenses, the present and the aorist; (3) the second aorist follows the present in the active and middle and the first aorist in the passive without the ϑ; (4) in the present and perfect the middle and passive forms are identical respectively; (5) αι at the end of a verb ending is a good clue since only the present and second aorist active forms do not have it.

2. Learn the translation for each form. Remember that the aorist is not a past tense but only indicates simple action. To bring out the continuous action of the present one can translate the infinitive by adding "to continue" before the "to," e.g., "to continue to loose."

Recognition and translation

1. ἔχειν
2. λῦσαι
3. λύεσθαι
4. ἐκβαλεῖν
5. λύειν
6. λελύσθαι
7. πιστευσαι
8. λιπεῖν
9. λύσασθαι
10. ἐλθεῖν
11. σωθῆναι
12. λελυκέναι
13. ἔρχεσθαι
14. λιπέσθαι
15. ἀποθανεῖν
16. λυθῆναι
17. δοξάζειν

LESSON 78

I JOHN 5:6-15

1. Read I John 5:6-15.

2. Reading helps

5:6   διά with genitive is translated "through."

μαρτυροῦν is a present active neuter nominative participle.
Contraction has taken place between the stem μαρτυρε and
the ending ον. The same thing has happened in 2:7:
μαρτυρε + οντες = μαρτυροῦντες.

5:7   If you check the King James Version you will notice that
it has part of vss. 7, 8 which are omitted in the Greek
text. This portion of the text was in the Latin Vulgate
but not in any of the Greek manuscripts till the fifteenth
or early sixteenth century. It was on the basis of this
one Greek manuscript that Erasmus added this passage into
his Greek text on which the KJV is ultimately based. It
is no longer included in recent translations.

5:8   εἰς τὸ ἕν. The predicate nominative and the predicate
accusative are sometimes replaced by εἰς with the accusative under Semitic influence. Thus this should be translated simply as "one."

5:10   εἰς τὸν υἱόν. The verb πιστεύω takes besides the dative,
εἰς and the thing believed. This should be translated
"in." Notice the second part of the verse where πιστεύω
takes the dative (τῷ θεῷ).

5:11   ζωὴν αἰώνιον ἔδωκεν ἡμῖν ὁ θεός. Notice where you have to
go to pick up the subject. This is not unusual at all for
Greek sentences. Always look for the nominative noun or
pronoun for your subject throughout the sentence before
translating. Only after you cannot find such do you look
for your subject in your verb.

5:13   εἰδῆτε comes from οἶδα not εἶδον.

πιστεύουσιν looks like a present indicative third person
plural but is a present participle in the dative plural
instead. Notice the τοῖς before it which signals a dative
participle with this form.

149

5:14 αἰτώμεθα is middle and has the sense "for ourselves."

ἡμῶν (also in vs. 15) is in the genitive but is the object of ἀκούει. The verb ἀκούω takes both the accusative and the genitive. Watch for this.

5:15 ᾐτήκαμεν is the perfect of αἰτέω. Notice that the diphthong αι has become ῃ for the augment, the ι of the diphthong becoming a subscript. No reduplication is possible with a verb beginning with a vowel. The α has lengthened to an η as usual before the consonantal ending.

3. Prepare a written translation of 1 John 5:6-15.

LESSON 79

GENERAL REVIEW 13

1. Study carefully the uses of the infinitive on pp. 301-302 in the Reader's Lexicon.

Translation.

1. ἐλθὲ πρὶν ἀποθανεῖν τὸ τέκνον μου.
2. οἶδεν γὰρ ὁ πατὴρ ὑμῶν πρὸ τοῦ ὑμᾶς αἰτῆσαι αὐτόν.
3. πρὸ τοῦ σε Φίλιππον φωνῆσαι, εἶδόν σε.
4. μετὰ δὲ τὸ ἐγερθῆναί με ἐλεύσομαι εἰς τὴν Γαλιλαίαν.
5. ἐπίστευσεν αὐτὸν διὰ τὸ εἶναι αὐτὸν ἐκ θεοῦ.
6. ἐν δὲ τῷ περιπατεῖν αὐτὸν εἶδεν τὸν ἀπόστολον.
7. ὁ υἱὸς ἦλθεν εἰς τὸ δοξασθῆναι.
8. ἐδίδαξεν ἡμᾶς ὥστε ἡμᾶς ἔχειν τὴν δύναμιν.
9. εἰσῆλθεν εἰς τὴν ἐκκλησίαν, λέγων ἑαυτὸν εἶναι προφήτην.

LESSON 80

1 JOHN 5:16-21; JOHN 1:1-5

1. Read 1 John 5:16-21; John 1:1-5.

2. Reading helps

5:16 ἴδῃ is the second aorist subjunctive of ὁράω.

5:18 γεννηθείς is the aorist passive masculine nominative participle of γεννάω. The nominative forms of λύω in the aorist passive participle are λυθείς, λυθέν, λυθεῖσα.

αὐτοῦ is genitive because ἅπτομαι takes the genitive object. It should be translated "him."

5:20 ἀληθινόν is an adjective used substantivally. It should not be translated "the truth" but "the true one."

5:21 φυλάξατε is the aorist imperative of φυλάσσω. For verbs of this kind the double σ becomes a ξ in the future and aorist.

ἑαυτά is the reflexive pronoun. The neuter is due to the fact that its antecedent is τεκνία.

1:1 ἦν is the imperfect third singular of the verb "to be."

θεός is translated as "a god" by the New World Translation, the Jehovah's Witnesses' version. According to Colwell, in Greek when the predicate nominative precedes the subject it never takes the article so that it is definite without the article. This is one explanation. Another is that the anarthrous (without the article) noun emphasizes the quality of the person or thing rather than his or its identity. Thus the quality is divinity and the translation should be "the Word was divine" or "the Word had Godhood." This is better because to say that the Word was God confuses the thought with the previous statement, "the Word was with God." Since two persons, the Word and God are distinguished, it would be confusing to say here that the Word was God. The Word obviously was not the God with whom He was but He was divine as God was divine. He possessed the same Godhood.

1:3 ἐγένετο is the second aorist of γίνομαι. This word is

152

translated variously, such as "come to be, come, become, originate; be made, created; happen, take place; appear" or as a substitute for εἰμί. The basic meaning is that of "becoming," i.e., of "coming into existence" referring to people, things, and events. Here the meaning is "were made" or "came into existence."

Verse 3 is usually punctuated with a period after γέγονεν. The UBS text, however, places the period after ἕν and thus joins the rest of the verse to the next verse. The period probably should be placed after γέγονεν.

γέγονεν is the perfect of γίνομαι.

3. Prepare a written translation of 1 John 5:16-21; John 1:1-5.

LESSON 81

GENERAL REVIEW 14

1. Review the participial forms on pp. 320-321 in the
Reader's Lexicon. This looks like an imposing list but don't let
that intimidate you. Notice that (1) the feminine forms throughout
are in the first declension; (2) the masculine and neuter take the
third declension in the active forms throughout; (3) the middle
forms throughout take the second declension in the masculine and
neuter (In the present and perfect the middle and passive forms
are identical so this holds true in the passive as well for these).
The forms of the verb "to be" are simply the endings of the present
active participle. The key to recognizing participles is the use
of the third declension endings on verbs, the -ντ- in the masculine active, the first declension endings on verbs, and the -μεν-
in middle participles. It is important to learn the nominative
forms throughout to place each participle under the right tense and
voice. Notice that the second aorist follows the present endings
in the active and middle.

Recognition

1. λελυμένην
2. ποιησάμενα
3. πιστεύσασα
4. λαμβάνοντι
5. λυομένου
6. λαβόντες
7. λυομένῃ
8. γινωσκούσῃ
9. διδασκούσαις
10. δόξαζον
11. ἐλθόν
12. λελυκυῖαν
13. ζητήσαντα

14. οὖσα
15. οὖσαις
16. ὄντα
17. ὄντι
18. ὄντες
19. ἔχοντας
20. θαυμάσασαν
21. λελυκότος
22. λυθεῖσα
23. λυθέντων
24. λυθείσῃ
25. ποιήσασι

LESSON 82

JOHN 1:6-16

1. Read John 1:6-16.

2. Reading helps

1:6 ἐγένετο can be translated as "came" or "appeared" here.

ἀπεσταλμένος is clearly a perfect participle of ἀποστέλλω. The augment in a participle shows that it is perfect. The lack of a thematic vowel (the o before the μενος), and the irregular accent are additional clues.

αὐτῷ is a dative of possession, translated "whose" here but usually "his." This is another use of the dative. This use is not too common.

1:7 εἰς μαρτυρίαν. The preposition εἰς frequently has the meaning "for the purpose of." Here an infinitive can be substituted for the two words--"to testify."

1:8 ἐκεῖνος is the subject.

ἀλλά is shortened to ἀλλ᾽ before a word beginning with a vowel.

1:9 ἐρχόμενον is better connected with φῶς rather than ἄνθρωπον. By its punctuation, the UBS text makes this connection.

1:11 τὰ ἴδια and οἱ ἴδιοι are not the same gender. The first is neuter and the second masculine. The first refers to his own country or home and the second to his own people.

1:12 ὅσοι is the nominative masculine plural of the correlative ὅσος, ὅσον, ὅση here meaning "as many as."

γενέσθαι is the second aorist deponent infinitive of γίνομαι. The changed stem indicates a second aorist. The second aorist infinitive takes the present endings.

1:14 ἐν ἡμῖν means "among us." The preposition ἐν here refers to the sphere where the Word dwelt, "in our midst."

μονογενοῦς is a genitive form following the declension of
ἀληθής.

1:15 κέκραγεν is the perfect of κράζω, I cry, but is a perfect
for a present. It should be translated "he cries out."

ὅν should be translated "about whom."

3. Prepare a written translation of John 1:6-16.

LESSON 83

GENERAL REVIEW 15

1. Study the uses of the participle on pp. 303-306 in the Reader's Lexicon.

Translation

1. εἶδεν τὸν ὄχλον ἀκολουθοῦντα αὐτῷ.
2. ἀκούσας ταῦτα ὁ Ἰησοῦς ἐθαύμασεν.
3. ἀπελθόντων δὲ τῶν ἀγγέλων, εἶπεν τῷ λαῷ.
4. οἱ Φαρισαῖοι οὐκ ἠκολούθησαν αὐτῷ, μὴ βαπτισθέντες ὑπ᾽ αὐτοῦ.
5. ὁ υἱὸς τοῦ ἀνθρώπου ἦλθεν ἐσθίων καὶ πίνων.
6. οἱ ἀπόστολοι οἱ ὄντες μετ᾽ αὐτοῦ ἐκήρυξαν τὸ εὐαγγέλιον.
7. οἱ διδαχθέντες ὑπὸ τοῦ κυρίου εἰσῆλθον εἰς τὴν ἐκκλησίαν.
8. ὁ ἀγαπῶν τὸν κύριον ἦν βαπτίζων τὸν δοῦλον αὐτοῦ.
9. ἡμᾶς δεῖ ἐργάζεσθαι τὰ ἔργα τοῦ πέμψαντός ἡμᾶς.
10. ταῦτα αὐτοῦ λαλοῦντος, πολλοὶ ἐπίστευσαν εἰς αὐτόν.
11. καθὼς ἐστιν γεγραμμένον, ἄρτον ἐκ τοῦ οὐρανοῦ ἔδωκεν αὐτοῖς φαγεῖν.
12. λαμβάνοντες δόξαν παρ᾽ ἀλλήλων, οὐ ζητεῖτε τὴν δόξαν παρὰ τοῦ θεοῦ.
13. οἱ ἀκούοντες ἔσονται υἱοὶ τοῦ θεοῦ.

LESSON 84

JOHN 1:17-28

1. Read John 1:17-28.

2. Reading helps

1:18 μονογενὴς θεός is read by the UBS text but some favor ὁ
μονογενὴς υἱός, the only Son. The manuscript evidence as
well as logic favors the UBS reading. It is easy to understand the changing of μονογενὴς θεός to ὁ μονογενὴς υἱός
rather than the other way around.

ὤν is the present participle of εἰμί.

1:19 Ἱεροσολύμων is a genitive plural. Sometimes it is in the
singular (2:13). Names of cities are frequently in the
plural but they should always be translated as singular.
Certain other nouns also have this characteristic.

εἰς τὸν κόλπον should be translated "in the bosom." The
preposition εἰς is frequently used for ἐν.

Λευίτας is "Levites."

ἱερεῖς is the accusative plural form of the third declension noun ἱερεύς.

1:20 ὅτι stands for the quotation mark.

1:21 ἀπεκρίθη is the aorist deponent of ἀποκρίνομαι. Deponents
may be either in the middle or passive forms. This same
word is also used in the middle form, ἀπεκρίνατο. Whatever
form they are in, deponents should always be translated
as actives.

1:22 εἶπαν is a second aorist with the first aorist ending
without the σ.

1:23 ἔφη, he said, is the second aorist of φημί.

The verb "am" is understood.

βοῶντος is a genitive participle. The words φωνῇ βοῶντος,
therefore, should not be translated "the voice crying,"
but "the voice of one crying."

158

εὐθύνατε comes from εὐθύνω which means it is a liquid verb. Thus it takes the first aorist without the σ.

1:24 ἀπεσταλμένοι ἦσαν is a periphrastic perfect and should be translated "they were sent."

1:26 ἀπεκρίθη takes the dative.

ἐν ὕδατι, "in water" or "with water." Probably it should be "with water."

ἕστηκεν is the perfect of ἵστημι but is translated as a present. Notice the rough breathing.

ὅν, "he whom."

1:28 ἐγένετο here means "occurred, took place."

ἦν. . .βαπτίζων is a periphrastic imperfect.

3. Vocabulary

πώποτε

4. Prepare a written translation of John 1:17-28.

LESSON 85

GENERAL REVIEW 16

1. Review the μι conjugation listed on pp. 106-118 of this grammar and Lessons 47-51. Notice that (1) the present and imperfect always have the reduplication with ι (in the case of ἵστημι, the ι with the rough breathing) in all the moods; (2) the aorist has the augment while the perfect the reduplication with ε or the augment in the indicative; (3) the stem without the reduplication with ι appears in all the aorist and future forms (these are not listed since they are regular); (4) the endings are basically the same as the ω verbs. Some things to watch for are (a) the third person singular of the present active indicative; (b) the third person plural of the imperfect active indicative; (c) the second person singular of the imperatives; (d) the infinitive endings, especially of the present active; (e) the second person singular of the present and imperfect middle; (f) the nominative endings of the participles. Ordinarily for recognition purposes, however, the student should have no difficulty if he keeps in mind the first four points.

2. If you have learned well how to translate the regular verbs, you should have no trouble with these.

Recognition and translation

1.	διδότω	14.	θεῖσα
2.	τιθέμενος	15.	ἱστάμεθα
3.	δόμενος	16.	ἱστάμενον
4.	δῶμεν	17.	τιθέντες
5.	διδῷ	18.	θέντες
6.	ἱστῆτε	19.	δοθῆναι
7.	δίδωσι	20.	δοῦναι
8.	τιθέασι	21.	τιθῶμαι
9.	τίθης	22.	διδόμεθα
10.	ἔθηκε	23.	ἐδιδόμην
11.	ἔστησαν	24.	ἵστην
12.	ἕστηκαν	25.	ἐδίδομεν
13.	δεδώκατε	26.	τέθεικας

LESSON 86

JOHN 1:29-39

1. Read John 1:29-39.

2. Reading helps

1:29 τῇ ἐπαύριον (ἡμέρᾳ understood), locative dative of time, "on the next day."

1:31 κἀγώ is a combination of καί and ἐγώ "and I." This is called crasis. Notice the breathing mark has not disappeared.

ᾔδειν is the pluperfect of οἶδα which is translated as an imperfect.

1:32 ἔμεινεν is the first aorist of μένω. Liquid verbs take first aorist forms without the σ.

1:33 ἐφ' comes from ἐπί. The ι drops out before a word beginning with a vowel and the π becomes a φ before the rough breathing.

ἐν ὕδατι. . . ἐν πνεύματι are both probably instrumental, "with water. . . with the Spirit."

1:35 εἱστήκει is the pluperfect of ἵστημι and is translated as an aorist, "stood."

δύο in translation should come before ἐκ τῶν μαθητῶν.

1:36 ἐμβλέψας is an aorist adverbial participle which takes the dative because of the ἐν which becomes ἐμ before β.

περιπατοῦντι is connected with τῷ Ἰησοῦ since both are masculine dative singular. Always observe carefully to what the participle is related.

1:37 αὐτοῦ does not go with μαθηταί but with ἤκουσαν. Remember that ἀκούω takes a genitive or accusative object. The adverbial participle λαλοῦντος is connected with αὐτοῦ.

The verb ἀκολουθέω takes the dative of association. We translate simply, "They followed Jesus."

161

1:38 στραφείς is a second aorist passive participle of στρέφω but does not have the passive sense. It is either a deponent in the passive or is used with a reflexive meaning. At any rate, it should not be translated in the usual passive way. Since it is an aorist adverbial participle we translate it "When Jesus turned."

οἱ is used as a pronoun. This is quite a frequent use of the article. Translate this as "they."

ὃ λέγεται μεθερμηνευόμενον, an idiomatic use of λέγω translated "which means, when translated."

1:39 ὄψεσθε is the future deponent of ὁράω.

ἦλθαν. . . εἶδαν. Notice the number of times second aorist verbs are taking first aorist endings without the σ.

ἔμειναν. What kind of verb is this?

3. Vocabulary

περιστερά, ἡ

4. Prepare a written translation of John 1:29-39.

LESSON 87

GENERAL REVIEW 17

1. Study well the "Miscellaneous Items" on pp. 308-312 in
the Reader's Lexicon.

Recognition and translation.

1. οἱ δὲ εἶπον.
2. ὁ αὐτὸς ἄνθρωπος ἦλθεν.
3. ὁ ἄνθρωπος αὐτὸς ἦλθεν.
4. ἠκολούθησαν δὲ αὐτῷ.
5. μὴ σὺ εἶ ὁ ἐρχόμενος;
6. αὐτοὶ ὑμεῖς μοι μαρτυρεῖτε ὅτι εἶπον ὅτι οὐκ εἰμὶ ἐγὼ
   ὁ χριστός.
7. εἰ γὰρ ἐπιστεύετε Μωϋσεῖ, ἐπιστεύετε ἂν ἐμοί.
8. ὄψεσθε μείζονα τούτων.
9. ὁ Ἰησοῦς πλείονας μαθητὰς ποιεῖ καὶ βαπτίζει ἢ Ἰωάννης.
10. πλείονας γὰρ οὗτος δόξαν παρὰ Μωϋσῆν λαμβάνει.
11. ἡ γυνὴ ἐκ τῆς Σαμαρείας ἦν.
12. ὁ Ἰησοῦς βαπτίσει ὑμᾶς ἐν πνεύματι.
13. ἤκουσαν αὐτοῦ.
14. προσκυνήσατε αὐτῷ.
15. γεύεται τοῦ ὕδατος.

1. Read John 1:40-51.

2. Reading helps

1:40 εἷς. Notice the rough breathing and the accent. This is not the preposition but the masculine nominative singular word meaning "one."

1:41 τὸν ἀδελφὸν τὸν ἴδιον, his own brother.

εὑρήκαμεν is the perfect of εὑρίσκω. Notice that it does not take a reduplication or an augment. A few verbs are like this. The κα however, indicates a perfect.

1:42 ἤγαγεν is the second aorist of ἄγω.

κληθήσῃ is from καλέω. This word shortens its stem to κλη in some of its forms.

1:43 ἠθέλησεν is the aorist of θέλω. Notice the irregularities: the augment with η and the first aorist ending with a liquid verb.

ἐξελθεῖν comes from ἐξέρχομαι. Therefore it is a second aorist with the second aorist stem. The second aorist infinitive takes the endings of the present infinitive.

ἀκολούθει bears close observation. It looks like a present active indicative third person singular but is instead a present imperative second person singular. In this case the accent is significant since that is the only difference between these two forms. The present is ἀκολουθεῖ and is a contraction of ἀκολουθέ + ει. With the long ει the acute accent changes to a circumflex. In the case of the present imperative ἀκολούθει, the contraction is between ἀκολούθε + ε. Since ε is short the acute accent goes back to the ultima ου. Thus the contracted form is ακολούθει. All verbs which contract with a short ending will be accented like ἀκολούθει. Watch for this.

1:45 ὅν is a relative without an antecedent. Translate as "he whom."

Μωϋσῆς ἐν τῷ νόμῳ καὶ οἱ προφῆται are compound subjects
of the verb ἔγραψεν. When there are several subjects, the
verb usually agrees with the first subject, especially if
the verb precedes the subject. In this sentence the verb
is singular even when there are two subjects because it
agrees with the first subject, Μωϋσῆς.

1:46 δύναται from δύναμαι can be translated as "is able" or
"can." It almost always takes the infinitive. If it is
translated "can," the infinitive drops the "to" before it.
The infinitive here is εἶναι, "to be."

τι is without the accent and, therefore, is the neuter indefinite pronoun, "anything, something."

ἔρχου is the present deponent imperative second singular
of ἔρχομαι.

1:48 ἀπεκρίθη is the deponent in the passive of ἀποκρίνομαι.
Notice its frequent use.

πρὸ τοῦ σὲ Φίλιππον φωνῆσαι is a preposition (πρό) with an
articular infinitive (τοῦ φωνῆσαι, the genitive article
is used because πρό takes the genitive) as its object and
two accusatives (σε and Φίλιππον). This construction
appears frequently enough with many different prepositions
so it is worth your while to master it. One should change
this prepositional phrase into an adverbial clause. The
preposition serves as the adverb, "before." The subject
of the sentence is always in the accusative case. However,
in this construction we have two words in the accusative.
One is the subject, the other the object of the verb.
There is no definite formula to determine which is the
subject except the context which should always be clear.
In this case the subject is "Philip" and the object is
"you." The infinitive becomes the verb in its regular
form. Thus the adverbial clause read, "before Philip called
you."

ὄντα is the participle of the verb, "to be," and agrees
with σε.

1:50 μείζω is the neuter accusative plural form of the comparative μείζων, greater. The regular form is μείζονα but it
frequently takes this form. The word τούτων is the genitive of comparison and is translated "than these" or "than
these things."

1:51 ἀνεῳγότα is the second perfect participle of ἀνοίγω.
Since this is a compound verb from the preposition ἀνά and

οἴγω the augment or reduplication should come after the
ἀνά. Since the main stem begins with a vowel, we should
look for an augment rather than reduplication. The augment
of οι is ῳ but there is also an ε preceding it. We have
a double augment.

3. Vocabulary

   ἑρμηνεύω

4. Prepare a written translation of John 1:40-51.

LESSON 89

GENERAL REVIEW 18

1. Study the basic rules of contractions on p. 316 of the
Reader's Lexicon. Give the resulting contractions of the
following:

1. ω + ο =   7. ο + α =
2. ο + ο =   8. ε + ευ =
3. ε + ε =   9. α + ει =
4. η + ο =   10. α + ε =
5. ε + α =   11. ε + ο =
6. ε + η =

2. Study the rules on accents on p. 317. Accent the
following verbs:

1. ἐρχομεθα   5. ποιουντα (ποιε + οντα)
2. ἠκολουθει (ἠκολουθε + ε)   6. ἐλαλει (ἐλαλε + ε)
3. ἀκολουθει (ἀκολουθε + ε)   7. ζητει (ζητε + ει)
4. ἠρωτων (ἠρωτα + ον)

Explain the following accented forms and give the original
uncontracted forms:

1. ἐζήτουν   4. ποιοῦν
2. ἀκολούθει   5. ἐλάλεις
3. ἠρώτας   6. ζητείτω

LESSON 90

JOHN 2:1-12

1. Read John 2:1-12.

2. Reading helps

2:1 τῇ ἡμέρᾳ τῇ τρίτῃ is a dative of time, "on the third day."

2:2 ἐκλήθη has the shortened stem of καλέω. It is a singular verb though it has a compound subject. See on 1:45.

καί . . . καί is translated both . . . and. Usually when καί is found before two nouns or pronouns, it will be translated as both. . . and.

2:3 ὑστερήσαντος οἴνου is a genitive absolute. The participle is not grammatically and by sense connected to any word in the main clause as the ordinary participle is. It also has a noun in the genitive case which serves as its subject. It is always adverbial, "when the wine ran out."

2:4 Τί ἐμοὶ καὶ σοί is idiomatic. "What have I to do with you?" The NEB translates "Your concern is not mine."

γύναι is the vocative of γυνή. In many instances the nominative serves as vocative but in some cases the regular vocative form appears as here. It is not worth the time to learn the vocative since they do not occur very frequently and when they do the context always helps to identify it.

2:5 ὅ τι ἄν. ὅ τι, what, sometimes combined into one word ὅτι, is the neuter singular form of ὅστις, and ἄν is "ever."

2:6 κείμεναι is the deponent participle modifying ὑδρίαι. χωροῦσαι is the present active feminine participle also modifying ὑδρίαι.

ἤ here means "or."

ὕδατος is a genitive of content and should be translated "with water" rather than "of water."

2:8 οἱ is used as a pronoun, "they."

168

ἤνεγκαν is the aorist of φέρω. It takes the first aorist endings with κ instead of σ.

2:9 ᾔδει is the pluperfect of οἶδα translated as an imperfect.

ἠντληκότες is the perfect participle of ἀντλέω. Notice the augment and the κ.

2:12 κατέβη is the second aorist of καταβαίνω. Notice the second aorist stem, βη. It has the regular second aorist endings except for the third person plural which is --βησαν, the same as the second aorist of γινώσκω, ἔγνων.

3. Vocabulary

ἕξ
χωρέω
ἄνω

4. Prepare a written translation of John 2:1-12.

LESSON 91

JOHN 2:13-25

1. Read John 2:13-25.

2. Reading helps

2:14 εὗρεν is from εὑρίσκω which tells you it has to be second aorist. Notice that it does not take an augment. Verbs beginning with ευ usually do not take an augment.

2:15 ἐξέβαλεν from ἐκβάλλω. Notice (1) the κ has become ξ because it precedes a vowel; (2) the augment comes after the preposition in a compound verb and before the main stem; (3) the stem has changed making this second aorist rather than imperfect. βάλλω takes a second aorist even though it is a liquid verb.

τε . . . καί or τε καί connects concepts usually of the same kind or corresponding as opposites, often together translated simply as "and."

τῶν κολλυβιστῶν is genitive connected with τὸ κέρμα.

ἐξέχεεν is the first aorist third singular without σ of ἐκχέω. The first person is ἐξέχεα. This form has the movable ν.

2:16 τοῖς is connected with πωλοῦσιν.

ἄρατε is a liquid first aorist of αἴρω.

2:17 ἐμνήσθησαν is the aorist deponent in the passive form of μιμνήσκομαι.

γεγραμμένον ἐστίν is a periphrastic perfect.

καταφάγεται is the future deponent of κατεσθίω. The second aorist of ἐσθίω has the same root, ἔφαγον.

2:19 ἐγερῶ and ἐγερεῖς have a different stem from the present
20 but more importantly are accented differently. Here again the accents are important. We have learned that liquid verbs (verbs ending in λ, μ, ν, and ρ) take the first aorist without the σ. We have learned further that in the future, they function like contract verbs. This shifts

170

the accent forward. The present in the first person is
ἐγείρω; the future ἐγερῶ. The present in the second person
is ἐγείρεις; the future ἐγερεῖς. In some verbs such as
μένω there is no change of stem in the future. Thus the
difference is only in the accent, present μένω, future
μενῶ. The accents need to be observed carefully in the
liquid futures and in the present imperative of the contract verbs.

2:20 ἔτεσιν is the dative plural of ἔτος, τό, a third declension noun. τεσσαράκοντα and ἕξ are non-declinable, "in
forty-six years."

2:21 σώματος is a genitive of apposition, so this phrase should
be translated "the temple, that is, his body," or "the temple
which is his body."

2:22 ἐμνήσθησαν is the aorist deponent in passive form of
μιμνήσκομαι.

2:23 Ἱεροσολύμοις is in the plural. See under 1:19.

ἐποίει is clearly an imperfect with the augment and present stem but the ending does not look like an imperfect.
It is due to the contraction of ἐποίε with ε which contracts to ἐποίει. Notice the short ending ε which leads
to an acute accent.

2:24 ἐπίστευεν is from πιστεύω which is usually translated
"believe" but it also means "trust" or "entrust" which is
the meaning here.

αὐτόν is the same as ἑαυτόν. It is not αὐτόν. Notice the
rough breathing which makes the difference.

διὰ τὸ αὐτὸν γινώσκειν πάντας is another preposition with
the articular infinitve which should be translated as an
adverbial clause. διά with the accusative (notice the τό)
means "because of, on account of." The subject is "αὐτόν"
and the object "πάντας" which is a masculine accusative
plural and the verb is "γινώσκειν." We translate this
"because (we drop the 'of' because it is not used as a
preposition but as an adverb) he knows all men."

2:25 εἶχεν, the imperfect of ἔχω.

3. Vocabulary

ἐντεῦθεν   ζῆλος, ὁ

4. Prepare a written translation of John 2:13-25.

171

JOHN 3:1-10

1. Read John 3:1-10.

2. Reading helps

3:1 ἦν δὲ ἄνθρωπος needs in English a preparatory "there," since there is no predicate nominative or adjective.

αὐτῷ is a dative of possession and should be translated "whose." The verb "to be" is understood, thus, "whose name was Nicodemus."

3:2 νυκτός is a genitive of time. The genitive being a descriptive case is emphasizing not some point at night which would be the dative or all during the night which would be the accusative but night time in contrast to day time, "at night."

ἐλήλυθας is the second perfect of ἔρχομαι.

δύναται. Always look for an infinitive after the verb δύναμαι.

ἐὰν μή is translated the same as εἰ μή, "except, unless."

ᾖ. Observe the accent and the iota subscript. These should distinguish it from the pronouns and define it as a subjunctive of εἰμί.

3:3 ἄνωθεν. John loves to use words which have double meanings and this is a case in point. It can mean "again" or "from above."

ἰδεῖν is the second aorist infinitive of ὁράω with the present ending.

3:4 ὤν is the participle of εἰμί.

μή in this interrogative sentence is due to the fact that a negative answer is expected. One can translate the force of this by, "A man cannot enter the womb of his mother the second time and be born, can he?"

3:6 τό is the generalizing and universalizing neuter.

3:7 μὴ θαυμάσῃς is an aorist subjunctive. The aorist subjunctive is used for the negative command in Greek and should be translated as an imperative, "Do not marvel." This is called the prohibitory subjunctive.

δεῖ ὑμᾶς γεννηθῆναι. δεῖ is always used with an infinitive in which case it is translated "it is necessary to_____," or "one must _____." Frequently it has an accusative noun or pronoun as in the above example. In such cases this clause should be translated "it is necessary for _____ to _____" or "_____ must _____." Thus the above is translated, "it is necessary for you to be born" or "you must be born."

3:9 γενέσθαι looks like a present but observe the stem.

3. Prepare a written translation of John 3:1-10.

LESSON 93

JOHN 3:11-21

1. Read John 3:11-21.

2. Reading helps

3:13 ἀναβέβηκεν is the perfect of ἀναβαίνω. Remember the stem of βαίνω is βη except for the present and imperfect forms.

καταβάς is the masculine aorist active participle of καταβαίνω. The genitive is καταβάντος. Only the masculine active forms of the participle are used in the NT. In the second aorist indicative καταβαίνω and ἀναβαίνω are declined like ἔγνων.

Aorist Active Indicative

	S	P
1	κατέβην	κατέβημεν
2	κατέβης	κατέβητε
3	κατέβη	κατέβησαν

The perfect active indicative is καταβέβηκα and the future is deponent, καταβήσομαι. In the subjunctive only the aorist active third person singular form, καταβῇ, is found in the NT. The aorist active participle nominative singular forms are καταβάς, καταβάν, and καταβᾶσα.

Aorist Active Imperative

	S	P
2	κατάβηθι	κατάβητε
3	καταβήτω	καταβήτωσαν

Aorist Active Infinitive

καταβῆναι

3:14 ὕψωσεν is an aorist indicative of ὑψόω. Notice it does not take the augment.

3:16 ἀπόληται with the single λ is the second aorist of ἀπόλλυμι and the η indicates a subjunctive.

3:18 κέκριται is clearly a perfect of κρίνω. The ν has dropped out.

3:19 ἐλήλυθεν is the second perfect indicative of ἔρχομαι.

ἤ is "than."

3:21 αὐτῶν πονηρὰ τὰ ἔργα. αὐτῶν goes with τὰ ἔργα even though they are separated by πονηρά. Notice also the singular verb with the neuter plural subject.

3:21 ἐστιν εἰργασμένα is a periphrastic perfect. εἰργασμένα is the perfect passive participle of ἐργάζομαι. Ordinarily since ἐργάζομαι is deponent it does not take a passive voice but this is not the case here. Notice it does not take the expected augment η but ει.

   3. Vocabulary

   ἐλέγχω

   4. Prepare a written translation of John 3:11-21.

LESSON 94

JOHN 3:22-30

1. Read John 3:22-30.

2. Reading helps

3:22 ἦλθεν, a singular verb with compound subject.

3:23 ἦν . . . βαπτίζων, a periphrastic participle.

ὕδατα πολλά. The Greek uses the plural where we would use the singular.

3:24 ἦν βεβλημένος, a periphrastic participle, with the perfect passive participle of βάλλω. Notice the stem is βλη.

3:26 ὅς, a relative without antecedent. Translate as "he who."

3:27 ἕν. Notice the breathing mark and the accent. This is not the preposition, ἐν, but the neuter for "one."

ᾖ δεδομένον, a periphrastic perfect with the perfect participle of δίδωμι. Notice the reduplication with δε.

3:28 αὐτοὶ ὑμεῖς. Ordinarily αὐτός is used as a third person singular personal pronoun. However, when it follows an article, it means "same," e.g. ὁ αὐτὸς ἄνθρωπος, "the same man." When it is used with a noun or pronoun and the article does not precede it, it means "oneself," e.g., αὐτὸς ἐγώ, "I myself," or ὁ ἄνθρωπος αὐτός, "the man himself." Thus, the above should be translated "you yourselves."

ἀπεσταλμένος εἰμί, another periphrastic participle. The participle is from ἀποστέλλω. The augment, lack of thematic vowel, and irregular accent obviously reveal its tense.

3:29 ἑστηκώς. The rough breathing which indicates the reduplication and the κ tell you that this is a perfect participle. Remember, however, that the perfect of ἵστημι always is translated as a present.

αὐτοῦ. Remember ἀκούω takes both an accusative and genitive object.

176

3:29 χαρᾷ χαίρει. The cognate dative (the same root word is used in the dative as is found in the verb χαίρει) influenced by the Hebrew infinitive absolute emphasizes the action of the verb. Thus "he rejoices greatly."

3:30 ἐλαττοῦσθαι, the passive infinitive used intransitively to mean "to diminish."

3. Vocabulary

νυμφίος, ὁ

4. Prepare a written translation of John 3:22-30.

177

JOHN 3:31-4:4

1. Read John 3:31-4:4.

2. Reading helps

3:33 λαβών is a second aorist participle. Second aorist participles take the present participle endings.

3:34 ὅν is a relative without antecedent, "he whom."

ἀπέστειλεν. What kind of verb is this? What kind of aorist does it take?

δίδωσιν is the third person <u>singular</u> of δίδωμι. The third person plural (all plurals take the o instead of the ω) is διδόασιν.

3:36 ὄψεται is deponent.

4:1 ἔγνω is the second aorist first person singular of γινώσκω.

πλείονας is a third declension comparative adjective, "more."

4:2 γε is connected with καίτοι and together are translated "and yet."

αὐτός, the reflexive use of αὐτός. See 3:28.

4:3 ἀφῆκεν, the first aorist (with κ) of ἀφίημι.

4:4 ἔδει, irregular imperfect of δεῖ.

3. Prepare a written translation of John 3:31-4:4.

JOHN 4:5-15

1. Read John 4:5-15.

2. Reading helps

4:7 δός is the aorist imperative second singular of δίδωμι.

πεῖν comes from πίνω, which means this has to be second aorist. Second aorist infinitives take the present endings.

4:8 ἀπεληλύθεισαν is the second pluperfect of ἀπέρχομαι. For the pluperfect endings see page 133.

4:9 ὤν. Most adverbial participles are translated as temporal participles. But the context must dictate what kind of adverbial participle it is. Here ὤν is clearly a concessive participle, meaning "although you are." "How is it that although you are a Jew."

γυναικὸς Σαμαρίτιδος οὔσης is a participle clause connected to ἐμοῦ.

συγχρῶνται is a contraction of συγχρα + ονται. It is not a subjunctive.

4:10 ᾔδεις, the pluperfect of οἶδα translated as an imperfect, here more smoothly translated simply as "you knew."

Εἰ ᾔδεις . . . , σὺ ἂν ᾔτησας αὐτὸν καὶ ἔδωκεν ἄν σοι ὕδωρ ζῶν is a second class contrary to fact condition. See page 133. The apodosis should be translated "You would have asked him and he would have given you living water." Remember the sign of the second class contrary to fact conditional is εἰ with the indicative in the protasis and the indicative with ἄν in the apodosis.

4:11 οὔτε is usually found in combination with another οὔτε, meaning "neither . . . nor," but it is used simply as a negative here.

4:12 μή introduces a question expecting a negative answer.

τοῦ πατρὸς ἡμῶν Ἰακώβ is the genitive of comparison after μείζων, "than our father Jacob."

ἔπιεν and πίη (4:14) come from πίνω, I drink. Observe the stem carefully.

4:14 οὗ is a genitive by attraction to its antecedent ὕδατος. Ordinarily we would expect ὅ.

οὐ μὴ . . . εἰς τὸν αἰῶνα. The double negative does not make a positive in Greek but strengthens the negative idea. This strong negative is further strengthened by the addition of εἰς τὸν αἰῶνα, "forever." Translate, "He shall never ever thirst."

γενήσεται is the deponent future of γίνομαι.

4:15 κύριε is the vocative form of κύριος.

3. Vocabulary

πηγή, ἡ

4. Prepare a written translation of John 4:5-15.

LESSON 97

JOHN 4:16-26

1. Read John 4:16-26.

2. Reading helps

4:16 ὕπαγε is the present imperative of ὑπάγω.

φώνησον is the aorist imperative of φωνέω.

ἐλθέ is from ἔρχομαι. Observe the stem and notice the ending is the same as ὕπαγε above.

4:17 ὅτι is used as a quotation mark. Do not translate.

4:18 ἔσχες is the second aorist of ἔχω.

εὕρηκας is the perfect of λέγω.

4:21 προσκυνέω takes the dative and accusative (4:22, 23).
23

4:23 τοιοῦτος, -αὕτη, -οῦτον is a pronominal adjective. Check vocabulary in Appendix I of the Lexicon.

4:25 ὁ λεγόμενος, "the one who is called."

ἀναγγελεῖ comes from ἀναγγέλλω. Notice that it is a liquid verb. Observe the accent and the difference in the stem. Liquid verbs, remember, act as contract verbs in the future. This causes the accent to shift toward the end of the verb.

4:26 ἐγώ εἰμί should be translated "I am he."

3. Vocabulary

ἀναγγέλλω

4. Prepare a written translation of John 4:16-26.

181

JOHN 4:27-38

1. Read John 4:27-38.

2. Reading helps

4:27 ἐλάλει, from λαλέω is obviously an imperfect since it has
an augment, the present stem, and no σ. The ending looks
peculiar but remember that λαλέω is a contract verb. The
contraction is between ἐλαλε and ε. With the short vowel
at the end the accent goes back to the antepenult in the
uncontracted form, thus the contraction is ἐλάλει. Be
sure you are able to recognize this form as well as the
first person form, ἐλάλουν.

4:29 δεῦτε is really an adverb but is used like an imperative.

μήτι is an interrogative participle expecting a negative
answer or which expresses doubt. This is the latter, "Is
this perhaps the Christ?"

4:31 ἠρώτων comes from ἐρωτάω. Notice the augment with the
present stem without the σ, showing it is clearly an
imperfect form. The ων in the ending is the result of
the contraction of ἠρωτα with ον.

φάγε is the second aorist of ἐσθίω. Notice the ending.

4:32 ὁ is used as a pronoun.

4:33 ἤνεγκεν is the first aorist with κ of φέρω.

4:34 ἐμόν, the pronominal adjective used for emphasis.

4:35 ἐπάρατε is from ἐπαίρω, a liquid verb. Thus the ending.

ἤδη is connected in the UBS text with verse 36. Some
connect it with verse 35.

4:37 ἄλλος. The first ἄλλος should be translated, "one."

3. Vocabulary

μέντοι

βρῶσις, ἡ
ἐπαίρω

4. Prepare a written translation of John 4:27-38.

JOHN 4:39-50

1. Read John 4:39-50.

2. Reading helps

4:39 τῶν Σαμαριτῶν is connected with πολλοί.

μαρτυρούσης is the present active feminine participle of μαρτυρέω.

4:40 μεῖναι and ἔμεινεν come from μένω, a liquid verb.

4:41 πολλῷ πλείους. The comparative πλείους is a masculine nominative third declension form and should be πλείονες but has contracted with the ν dropped out to πλείους. It is the subject of the sentence. The πολλῷ heightens the comparative to "much more" or "still more," and is a dative of degree.

4:42 σήν is the pronominal adjective used for emphasis.

4:45 ἐδέξαντο is the aorist deponent of δέχομαι, I receive.

ἑωρακότες is the perfect participle of ὁράω.

4:46 οὗ is the genitive relative, "of whom." Translate as "whose" here.

ἠσθένει is from ἀσθενέω, a contract verb; thus the ending.

4:47 ἠρώτα is from ἐρωτάω, a contract verb. The α + ε becomes α.

ἤμελλεν, imperfect from μέλλω. Notice the irregular augment.

4:48 οὐ μή, the strong negative with the subjunctive is the subjunctive of emphatic negation and should be translated as a future, "You shall never believe."

4:49 κατάβηθι is the second aorist active imperative second singular of καταβαίνω. It follows ἵστημι and γινώσκω in their second aorist endings, whose respective imperative forms are στῆθι and γνῶθι.

184

πρὶν ἀποθανεῖν τὸ παιδίον μου is a prepositional phrase with the infinitive (without the article). The accusative (τὸ παιδίον μου) called the accusative of general reference becomes the subject of the adverbial clause. "Before my child dies." The infinitive is aorist but kind of action is emphasized rather than time. The time is derived from the context.

4:50 πορεύου is the present imperative of the deponent verb πορεύομαι.

3. Vocabulary

πρίν

4. Prepare a written translation of John 4:39-50.

LESSON 100

JOHN 4:51-5:7

1. Read John 4:51-5:7.

2. Reading helps

4:51 αὐτοῦ καταβαίνοντος is a genitive absolute in the present tense. Translate with "while" and αὐτοῦ is the subject.

4:52 κομψότερον ἔσχεν, literally, "he had better," but more smoothly translated, "he became better."

ἀφῆκεν is first aorist with κ.

4:53 ἔγνω is the second aorist third singular of γινώσκω.

5:2 'Εβραϊστί, "in Hebrew."

5:6 γνούς, second aorist participle masculine nominative singular of γινώσκω. The second aorist nominative forms are γνούς, γνόν, γνοῦσα.

5:7 ταραχθῇ. Notice the θ and the long ending.

βάλῃ. Notice the stem and the long ending.

ἐν ᾧ, idiomatic for "while," from ἐν τῷ χρόνῳ ᾧ.

3. Vocabulary

ὑπαντάω

4. Prepare a written translation of John 4:51-5:7.

LESSON 101

JOHN 5:8-18

1. Read John 5:8-18.

2. Reading helps

5:8 ἆρον, first aorist active imperative of the liquid verb αἴρω. This verb occurs several times in different forms in this section. The ι of the diphthong disappears in the aorist forms. Watch for it in 5:9, 10, 11, 12.

περιπάτει (also in 5:9, 11, 12). Notice the accent. What is the difference between this form and περιπατεῖ? What kind of verb is περιπατέω? The accent has shifted from the ει to the α. This means that the first has a short ending, in this case the ε of the present imperative.

5:13 ὄχλου ὄντος is a genitive absolute. ὄντος is a causal adverbial participle, "because there was a crowd."

5:14 χεῖρον is the neuter comparative of χείρων, worse.

5:15 ἀνήγγειλεν is a liquid verb from ἀναγγέλλω.

5:16 ἐποίει has an augment and the present ending without the σ. Why does it have that kind of ending?

ἀπεκρίνατο is translated the same as ἀπεκρίθη.

5:18 ἐζήτουν, from ζητέω, has the augment and the present stem without σ. Why does it have that kind of ending?

ἀποκτεῖναι is from ἀποκτείνω. Why does it have no σ?

3. Vocabulary

   κράβατος, ὁ

4. Prepare a written translation of John 5:8-18.

LESSON 102

JOHN 5:19-29

1. Read John 5:19-29.

2. Reading helps

5:20 δείκνυσιν is the present active indicative third person singular of δείκνυμι. Only the singular form is found in the present in the NT.

μείζονα goes with ἔργα. Why is τούτων in the genitive?

δείξει, the future of δείκνυμι.

5:25 ἀκούσαντες is an aorist active participle but is translated as an aoristic present, "those who hear." The context decides this.

3. Prepare a written translation of John 5:19-29.

LESSON 103

JOHN 5:30-40

1. Read John 5:30-40.

2. Reading helps

5:34 σωθῆτε. In this form σώζω has dropped the ζ. The θ with the long ending without the augment clearly indicates an aorist passive subjunctive.

5:35 καιόμενος. The active means "to cause something to burn" and the passive "to be lit, burn."

ἠθελήσατε. Notice the augment with η and the first aorist ending with σ of this liquid verb.

ἀγαλλιαθῆναι comes from ἀγαλλιάω, but is usually deponent, ἀγαλλιάομαι. This passive infinitive is obviously deponent.

5:36 μείζω is the short form of μείζονα which is masculine or feminine.

αὐτὰ τὰ ἔργα, the reflexive use of αὐτός.

5:37 ὁ πέμψας με πατὴρ ἐκεῖνος is the same as ἐκεῖνος ὁ πατὴρ ὁ πέμψας με.

5:39 ἐραυνᾶτε is the same as ἐρευνᾶτε, the classical form. It is a contract verb. Since in the present tense, the indicative and imperative are identical in form, the context must decide which it is. Commentators generally accept it as indicative.

3. Vocabulary

πώποτε

4. Prepare a written translation of John 5:30-40.

189

LESSON 104

JOHN 5:41-6:4

1. Read John 5:41-6:4.

2. Reading helps

5:41 ἔγνωκα, perfect of γινώσκω. Remember γινώσκω has a second aorist, ἔγνων.

5:43 ἐλήλυθα. You should know this by now as the perfect of ἔρχομαι.

λήμφεσθε is the future deponent of λαμβάνω.

5:45 ὑμῶν. κατηγορέω takes the genitive of the person accused.

5:46 What kind of condition is this? How do you translate the apodosis?

6:2 ἠκολούθει and ἐποίει from ἀκολουθέω and ποιέω have the augment with the present stem without the σ. How do we get the ει ending?

ἐθεωροῦν, from θεωρέω, I see, is the same form as the previous verbs except that it has an ουν ending. How do we get this?

3. Prepare a written translation of John 5:41-6:4.

JOHN 6:5-15

1. Read John 6:5-15.

2. Reading helps

6:5 ἐπάρας comes from the liquid verb, ἐπαίρω. The ending is
the aorist active participle corresponding to λύσας without the σ. The nominative forms of the aorist active
participle are λύσας, λῦσαν, λύσασα.

6:7 ἄρτοι. The Greek uses the plural for bread. We translate
as "loaves of bread."

6:10 ἀναπεσεῖν and ἀνάπεσαν. πες is the second aorist stem of
πίπτω. Remember that second aorists take present endings
in the infinitive.

6:12 συναγάγετε comes from συνάγω. Look at the stem. Clearly
it is second aorist indicative of συνάγω. What mood is
this?

ἀπόληται comes from ἀπόλλυμι. Look at the stem and the
lengthened ending and you have the clues for a second
aorist subjunctive.

6:13 βεβρωκόσιν has the reduplication with ε, the κ and the
participle ending. It can only be the perfect active
participle masculine dative plural.

6:15 γνούς. See 5:6.

3. Vocabulary

ἐπαίρω   ἀναπίπτω
ὀψάριον, τό   ἀνακεῖμαι
τοσοῦτος

4. Prepare a written translation of John 6:5-15.

191

LESSON 106

JOHN 6:16-26

1. Read John 6:16-26.

2. Reading helps

6:16 κατέβησαν. Notice that this second aorist verb has a
first aorist ending. This is only true in the third
person plural of this verb, in γινώσκω, and in the second
aorist of ἴστημι.

6:17 ἐμβάντες is the aorist participle of ἐμβαίνω. The ἐν
becomes ἐμ before β. The nominative aorist participle
forms in the active are ἐμβάς, ἐμβάν, ἐμβᾶσα.

ἐγεγόνει and ἐληλύθει are both pluperfect. Notice the
augment with the reduplication and augment and the ει
ending.

6:18 τε here connects this sentence with the previous one.
Translate as "and."

ἀνέμου μεγάλου πνέοντος is a genitive absolute. Translate
it as a causal adverbial in the same time as the main
verb. "Because a strong wind was blowing."

6:19 ἐληλακότες is the perfect participle of ἐλαύνω.

ἐφοβήθησαν and φοβεῖσθε come from φοβέω. "I cause (someone)
to be afraid, terrify," but it is used only as a passive
in the NT in the sense "be afraid, fear."

6:22 ἑστηκώς is the perfect participle of ἴστημι. Translate as
a past tense here.

6:23 ἔφαγον is from ἐσθίω.

εὐχαριστήσαντος τοῦ κυρίου is a genitive absolute.

6:24 ἔστιν. Translate as "was." Greek often especially in
indirect discourses uses the present where English uses
a past tense.

ἐνέβησαν. See 6:16 and 6:17 above.

6:25 εὑρόντες is from εὑρίσκω. Notice the stem and the present
ending.

3. Vocabulary

πλοιάριον, τό
ἐμβαίνω

4. Prepare a written translation of John 6:16-26.

LESSON 107

JOHN 6:27-37

1. Read John 6:27-37.

2. Reading helps

6:31 ἐστιν γεγραμμένον is a periphrastic perfect.

6:33 διδούς is the present active participle masculine nominative singular of δίδωμι. The nominative forms for the
neuter and feminine are διδόν, διδοῦσα.

6:34 δός is the aorist active second singular imperative of
δίδωμι.

οὐ μὴ πεινάσῃ is the subjunctive of emphatic negation.
Translate as future "shall never hunger."

3. Prepare a written translation of John 6:27-37.

LESSON 108

JOHN 6:38-48

1. Read John 6:38-48.

2. Reading helps

6:38 καταβέβηκα comes from καταβαίνω. You should recognize this form.

6:39 ἀπολέσω is the future of ἀπόλλυμι.

6:41 καταβάς comes from καταβαίνω. See 6:17.

6:44 κἀγώ is a crasis of καί and ἐγώ.

3. Vocabulary

ἑλκύω

4. Prepare a written translation of John 6:38-48.

LESSON 109

JOHN 6:49-59

1. Read John 6:49-59.

2. Reading helps

6:52 δοῦναι is the aorist active infinitive of δίδωμι. Notice that it does not have the reduplication with δι.

6:53 πίητε. What does it come from? Examine its stem. What kind of ending does it have?

6:57 κἀκεῖνος is a crasis of καί and ἐκεῖνος.

3. Vocabulary

τρώγω

4. Prepare a written translation of John 6:49-59.

LESSON 110

JOHN 6:60-71

1. Read John 6:60-71.

2. Reading helps

6:61 εἰδώς comes from οἶδα. It is the second perfect participle.

6:62 ζῳοποιοῦν comes from ζωοποιέω. It is the neuter present participle. What have contracted?

6:64 οὕ. Notice the accent. It is not an article but a relative pronoun.

παραδώσων is a future participle of παραδίδωμι. The endings of the future are the same as those of the present.

6:65 εἴρηκα is the perfect of λέγω.

6:66 εἰς τὰ ὀπίσω is an idiom. Translate simply as "back."

περιεπάτουν. Observe the augment after the preposition and the present stem without the σ. What is the cause for the ουν ending? The preposition περί does not drop its final vowel when it is followed by a vowel.

6:68 ἀπελευσόμεθα. The future of ἔρχομαι is ἐλεύσομαι.

6:70 ἐξελεξάμην. Observe the augment and the σ (in the ξ; γ + σ = ξ). Remember that this is a deponent verb.

6:71 παραδιδόναι is the present infinitive of παραδίδωμι.

3. Vocabulary

πρότερος
ζωοποιέω
ἐκλέγομαι

4. Prepare a written translation of John 6:60-71.

LESSON 111

JOHN 7:1-11

1. Read John 7:1-11.

2. Reading helps

7:1 περιεπάτει. The augment with the present stem without the
tells you what form this is. Why the ει ending?

ἀποκτεῖναι is a liquid verb. What kind of ending is that?

7:3 μετάβηθι is the second aorist imperative second singular
of μεταβαίνω.

7:4 ἐν παρρησίᾳ εἶναι, "to be known publicly."

φανέρωσον. Remember the σον ending is the aorist active
imperative second singular.

7:8 ἀνάβητε is the second aorist imperative of ἀναβαίνω.

3. Vocabulary

ἐντεῦθεν
κρυπτός

4. Prepare a written translation of John 7:1-11.

LESSON 112

JOHN 7:12-24

1. Read John 7:12-24.

2. Reading helps

7:12 μὲν . . . δέ, "on the one hand . . . on the other hand."

οὔ. With the accent οὔ is the negative answer "no."

7:14 τῆς ἑορτῆς μεσούσης. What kind of participle clause is this? What is the function of τῆς ἑορτῆς? What tense is μεσούσης?

7:17 γνώσεται. Remember that γινώσκω is deponent in the future.

7:21 ἕν. Notice the rough breathing and the accent. This is not the preposition but the word "one" in the neuter.

3. Prepare a written translation of John 7:12-24.

JOHN 7:25-36

1. Read John 7:25-36.

2. Reading helps

7:25 Ἱεροσολυμιτῶν, "Jerusalemites" or "inhabitants of Jerusalem."

7:26 παρρησίᾳ. Notice the dative form, "in openness" or "openly."

7:28 ἔκραξεν is from κράζω. Check Appendix I in Reader's Lexicon. Notice that the ζ becomes a ξ when it combines with σ.

κἀμέ is a crasis of καί and ἐμέ.

7:29 κἀκεῖνος is a crasis of καί and ἐκεῖνος.

7:30 πιάσαι and πιάσωσιν (7:32). Check the Special Vocabulary. Notice that the ζ drops here before the σ.

ἐληλύθει. Notice the ει ending on the perfect stem, the sign of the pluperfect.

7:31 πλείονα is from πλείων.

ὧν is the genitive of comparison but also serves as the relative pronoun which is the object of the verb ἐποίησεν. The full expression would be ἐκείνων ἅ.

7:32 τοῦ ὄχλου is not genitive because it is part of a genitive absolute but because it is the object of ἤκουσαν. Remember that ἀκούω takes accusative as well as genitive objects. γογγύζοντος is in the genitive because it modifies ὄχλου which is in the genitive.

ὑπηρέτας. Check the Special Vocabulary.

7:34 εὑρήσετε and εὑρήσομεν (7:35) are obviously the future forms of εὑρίσκω.

7:36 τίς is the interrogative pronoun, "who" or "what." Here though it is masculine, it should be "what" because it modifies ὁ λόγος and not a person.

3. Prepare a written translation of John 7:25-36.

LESSON 114

JOHN 7:37-47

1. Read John 7:37-47.

2. Reading helps

7:37 εἰστήκει is the pluperfect of ἵστημι used as an aorist, "stood."

ἐρχέσθω and πινέτω. εσθω and ετω are sure signs of the imperative in the third person singular. The first is the middle form but in this case it is deponent. Always translate the third person imperative beginning with "let."

7:38 ὕδατος ζῶντος is connected with ποταμοί.

7:40 ἐκ τοῦ ὄχλου. The word "some" must be added before this phrase.

7:41 οἱ is the article used as a pronoun, usually as "they," but here as "some."

μή. Notice how frequently μή is used with a question expecting a negative answer. Watch for this in this section.

7:42 ἔρχεται. As in English the present can be used as a future.

7:45 διὰ τί is literally "because of what" but it is more simple to translate it, "why."

ἠγάγετε is from ἄγω.

3. Vocabulary

σχίσμα, τό

4. Prepare a written translation of 7:37-47.

202

LESSON 115

JOHN 7:48-8:16

1. Read John 7:48-8:16.

2. Reading helps

7:50 ὤν is the participle of εἰμί.

7:51 γνῷ is the subjunctive of γινώσκω.

8:12 οὐ μὴ περιπατήσῃ is the subjunctive of emphatic negation. Translate as future with "never."

ἕξει is the future of ἔχω. Notice the rough breathing.

8:14 κἄν is crasis of καί and ἐάν.

8:15 οὐδένα is the accusative of οὐδείς.

3. Prepare a written translation of John 7:48-8:16.

LESSON 116

JOHN 8:12-25

1. Read John 8:12-25.

2. Reading helps

8:17 γέγραπται is the perfect passive indicative of γράφω.

8:19 ἂν ᾖδειτε is the second class contrary to fact condition.
"You would have known."

8:21 ἀποθανεῖσθε is the liquid deponent future of ἀποθνῄσκω.
The first person is ἀποθανοῦμαι. Remember that liquid
verbs act like contract verbs in the future.

8:22 μήτι is a negative interrogative particle expecting a
negative answer.

ἀποκτενεῖ is the liquid future of ἀποκτείνω. The first
person is ἀποκτενῶ.

8:25 τὴν ἀρχὴν ὅ τι (or ὅτι) καὶ λαλῶ ὑμῖν. Some take the τὴν
ἀρχήν as having the meaning "at all" and ὅτι as "why" and
translate this clause, "Why do I speak to you at all?"
Others take the τὴν ἀρχήν adverbially to mean "from the
beginning" and ὅ τι as "what" and translate this, "(I am)
what I tell you from the beginning ." From the context
it probably should be "From the beginning what I tell you."

3. Vocabulary

ἄνω

4. Prepare a written translation of John 8:17-25.

LESSON 117

JOHN 8:26-38

1. Read John 8:26-38.

2. Reading helps

8:29 ἀφῆκεν is the first aorist active with κ of ἀφίημι.

8:30 αὐτοῦ λαλοῦντος. What kind of construction is this?

8:31 πεπιστευκότας is the perfect active participle of πιστεύω.

8:33 οὐδενί is the dative of οὐδείς.

γενήσεσθε is the future deponent of γίνομαι. The first
person form is γενήσομαι.

3. Prepare a written translation of John 8:26-38.

LESSON 118

JOHN 8:39-47

1. Read John 8:39-47.

2. Reading helps

8:39 ἐποιεῦτε. Notice the augment and the present ending
without the σ. What is the reason for the ειτε ending?

8:41 ἕνα is the masculine accusative of εἷς.

8:42 ἠγαπᾶτε ἂν ἐμέ is the second class contrary to fact
condition. "You would have loved me."

8:43 διὰ τί (also 8:46), "on account of what," or "why."

8:44 ἕστηκεν is probably the perfect of ἵστημι whether written
ἕστηκεν or ἔστηκεν. Ordinarily the former would be the
imperfect of στήκω and the latter the perfect of ἵστημι.
Translate as a present.

3. Prepare a written translation of John 8:39-47.

LESSON 119

JOHN 8:48-59

1. Read John 8:48-59.

2. Reading helps

8:50 ἔστιν. Translate as "there is one."

8:51 οὐ μὴ θεωρήσῃ εἰς τὸν αἰῶνα is a subjunctive of emphatic negation with εἰς τὸν αἰῶνα, "he will never ever see."

8:52 οὐ μὴ γεύσηται is the same as above.

θανάτου. γεύομαι takes the genitive.

8:53 ὅστις is an indefinite relative mainly used as a simple relative.

8:55 κἄν is crasis of καί and ἐάν.

ὑμῖν is dative following ὅμοιος.

8:56 ἐχάρη is the second aorist passive of χαίρω, "I rejoice, am glad." The passive is translated as an active.

8:58 πρὶν Ἀβραὰμ γενέσθαι is a preposition with the infinitive. Translate as an adverbial clause with Ἀβραάμ as subject, "Before Abraham came into existence."

8:59 ἐκρύβη. The passive of this verb is translated as "to hide or conceal oneself."

3. Vocabulary

πρίν

4. Prepare a written translation of John 8:48-59.

JOHN 9:1-12

1. Read John 9:1-12.

2. Reading helps

9:2 ἥμαρτεν is from ἀμαρτάνω. Notice the stem.

ἤ, "or."

9:4 ἕως is usually "till, until," but here "while" is better.

9:5 ὦ is the subjunctive of εἰμί.

9:7 νίψαι (also 9:11) is from νίπτω, "I wash" (See Special Vocabulary). It is the aorist middle imperative second singular, "wash yourself." Notice the other aorist forms used in this section: ἐνίψατο (9:7); νιψάμενος (9:11); ἐνιψάμην (9:15). When it refers to oneself, it is always in the middle.

εἰς is used for ἐν.

9:8 οἱ θεωροῦντες in the context must be translated in the imperfect, "used to see."

οὐχ is used instead of οὐ before a word with a rough breathing. It is used here to indicate that a positive answer is expected.

9:9 οὐχί is the strengthened form of οὔ, "no."

αὐτῷ is dative following ὅμοιος.

9:10 ἠνεῴχθησαν is from ἀνοίγω. Notice the irregular augment before the preposition ἀν, the double augment before the stem (εῳ), the change of the γ to χ before the θ. The augment and the θη is a clear clue to what it is.

9:11 ὁ λεγόμενος, "who is called."

3. Vocabulary   πηλός, ὁ

4. Prepare a written translation of John 9:1-12

LESSON 121

JOHN 9:13-23

1. Read John 9:13-23.

2. Reading helps

9:14 ᾗ. What is this form? It is not the article since it has an accent and an iota sybscript. Neither is it the subjunctive of εἰμί (ᾖ) since it has a rough breathing. It is the feminine dative relative pronoun. In Greek it is literally "on which day." However, it stands for ἐν τῇ ἡμέρᾳ ἐν ᾗ and should be translated "on the day on which."

ἀνέῳξεν is the aorist active of ἀνοίγω with the double augment. The aorist is also found in the form ἤνοιξεν (9:26, 32) with the irregular augment before the preposition ἀν.

9:15 ἠρώτων is from ἐρωτάω. This form has the augment with the present stem without σ. How is the ων ending to be explained?

9:16 ἄνθρωπος ἁμαρτωλός. Translate simply as "sinner."

ἐν αὐτοῖς, "among them."

9:18 ἕως ὅτου, "until."

αὐτοῦ is redundant. Do not translate.

9:21 ἡλικίαν ἔχει (also 9:23) is literally, "he has age," but translate as "he is of age."

9:22 συνετέθειντο is pluperfect middle of συντίθημι, I place, which in the middle means, I agree. "The Jews had agreed."

3. Vocabulary

ἀποσυνάγωγος

4. Prepare a written translation of John 9:13-23.

209

LESSON 122

JOHN 9:24-34

1. Read John 9:24-34.

2. Reading helps

9:24 ἐκ δευτέρου, "for the second time."

δός is from δίδωμι, the aorist active imperative second singular.

9:24 ἕν is the neuter of "one."

ὤν is a concessive participle, "though I was blind."

9:29 Μωϋσεῖ is dative. It is declined as follows:

$$
\begin{array}{ll}
N & Μωϋσῆς \\
G & Μωϋσέως \\
D & Μωϋσεῖ \\
A & Μωϋσῆν
\end{array}
$$

9:31 ἁμαρτωλῶν and τούτου are the objects of ἀκούει.

9:32 ἐκ τοῦ αἰῶνος, "since the world began"; literally, "from the age."

9:33 ἠδύνατο. Notice the irregular η augment for δύναμαι. This is an imperfect deponent.

3. Prepare a written translation of John 9:24-34.

LESSON 123

JOHN 9:35-10:3

1. Read John 9:35-10:3.

2. Reading helps

9:38 ὁ is an article used as a pronoun.

ἔφη is the second aorist of φημί, I say.

αὐτῷ is the dative after προσκυνέω. This verb also takes the accusative.

9:40 οἱ is connected with ὄντες.

9:41 οὐκ ἂν εἴχετε is a second class contrary to fact condition, "you would not have." εἴχετε is imperfect of ἔχω.

10:3 τῆς φωνῆς is the object of ἀκούει.

3. Prepare a written translation of 9:35-10:3.

APPENDIX 1

RULES FOR ACCENTS

We have provided only the basic rules in the text. We present now a more comprehensive treatment of the rules as a source of reference for the student who wishes to understand certain phenomena which he observes. The basic rules given on page 8 should be reviewed.

1. Verbs

The basic rule for verbs is that the accent goes as far back as the rules allow (recessive). This means that if there is a short ultima, the accent (acute) will fall on the antepenult. If the verb has only two syllables the acute will fall on the penult if the penult is short. If it is long, the circumflex will fall on the penult. If the ultima is long the accent (acute) will fall on the penult. The application of this rule has a slight modification in the case of contract verbs which is provided on page 27.

a. In compound verbs the accent does not go back of the augment, i.e., the preposition never takes the accent.

b. After οὐκ, ἐστι takes the accent on the first syllable.

c. The second aorist middle imperative second person singular is irregular in that the accent falls on the ultima; it is not recessive.

d. The accenting on the perfect active, middle, and passive infinitive is irregular, λελυκέναι, λελύσθαι, since one would expect it to fall on the antepenult with a short ultima.

e. The accenting on the present active infinitive of δίδωμι, διδόναι, is irregular.

2. Nouns

The basic rule for nouns is that the accent will remain where it is in the nominative singular form if the rules allow it. The accent on the nominative singular form

212

can fall on any of the last three syllables. This must be learned separately for each noun.

Some modifications or exceptions to this rule:

a. In the first and second declension, if the accent falls on the ultima the genitive and dative forms in both the singular and plural take the circumflex but the other forms take the acute.

b. Nouns of the first declension take the circumflex on the ultima of the genitive plural regardless of where the accent falls on the nominative singular.

c. Monosyllabic third declension nouns take the accent on the ultima in the genitive and dative of the singular and plural (circumflex in the genitive plural).

d. The accent (acute on the antepenult) on the genitive singular and plural of the third declension nouns ending in -ις goes against the rule that states that the antepenult cannot be accented when the ultima is long.

3. Enclitics

An enclitic is a word that is so closely connected with the preceding word that it normally has no accent of its own, e.g., μου, με, ἐστιν.

a. An acute on the ultima of the word that precedes an enclitic does not turn to a grave.

b. If the word preceding the enclitic has an acute on the antepenult or a circumflex on the penult, it takes an additional accent (acute) on the ultima.

c. If the word preceding the enclitic is itself an enclitic or proclitic, it takes an acute on the ultima.

d. If the enclitic of two syllables follows a word that has an acute on the penult it retains its own accent.

e. If the enclitic has emphasis or begins a clause, it retains its accent.

4. Participles

a. The genitive plural of feminine present active participles follows 2b above.

213

b. The accent of the aorist passive participle is not recessive. It takes the acute on the ultima and follows the rule of noun accent. In the genitive plural of the feminine, it follow 1a above.

c. The accenting on the perfect active, middle, passive participle λελυκώς, λελυκός, λελυκυῖα, λελυμένος, λελυμένον, λελυμένη, is irregular.

d. The accenting of the present participle of δίδωμι, διδούς, διδόν, διδοῦσα, is not recessive.

5. Miscellaneous

The accent of ὥστε appears irregular but this is due to the fact that τε was an enclitic separate from ὡς. Thus actually it follows rule 2c.

APPENDIX 2. THE VERB CHART

	Present	Future	Imperfect	2 Aorist	1 Aorist	1 Perfect
I	λύω	λύσω	ἔλυον	ἔλιπον	ἔλυσα	λέλυκα
N	λύεις	λύσεις	ἔλυες	ἔλιπες	ἔλυσας	λέλυκας
D.	λύει	λύσει	ἔλυε(ν)	ἔλιπε(ν)	ἔλυσε(ν)	λέλυκε(ν)
A	λύομεν	λύσομεν	ἐλύομεν	ἐλίπομεν	ἐλύσαμεν	λελύκαμεν
C	λύετε	λύσετε	ἐλύετε	ἐλίπετε	ἐλύσατε	λελύκατε
T.	λύουσι(ν)	λύσουσι(ν)	ἔλυον	ἔλιπον	ἔλυσαν	λελύκασι(ν) -καν

	Present	2 Aorist	1 Aorist
S	λύω	λίπω	λύσω
U	λύῃς	λίπῃς	λύσῃς
B.	λύῃ	λίπῃ	λύσῃ
A	λύωμεν	λίπωμεν	λύσωμεν
C	λύητε	λίπητε	λύσητε
T.	λύωσι(ν)	λίπωσι(ν)	λύσωσι(ν)

	Present	Future	Imperfect	2 Aorist	1 Aorist	1 Perfect
I	λύομαι	λύσομαι	ἐλυόμην	ἐλιπόμην	ἐλυσάμην	λέλυμαι
N	λύῃ	λύσῃ	ἐλύου	ἐλίπου	ἐλύσω	λέλυσαι
D.	λύεται	λύσεται	ἐλύετο	ἐλίπετο	ἐλύσατο	λέλυται
M	λυόμεθα	λυσόμεθα	ἐλυόμεθα	ἐλιπόμεθα	ἐλυσάμεθα	λελύμεθα
I	λύεσθε	λύσεσθε	ἐλύεσθε	ἐλίπεσθε	ἐλύσασθε	λέλυσθε
D.	λύονται	λύσονται	ἐλύοντο	ἐλίποντο	ἐλύσαντο	λέλυνται

	Present	2 Aorist	1 Aorist
S	λύωμαι	λίπωμαι	λύσωμαι
U	λύῃ	λίπῃ	λύσῃ
B.	λύηται	λίπηται	λύσηται
M	λυώμεθα	λιπώμεθα	λυσώμεθα
I	λύησθε	λίπησθε	λύσησθε
D.	λύωνται	λίπωνται	λύσωνται

	Present	Future	Imperfect	2 Aorist	1 Aorist	1 Perfect
I	λύομαι	λυθήσομαι	ἐλυόμην	ἐγράφην[1]	ἐλύθην	λέλυμαι
N	λύῃ	λυθήσῃ	ἐλύου	ἐγράφης	ἐλύθης	λέλυσαι
D.	λύεται	λυθήσεται	ἐλύετο	ἐγράφη	ἐλύθη	λέλυται
P	λυόμεθα	λυθησόμεθα	ἐλυόμεθα	ἐγράφημεν	ἐλύθημεν	λελύμεθα
A	λύεσθε	λυθήσεσθε	ἐλύεσθε	ἐγράφητε	ἐλύθητε	λέλυσθε
S	λύονται	λυθήσονται	ἐλύοντο	ἐγράφησαν	ἐλύθησαν	λέλυνται

	Present	2 Aorist	1 Aorist
S	λύωμαι	λιπῶ	λυθῶ
U	λύῃ	λιπῇς	λυθῇς
B.	λύηται	λιπῇ	λυθῇ
P	λυώμεθα	λιπῶμεν	λυθῶμεν
A	λύησθε	λιπῆτε	λυθῆτε
S.	λύωνται	λιπῶσι(ν)	λυθῶσι(ν)

---

[1]λείπω is not a second aorist in the passive so we have substituted γράφω instead.

	Present	Future	Imperfect	2 Aorist	1 Aorist	1 Perfect
I						
M	λῦε			λίπε	λῦσον	
P.	λυέτω			λιπέτω	λυσάτω	
A						
C	λύετε			λίπετε	λύσατε	
T.	λυέτωσαν			λιπέτωσαν	λυσάτωσαν	
I						
M	λύου			λιποῦ	λῦσαι	
P.	λυέσθω			λιπέσθω	λυσάσθω	
M						
I	λύεσθε			λίπεσθε	λύσασθε	
D.	λυέσθωσαν			λιπέσθωσαν	λυσάσθωσαν	
I						
M	λύου			λίπηθι	λύθητι	
P.	λυέσθω			λιπήτωσαν	λυθήτω	
P						
A	λύεσθε			λίπητε	λύθητε	
S.	λυέσθωσαν			λιπήτωσαν	λυθήτωσαν	
I						
N						
F						
A.	λύειν			λιπεῖν	λῦσαι	λελυκέναι
M.	λύεσθαι			λίπεσθαι	λύσασθαι	λέλυσθαι
P.	λύεσθαι			λιπῆναι	λυθῆναι	λέλυσθαι

Pluperfect Active Indicative

	Singular	Plural
1	(ε)λελύκειν	(ε)λελύκειμεν
2	(ε)λελύκεις	(ε)λελύκειτε
3	(ε)λελύκει	(ε)λελύκεισαν

Contract Verbs

-αω	-εω	-οω	-αω	-εω	-οω

Present Indicative

Active			Middle and Passive		
ἀγαπῶ	ποιῶ	πληρῶ	ἀγαπῶμαι	ποιοῦμαι	πληροῦμαι
ἀγαπᾷς	ποιεῖς	πληροῖς	ἀγαπᾷ	ποιῇ	πληροῖ
ἀγαπᾷ	ποιεῖ	πληροῖ	ἀγαπᾶται	ποιεῖται	πληροῦται
ἀγαπῶμεν	ποιοῦμεν	πληροῦμεν	ἀγαπώμεθα	ποιούμεθα	πληρούμεθα
ἀγαπᾶτε	ποιεῖτε	πληροῦτε	ἀγαπᾶσθε	ποιεῖσθε	πληροῦσθε
ἀγαπῶσι(ν)	ποιοῦσι(ν)	πληροῦσι(ν)	ἀγαπῶνται	ποιοῦνται	πληροῦνται

Imperfect Indicative

	Active			Middle and Passive		
1	ἠγάπων	ἐποίουν	ἐπλήρουν	ἠγαπώμην	ἐποιούμην	ἐπληρούμην
2	ἠγάπας	ἐποίεις	ἐπλήρους	ἠγαπῶ	ἐποιοῦ	ἐπληροῦ
3	ἠγάπα	ἐποίει	ἐπλήρου	ἠγαπᾶτο	ἐποιεῖτο	ἐπληροῦτο
1	ἠγαπῶμεν	ἐποιοῦμεν	ἐπληροῦμεν	ἠγαπώμεθα	ἐποιούμεθα	ἐπληρούμεθα
2	ἠγαπᾶτε	ἐποιεῖτε	ἐπληροῦτε	ἠγαπᾶσθε	ἐποιεῖσθε	ἐπληροῦσθε
3	ἠγάπων	ἐποίουν	ἐπλήρουν	ἠγαπῶντο	ἐποιοῦντο	ἐπληροῦντο

Present Subjunctive

1	ἀγαπῶ	ποιῶ	πληρῶ	ἀγαπῶμαι	ποιῶμαι	πληρῶμαι
2	ἀγαπᾷς	ποιῇς	πληροῖς	ἀγαπᾷ	ποιῇ	πληροῖ
3	ἀγαπᾷ	ποιῇ	πληροῖ	ἀγαπᾶται	ποιῆται	πληρῶται
1	ἀγαπῶμεν	ποιῶμεν	πληρῶμεν	ἀγαπώμεθα	ποιώμεθα	πληρώμεθα
2	ἀγαπᾶτε	ποιῆτε	πληρῶτε	ἀγαπᾶσθε	ποιῆσθε	πληρῶσθε
3	ἀγαπῶσι(ν)	ποιῶσι(ν)	πληρῶσι(ν)	ἀγαπῶνται	ποιῶνται	πληρῶνται

Present Imperative

2	ἀγάπα	ποίει	πλήρου	ἀγαπῶ	ποιοῦ	πληροῦ
3	ἀγαπάτω	ποιείτω	πληρούτω	ἀγαπάσθω	ποιείσθω	πληρούσθω
2	ἀγαπᾶτε	ποιεῖτε	πληροῦτε	ἀγαπᾶσθε	ποιεῖσθε	πληροῦσθε
3	ἀγαπάτωσαν	ποιείτωσαν	πληρούτωσαν	ἀγαπάσθωσαν	ποιεισθωσαν	πληρουσθωσαν

Present Infinitive

ἀγαπᾶν	ποιεῖν	πληροῦν	ἀγαπᾶσθαι	ποιεῖσθαι	πληροῦσθαι

Present Participle

M	ἀγαπῶν	ποιῶν	πληρῶν	ἀγαπώμενος	ποιούμενος	πληρούμενος
N	ἀγαπῶν	ποιοῦν	πληροῦν	ἀγαπώμενον	ποιούμενον	πληρούμενον
F	ἀγαπῶσα	ποιοῦσα	πληροῦσα	ἀγαπωμένη	ποιουμένη	πληρουμένη

The Verb To Be

	Present Indicative	Future Indicative	Imperfect Indicative
1	εἰμί	ἔσομαι	ἤμην
2	εἶ	ἔσῃ	ἦς, ἦσθα
3	ἐστί(ν)	ἔσται	ἦν
1	ἐσμέν	ἐσόμεθα	ἦμεν, ἤμεθα
2	ἐστέ	ἔσεσθε	ἦτε
3	εἰσί(ν)	ἔσονται	ἦσαν

Present Subjunctive   Present Imperative   Present Infinitive

1	ὦ		εἶναι
2	ἦς	ἴσθι	
3	ἦ	ἔστω	
1	ὦμεν		
2	ἦτε	ἔστε	
3	ὦσι(ν)	ἔστωσαν	

Participles

The Verb To Be

	Singular			Plural		
	M	N	F	M	N	F
N	ὤν	ὄν	οὖσα	ὄντες	ὄντα	οὖσαι
G	ὄντος	ὄντος	οὔσης	ὄντων	ὄντων	οὐσῶν
D	ὄντι	ὄντι	οὔσῃ	οὖσι(ν)	οὖσι(ν)	οὔσαις
A	ὄντα	ὄν	οὖσαν	ὄντας	ὄντα	οὔσας

The forms of the participle follow the third declension in the masculine and neuter active and passive forms, the second declension in the masculine and neuter middle forms, and the first declension in all the feminine forms throughout. The active endings are the same as those of εἰμί. The μενος, μενον, μενη endings are clear signs of the participle endings in the middle and for the present and perfect in the passive as well.

Present Active

	Singular			Plural		
	M	N	F	M	N	F
N	λύων	λῦον	λύουσα	λύοντες	λύοντα	λύουσαι
G	λύοντος	λύοντος	λυούσης	λυόντων	λυόντων	λυουσῶν
D	λύοντι	λύοντι	λυούσῃ	λύουσι(ν)	λύουσι(ν)	λυούσαις
A	λύοντα	λῦον	λύουσαν	λύοντας	λύοντα	λυούσας

Present Middle and Passive

N	λυόμενος	λυόμενον	λυομένη	λυόμενοι	λυόμενα	λυόμεναι
G	λυομένου	λυομένου	λυομένης	λυομένων	λυομένων	λυομένων
D	λυομένῳ	λυομένῳ	λυομένῃ	λυομένοις	λυομένοις	λυομέναις
A	λυόμενον	λυόμενον	λυομένην	λυομένους	λυόμενα	λυομένας

2 Aorist Active

N	λιπών	λιπόν	λιποῦσα	λιπόντες	λιπόμενα	λιπόμεναι
G	λιπόντος	λιπόντος	λιπούσης	λιπόντων	λιπομένων	λιπομένων
D	λιπόντι	λιπόντι	λιπούσῃ	λιποῦσι(ν)	λιπομένοις	λιπομέναις
A	λιπόντα	λιπόν	λιποῦσαν	λιπόντας	λιπόμενα	λιπομένας

2 Aorist Middle

	Singular			Plural		
	M	N	F	M	N	F
N	λιπόμενος	λιπόμενον	λιπομένη	λιπόμενοι	λιπόμενα	λιπόμεναι
G	λιπομένου	λιπομένου	λιπομένης	λιπομένων	λιπομένων	λιπομένων
D	λιπομένῳ	λιπομένῳ	λιπομένῃ	λιπομένοις	λιπομένοις	λιπομέναις
A	λιπόμενον	λιπόμενον	λιπομένην	λιπομένους	λιπόμενα	λιπομένας

2 Aorist Passive

N	λιπείς	λιπέν	λιπεῖσα	λιπέντες	λιπέντα	λιπεῖσαι
G	λιπέντος	λιπέντος	λιπείσης	λιπέντων	λιπέντων	λιπεισῶν
D	λιπέντι	λιπέντι	λιπείσῃ	λιπεῖσι(ν)	λιπεῖσι(ν)	λιπείσαις
A	λιπέντα	λιπέν	λιπεῖσαν	λιπέντας	λιπέντα	λιπείσας

1 Aorist Active

N	λύσας	λῦσαν	λύσασα	λύσαντες	λύσαντα	λύσασαι
G	λύσαντος	λύσαντος	λυσάσης	λυσάντων	λυσάντων	λυσασῶν
D	λύσαντι	λύσαντι	λυσάσῃ	λύσασι(ν)	λύσασι(ν)	λυσάσαις
A	λύσαντα	λῦσαν	λύσασαν	λύσαντας	λύσαντα	λύσασας

1 Aorist Middle

N	λυσάμενος	λυσάμενον	λυσαμένη	λυσάμενοι	λυσάμενα	λυσάμεναι
G	λυσαμένου	λυσαμένου	λυσαμένης	λυσαμένων	λυσαμένων	λυσαμένων
D	λυσαμένῳ	λυσαμένῳ	λυσαμένη	λύσασι(ν)	λυσαμένοις	λυσαμέναις
A	λυσάμενον	λυσάμενον	λυσαμένην	λύσαντας	λυσάμενα	λυσαμένας

1 Aorist Passive

N	λυθείς	λυθέν	λυθεῖσα	λυθέντες	λυθέντα	λυθεῖσαι
G	λυθέντος	λυθέντος	λυθείσης	λυθέντων	λυθέντων	λυθεισῶν
D	λυθέντι	λυθέντι	λυθείσῃ	λυθεῖσι(ν)	λυθεῖσι(ν)	λυθείσαις
A	λυθέντα	λυθέν	λυθεῖσαν	λυθέντας	λυθέντα	λυθείσας

1 Perfect Active

N	λελυκώς	λελυκός	λελυκυῖα	λελυκότες	λελυκότα	λελυκυῖαι
G	λελυκότος	λελυκότος	λελυκυίας	λελυκότων	λελυκότων	λελυκυιῶν
D	λελυκότι	λελυκότι	λελυκυίᾳ	λελυκόσι(ν)	λελυκόσι(ν)	λελυκυίαις
A	λελυκότα	λελυκός	λελυκυῖαν	λελυκότας	λελυκότα	λελυκυίας

1 Perfect Middle and Passive

N	λελυμένος	λελυμένον	λελυμένη	λελυμένοι	λελυμένα	λελυμέναι
G	λελυμένου	λελυμένου	λελυμένης	λελυμένων	λελυμένων	λελυμένων
D	λελυμένῳ	λελυμένῳ	λελυμένη	λελυμένοις	λελυμένοις	λελυμέναις
A	λελυμένον	λελυμένον	λελυμένην	λελυμένους	λελυμένα	λελυμένας

μι Conjugation

Active

	Present			Imperfect		
I	ἵστημι	τίθημι	δίδωμι	ἵστην	ἐτίθην	ἐδίδουν
N	ἵστης	τίθης	δίδως	ἵστης	ἐτίθεις	ἐδίδους
D.	ἵστησι	τίθησι	δίδωσι	ἵστη	ἐτίθει	ἐδίδου
	ἵσταμεν	τίθεμεν	δίδομεν	ἵσταμεν	ἐτίθεμεν	ἐδίδομεν
	ἵστατε	τίθετε	δίδοτε	ἵστατε	ἐτίθετε	ἐδίδοτε
	ἵστασι	τιθέασι	διδόασι	ἵστασαν	ἐτίθεσαν	ἐδίδοσαν

	1 Aorist			Perfect		
I	ἔστησα	ἔθηκα	ἔδωκα	ἔστηκα	τέθεικα	δέδωκα
N	ἔστησας	ἔθηκας	ἔδωκας	ἔστηκας	τέθεικας	δέδωκας
D.	ἔστησε	ἔθηκε	ἔδωκε	ἔστηκε	τέθεικε	δέδωκε
	ἐστήσαμεν	ἐθήκαμεν	ἐδώκαμεν	ἐστήκαμεν	τεθείκαμεν	δεδώκαμεν
	ἐστήσατε	ἐθήκατε	ἐδώκατε	ἐστήκατε	τεθείκατε	δεδώκατε
	ἔστησαν	ἔθηκαν	ἔδωκαν	ἔστηκαν	τέθεικαν	δέδωκαν

2 Aorist of ἵστημι

ἔστην	ἔστημεν
ἔστης	ἔστητε
ἔστη	ἔστησαν

	Present			2 Aorist		
S	ἱστῶ	τιθῶ	διδῶ	στῶ	θῶ	δῶ
U	ἱστῆς	τιθῇς	διδῷς	στῇς	θῇς	δῷς
B	ἱστῇ	τιθῇ	διδῷ	στῇ	θῇ	δῷ
J.	ἱστῶμεν	τιθῶμεν	διδῶμεν	στῶμεν	θῶμεν	δῶμεν
	ἱστῆτε	τιθῆτε	διδῶτε	στῆτε	θῆτε	δῶτε
	ἱστῶσι	τιθῶσι	διδῶσι	στῶσι	θῶσι	δῶσι

	Present			2 Aorist		
I						
M	ἵστη	τίθει	δίδου	στῆθι	θές	δός
P.	ἱστάτω	τιθέτω	διδότω	στήτω	θέτω	δότω
	ἵστατε	τίθετε	δίδοτε	στῆτε	θέτε	δότε
	ἱστάτωσαν	τιθέτωσαν	διδότωσαν	στήτωσαν	θέτωσαν	δότωσαν

I						
N	ἱστάναι	τιθέναι	διδόναι	στῆναι	θεῖναι	δοῦναι
F.						

Middle and Passive

	Present			Imperfect		
I	ἵσταμαι	τίθεμαι	δίδομαι	ἱστάμην	ἐτιθέμην	ἐδιδόμην
N	ἵστασαι	τίθεσαι	δίδοσαι	ἵστασο	ἐτίθεσο	ἐδίδοσο
D.	ἵσταται	τίθεται	δίδοται	ἵστατο	ἐτίθετο	ἐδίδοτο
	ἱστάμεθα	τιθέμεθα	διδόμεθα	ἱστάμεθα	ἐτιθέμεθα	ἐδιδόμεθα
	ἵστασθε	τίθεσθε	δίδοσθε	ἵστασθε	ἐτίθεσθε	ἐδίδοσθε
	ἵστανται	τίθενται	δίδονται	ἵσταντο	ἐτίθεντο	ἐδίδοντο

2 Aorist Middle			Aorist Passive		
I	ἐθέμην	ἐδόμην	ἐστάθην	ἐτέθην	ἐδόθην
N	ἔθου	ἔδου	ἐστάθης	ἐτέθης	ἐδόθης
D.	ἔθετο	ἔδοτο	ἐστάθη	ἐτέθη	ἐδόθη
	ἐθέμεθα	ἐδόμεθα	ἐστάθημεν	ἐτέθημεν	ἐδόθημεν
	ἔθεσθε	ἔδοσθε	ἐστάθητε	ἐτέθητε	ἐδόθητε
	ἔθεντο	ἔδοντο	ἐστάθησαν	ἐτέθησαν	ἐδόθησαν

	Middle and Passive Present			Middle 2 Aorist	
S	ἱστῶμαι	τιθῶμαι	διδῶμαι	θῶμαι	δῶμαι
U	ἱστῇ	τιθῇ	διδῷ	θῇ	δῷ
B	ἱστῆται	τιθῆται	διδῶται	θῆται	δῶται
J.	ἱστώμεθα	τιθώμεθα	διδώμεθα	θώμεθα	δώμεθα
	ἱστῆσθε	τιθῆσθε	διδῶσθε	θῆσθε	δῶσθε
	ἱστῶνται	τιθῶνται	διδῶνται	θῶνται	δῶνται

	Present Middle and Passive			2 Aorist Middle	
I					
M	ἵστασο	τίθεσο	δίδοσο	θοῦ	δοῦ
P.	ἱστάσθω	τιθέσθω	διδόσθω	θέσθω	δόσθω
	ἵστασθε	τίθεσθε	δίδοσθε	θέσθε	δόσθε
	ἱστάσθωσαν	τιθέσθωσαν	διδόσθωσαν	θέσθωσαν	δόσθωσαν

	Aorist Passive		
I			
M	στάθητι	τέθητι	δόθητι
P.	σταθήτω	τεθήτω	δοθήτω
	στάθητε	τέθητε	δόθητε
	σταθήτωσαν	τεθήτωσαν	δοθήτωσαν

	Present Middle and Passive			2 Aorist Middle	
I					
N	ἵστασθαι	τίθεσθαι	δίδοσθαι	θέσθαι	δόσθαι
F.					

	Aorist Passive		
I			
N	σταθῆναι	τεθῆναι	δοθῆναι
F.			

The nominative singular forms of the participles in the μι conjugation are:

	Present Active			2 Aorist Active		
M	ἱστάς	τιθείς	διδούς	στάς	θείς	δούς
N	ἱστάν	τιθέν	διδόν	στάν	θέν	δόν
F	ἱστᾶσα	τιθεῖσα	διδοῦσα	στᾶσα	θεῖσα	δοῦσα

221

Present Middle and Passive

```
  M  ἱστάμενος  τιθέμενος  διδόμενος
  N  ἱστάμενον  τιθέμενον  διδόμενον
  F  ἱσταμένη   τιθεμένη   διδομένη
```

2 Aorist Active

```
  θέμενος  δόμενος
  θέμενον  δόμενον
  θεμένη   δομένη
```

γινώσκω (2 Aorist Forms)

We include the second aorist forms of γινώσκω and βαίνω here since they follow exactly the second aorist forms of ἵστημι.

Indicative	Subjunctive	Imperative	Infinitive	Participle
ἔγνων	γνῶ		γνῶναι	M γνούς
ἔγνως	γνῷς	γνῶθι		N γνόν
ἔγνω	γνῷ (γνοῖ)	γνώτω		F γνοῦσα
ἔγνωμεν	γνῶμεν			
ἔγνωτε	γνῶτε	γνῶτε		
ἔγνωσαν	γνῶσι	γνώτωσαν		

βαίνω (2 Aorist Forms)

βαίνω occurs only in compound form in the NT. We give here the forms of the root only.

Indicative	Subjunctive	Imperative	Infinitive	Participle
ἔβην	βῆ		βῆναι	M βάς
ἔβης	βῇς	βῆθι, βα		N βάν
ἔβη	βῇ	βήτω		F βᾶσα
ἔβημεν	βῆμεν			
ἔβητε	βῆτε	βῆτε		
ἔβησαν	βῆσι	βήτωσαν		

It takes a future deponent form, βήσομαι.

The Article

	Singular			Plural		
	M	N	F	M	N	F
N	ὁ	τό	ἡ	οἱ	τά	αἱ
G	τοῦ	τοῦ	τῆς	τῶν	τῶν	τῶν
D	τῷ	τῷ	τῇ	τοῖς	τõις	ταῖς
A	τόν	τό	τήν	τούς	τά	τάς

Noun Declensions

1. First Declension

a. Feminine nouns

	Singular			Plural		
N	ἡμέρα	δόξα	γραφή	ἡμέραι	δόξαι	γραφαί
G	ἡμέρας	δόξης	γραφῆς	ἡμερῶν	δοξῶν	γραφῶν
D	ἡμέρᾳ	δόξῃ	γραφῇ	ἡμέραις	δόξαις	γραφαῖς
A	ἡμέραν	δόξαν	γραφήν	ἡμέρας	δόξας	γραφάς

　　　　When a first declension noun ends in an α in the nominative
singular and is preceded by ε, ι, or ρ, it maintains the α throughout. Otherwise the genitive and dative take the η as in δόξα. If
the noun ends in η in the nominative, it maintains the η throughout.
The plural forms are all alike. Notice that the genitive plural
always takes a circumflex on the ultima.

b. Masculine nouns

	Singular		Plural	
N	προφήτης	νεανίας	προφῆται	νεανίαι
G	προφήτου	νεανίου	προφητῶν	νεανιῶν
D	προφήτῃ	νεανίᾳ	προφήταις	νεανίαις
A	προφήτην	νεανίαν	προφήτας	νεανίας

　　　　Nouns of this type will take the α in the nominative,
dative and accusative when the ending is preceded by ε, ι, or ρ.
Otherwise it will take an η. The genitive singular forms of both
types have ου since the nominative forms are like the genitive
forms of the feminine nouns.

2. Second Declension

a. Masculine nouns

	Singular	Plural	Singular	Plural
N	ἄνθρωπος	ἄνθρωποι	τέκνον	τέκνα
G	ἀνθρώπου	ἀνθρώπων	τέκνου	τέκνων
D	ἀνθρώπῳ	ἀνθρώποις	τέκνῳ	τέκνοις
A	ἄνθρωπον	ἀνθρώπους	τέκνον	τέκνα

3. Third Declension

a. Mute endings, feminine nouns: νυκτ-, ἐλπιδ-, χαριτ-

	Singular			Plural		
N	νύξ	ἐλπίς	χάρις	νύκτες	ἐλπίδες	χάριτες
G	νυκτός	ἐλπίδος	χάριτος	νυκτῶν	ἐλπίδων	χαρίτων
D	νυκτί	ἐλπίδι	χάριτι	νυξί(ν)	ἐλπίσι(ν)	χάρισι(ν)
A	νύκτα	ἐλπίδα	χάριν	νύκτας	ἐλπίδας	χάριτας

Masculine noun: ἀρχοντ-   Neuter noun: ὀνοματ-

	Singular	Plural	Singular	Plural
N	ἄρχων	ἄρχοντες	ὄνομα	ὀνόματα
G	ἄρχοντος	ἀρχόντων	ὀνόματος	ὀνομάτων
D	ἄρχοντι	ἄρχουσι(ν)	ὀνόματι	ὀνόμασι(ν)
A	ἄρχοντα	ἄρχοντας	ὄνομα	ὀνόματα

b. Nasal endings: ὁ δαιμον-, ὁ ποιμεν-, ὁ αἰων-

	Singular			Plural		
N	δαίμων	ποιμήν	αἰών	δαίμονες	ποιμένες	αἰῶνες
G	δαίμονος	ποιμένος	αἰῶνος	δαιμόνων	ποιμένων	αἰώνων
D	δαίμονι	ποιμένι	αἰῶνι	δαίμοσι(ν)	ποιμέσι(ν)	αἰῶσι(ν)
A	δαίμονα	ποιμένα	αἰῶνα	δαίμονας	ποιμένας	αἰῶνας

Notice that the dative plurals drop the ν before the σ.

c. Liquid endings: ὁ πατερ-, ἡ χειρ-, ὁ σωτηρ-

	Singular			Plural		
N	πατήρ	χείρ	σωτήρ	πατέρες	χεῖρες	σωτῆρες
G	πατρός	χειρός	σωτῆρος	πατέρων	χειρῶν	σωτήρων
D	πατρί	χειρί	σωτῆρι	πατράσι(ν)	χερσί(ν)	σωτῆρσι(ν)
A	πατέρα	χεῖρα	σωτῆρα	πατέρας	χεῖρας	σωτῆρας

d. σ endings: τὸ τελεσ-, ὁ συγγενεσ-

	Singular		Plural	
N	τέλος	συγγενής	τέλη=ε(σ)α	συγγενεῖς=ε(σ)ες
G	τέλους=ε(σ)ος	συγγενοῦς	τελῶν=ε(σ)ων	συγγενῶν
D	τέλει=ε(σ)ι	συγγενεῖ	τέλεσι=εσ(σ)ι	συγγενέσι(ν)
A	τέλος	συγγενῆ=ε(σ)α	τέλη=ε(σ)α	συγγενεῖς

e. Semi-vowel endings: ἡ πολει(ι)-, ἡ ισχυ-, ὁ βασιλευ-

N	πόλις	ἰσχύς	βασιλεύς	πόλεις	ἰσχύες	βασιλεῖς
G	πόλεως	ἰσχύος	βασιλέως	πόλεων	ἰσχύων	βασιλέων
D	πόλει	ἰσχύϊ	βασιλεῖ	πόλεσι(ν)	ἰσχύσι(ν)	βασιλεῦσι(ν)
A	πόλιν	ἰσχύν	βασιλέα	πόλεις	ἰσχύας	βασιλεῖς

Note the basic endings of the third declension are:

	Singular		Plural	
	MF	N	MF	N
N	ς		ες	α
G	ος	ος	ων	ων
D	ι	ι	σι	σι
A	α		ας	α

Adjectives

	Singular			Plural		
	M	N	F	M	N	F
N	ἀγαθός	ἀγαθόν	ἀγαθή	ἀγαθοί	ἀγαθά	ἀγαθαί
G	ἀγαθοῦ	ἀγαθοῦ	ἀγαθῆς	ἀγαθῶν	ἀγαθῶν	ἀγαθῶν
D	ἀγαθῷ	ἀγαθῷ	ἀγαθῇ	ἀγαθοῖς	ἀγαθοῖς	ἀγαθαῖς
A	ἀγαθόν	ἀγαθόν	ἀγαθήν	ἀγαθούς	ἀγαθά	ἀγαθάς

N	μικρός	μικρόν	μικρά	μικροί	μικρά	μικραί
G	μικροῦ	μικροῦ	μικρᾶς	μικρῶν	μικρῶν	μικρῶν
D	μικρῷ	μικρῷ	μικρᾷ	μικροῖς	μικροῖς	μικραῖς
A	μικρόν	μικρόν	μικράν	μικρούς	μικρά	μικράς

N	δίκαιος	δίκαιον	δικαία	δίκαιοι	δίκαια	δίκαιαι
G	δικαίου	δικαίου	δικαίας	δικαίων	δικαίων	δικαίων
D	δικαίῳ	δικαίῳ	δικαίᾳ	δικαίοις	δικαίοις	δικαίαις
A	δίκαιον	δίκαιον	δικαίαν	δικαίους	δίκαια	δικαίας

The declension of ἀληθής, true. Notice that the masculine and feminine forms are identical.

	Plural		Plural	
	MF	N	MF	N
N	ἀληθής	ἀληθές	ἀληθεῖς	ἀληθῆ
G	ἀληθοῦς	ἀληθοῦς	ἀληθῶν	ἀληθῶν
D	ἀληθεῖ	ἀληθεῖ	ἀληθέσι(ν)	ἀληθέσι(ν)
A	ἀληθῆ	ἀληθές	ἀληθεῖς	ἀληθῆ

The declension of μέγας, great.

Singular   Plural

225

	M	N	F	M	N	F
N	μέγας	μέγα	μεγάλη	μεγάλοι	μεγάλα	μεγάλαι
G	μεγάλου	μεγάλου	μεγάλης	μεγάλων	μεγάλων	μεγάλων
D	μεγάλῳ	μεγάλῳ	μεγάλῃ	μεγάλοις	μεγάλοις	μεγάλαις
A	μέγαν	μέγα	μεγάλην	μεγάλους	μεγάλα	μεγάλας

The declension of μείζων, greater.

	Singular		Plural	
	MF	N	MF	N
N	μείζων	μεῖζον	μείζονες/μείζους	μείζονα/μείζω
G	μείζονος	μείζονος	μειζόνων	μειζόνων
D	μείζονι	μείζονι	μείζοσι(ν)	μείζοσι(ν)
A	μειζονα/μείζω	μεῖζον	μείζονας/μείζους	μείζονα/μείζω

The declension of πολύς, much.

	Singular			Plural		
	M	N	F	M	N	F
N	πολύς	πολύ	πολλή	πολλοί	πολλά	πολλαί
G	πολλοῦ	πολλοῦ	πολλῆς	πολλῶν	πολλῶν	πολλῶν
D	πολλῷ	πολλῷ	πολλῇ	πολλοῖς	πολλοῖς	πολλαῖς
A	πολύν	πολύ	πολλήν	πολλούς	πολλά	πολλάς

The declension of πᾶς, every, all.

	Singular			Plural		
	M	N	F	M	N	F
N	πᾶς	πᾶν	πᾶσα	πάντες	πάντα	πᾶσαι
G	παντός	παντός	πάσης	πάντων	πάντων	πασῶν
D	παντί	παντί	πάσῃ	πᾶσι(ν)	πᾶσι(ν)	πάσαις
A	πάντα	πᾶν	πᾶσαν	πάντας	πάντα	πάσας

The declension of εἷς, one.

N	εἷς	ἕν	μία
G	ἑνός	ἑνός	μιᾶς
D	ἑνί	ἑνί	μιᾷ
A	ἑνά	ἕν	μίαν

Pronouns

1. Personal pronouns

	Singular			Plural		
	1	2	3	1	2	3
N	ἐγώ	σύ	αὐτός, ο, η	ἡμεῖς	ὑμεῖς	αὐτοί, α, αι
G	ἐμοῦ (μου)	σοῦ (σου)	αὐτοῦ, ου, ης	ἡμῶν	ὑμῶν	αὐτῶν, ων, ων
D	ἐμοί (μοι)	σοί (σοι)	αὐτῷ, ῷ, ῇ	ἡμῖν	ὑμῖν	αὐτοῖς, οις, αις
A	ἐμέ (με)	σέ (σε)	αὐτόν, ο, ην	ἡμᾶς	ὑμᾶς	αὐτούς, α, ας

2. Demonstrative Pronouns

	Singular			Plural		
	M	N	F	M	N	F
N	οὗτος	τοῦτο	αὕτη	οὗτοι	ταῦτα	αὗται
G	τούτου	τούτου	ταύτης	τούτων	τούτων	τούτων
D	τούτῳ	τούτῳ	ταύτῃ	τούτοις	τούτοις	ταύταις
A	τοῦτον	τοῦτο	ταύτην	τούτους	ταῦτα	ταύτας

3. Relative Pronouns

	Singular			Plural		
	M	N	F	M	N	F
N	ὅς	ὅ	ἥ	οἵ	ἅ	αἵ
G	οὗ	οὗ	ἧς	ὧν	ὧν	ὧν
D	ᾧ	ᾧ	ᾗ	οἷς	οἷς	αἷς
A	ὅν	ὅ	ἥν	οὕς	ἅ	ἅς

4. Interrogative Pronouns

	Singular		Plural	
	MF	S	MF	N
N	τίς	τί	τίνες	τίνα
G	τίνος	τίνος	τίνων	τίνων
D	τίνι	τίνι	τίσι(ν)	τίσι(ν)
A	τίνα	τί	τίνας	τίνα

5. Indefinite Pronouns

The indefinite pronoun, something, someone, has the same forms as the interrogative pronoun but is normally unaccented.

6. Reflexive Pronouns

The first and second person singular reflexive pronoun: myself, yourself.

	M	F	M	F
G	ἐμαυτοῦ	ἐμαυτῆς	σεαυτοῦ	σεαυτῆς
D	ἐμαυτῷ	ἐμαυτῇ	σεαυτῷ	σεαυτῇ
A	ἐμαυτόν	ἐμαυτήν	σεαυτόν	σεαυτήν

The third person singular reflexive pronoun has three genders: himself, itself, herself.

	M	N	F
G	ἑαυτοῦ	ἑαυτοῦ	ἑαυτῆς
D	ἑαυτῷ	ἑαυτῷ	ἑαυτῇ
A	ἑαυτόν	ἑαυτό	ἑαυτήν

There is only one set of plural endings which serve for all three persons: ourselves, yourselves, themselves.

	M	N	F
G	ἑαυτῶν	ἑαυτῶν	ἑαυτῶν
D	ἑαυτοῖς	ἑαυτοῖς	ἑαυταῖς
A	ἑαυτούς	ἑαυτά	ἑαυτάς

ἀγαθός, ον η good
ἀγαπάω I love
ἀγάπη, ἡ love
ἀγαπητός, ον η beloved
ἄγγελος, ὁ messenger, angel
ἅγιος, ον, α holy
ἄγω I lead
ἀδελφή, ἡ sister
ἀδελφός, ὁ brother
αἷμα, αἵματος, τό blood
αἴρω I take up, take away
αἰτέω I ask
αἰών, αἰῶνος, ὁ age
αἰώνιος, ον, ος eternal
ἀκολουθέω I follow
ἀκούω I hear
ἀλήθεια, ἡ truth
ἀληθής, ες, η true
ἀληθινός, ον, η true, genuine
ἀληθῶς truly
ἀλλά but, except
ἀλλήλων of one another (gen. plural); ἀλλήλοις to or for one another (dat. plural); ἀλλήλους one another (acc. plural)
ἄλλος, ο, η other, another
ἁμαρτάνω I sin
ἁμαρτία, ἡ sin
ἁμαρτωλός, ον, η sinful; as a noun, sinner
ἀναβαίνω I go up
ἀνάστασις, ἡ resurrection
ἀνήρ, ἀνδρός, ὁ man, husband
ἄνθρωπος, ὁ man
ἀνοίγω I open
ἀπέρχομαι I go away, depart
ἀπό from (with genitive)
ἀποθνήσκω I die
ἀποκρίνομαι I answer
ἀποκτείνω I kill
ἀπόλλυμι I destroy; pass. I die
ἀπολύω I release
ἀποστέλλω I send
ἀπόστολος, ὁ apostle
ἄρα then
ἄρτι now
ἄρτος, ὁ bread
ἀρχιερεύς, ἀρχιερέως, ὁ high priest

ἀρχή, ἡ beginning
ἄρχομαι I begin
ἄρχων, ἄρχοντος, ὁ ruler
ἀσθενέω I am sick, weak
ἀσπάζομαι I greet, salute
ἀφίημι I leave, permit, forgive
ἄχρι, ἄχρις as far as, up to (with genitive); on account of, because of (with accusative)

βάλλω I cast, throw
βαπτίζω I baptize
βασιλεία, ἡ kingdom
βασιλεύς, βασιλέως, ὁ king
βασιλεύω I reign, rule
βλασφημέω I blaspheme, revile
βλέπω I see

γάρ for (postpositive)
γεννάω I beget
γένος, γένους, τό race
γῆ, ἡ earth
γίνομαι I become, come into existence, appear
γινώσκω I know
γλῶσσα, ἡ tongue, language
γονεύς, γονέως, ὁ begetter, pl. parents
γραμματεύς, γραμματέως, ὁ scribe
γραφή, ἡ writing, Scripture
γράφω I write
γυνή, γυναικός, ἡ woman, wife

δαιμόνιον, τό demon
δέ but, and (postpositive)
δεῖ it is necessary
δείκνυμι I show
δεξιός, ον, α right
δεύτερος, ον, α second
δέχομαι I receive
δέω I bind
διά through (with genitive); on account of, because of (with accusative)
διάβολος, ὁ devil
διαθήκη, ἡ covenant, will
διδάσκαλος, ὁ teacher
διδάσκω I teach
διδαχή, ἡ teaching

δίδωμι I give
δίκαιος, ον, α just
δικαιοσύνη, ἡ righteousness
διό wherefore
διψάω I thirst
διώκω I pursue, persecute
δοκέω I think, seem
δόξα, ἡ glory
δοξάζω I glorify
δοῦλος, ὁ slave, servant
δύναμαι I am able
δύναμις, δυνάμεως, ἡ power
δύο two

ἐγγίζω I come near
ἐγγύς near
ἐγείρω I raise up
ἐγώ I
ἔθνος, ἔθνους, τό nation; pl.
 Gentiles
εἰ if
εἶδον I saw
εἶπον I said
εἰρήνη, ἡ peace
εἰς into (with accusative)
εἰσέρχομαι I go in, come in
ἐκ, ἐξ out of, from (with genitive only; the second form is
used before a word beginning
with a vowel)
ἕκαστος, ον, η each
ἐκβάλλω I cast out
ἐκεῖ there
ἐκκλησία, ἡ church
ἐκπορεύομαι I go out
ἐλπίζω I hope
ἐλπίς, ἐλπίδος, ἡ hope
ἐμαυτοῦ myself
ἔμπροσθεν before, in front of
 (with genitive)
ἐν in (with dative)
ἐντολή, ἡ commandment
ἐνώπιον before (with genitive)
ἑορτή, ἡ feast, festival
ἐπαγγελία, ἡ promise
ἐπερωτάω I ask, demand
ἐπί over, on (with gen.); at,
 on the basis of (with dative);
 on, to, against (with acc.)
ἐπιστολή, ἡ letter
ἑπτά seven

ἐξέρχομαι I go out
ἔξεστι(ν) it is lawful
ἐξουσία, ἡ authority
ἔξω adv. without; prep. outside
 (with genitive)
ἐργάζομαι I work, labor
ἔργον work
ἔρημος, ον, η solitary, deserted;
 as a noun, desert, wilderness
ἔρχομαι I come, go
ἐρῶ I shall say, speak
ἐρωτάω I ask, request
ἐσθίω I eat
ἔσχατος, ον, η last
ἕτερος, ον, α other
ἔτι yet, still, even
ἕτοιμος, ον, η ready, prepared
ἔτος, ἔτους, τό year
εὐαγγελίζω I preach good tidings;
 usually deponent
εὐαγγέλιον, τό gospel
εὐθύς immediately
εὐλογέω I bless
εὑρίσκω I find
εὐχαριστέω I give thanks
ἔχω I have
ἕως until

ζητέω I seek
ζωή, ἡ life

ἤ or, than
ἤδη already, now
ἡμέρα, ἡ day

θάλασσα, ἡ sea
θάνατος, ὁ death
θαυμάζω I marvel, wonder
θεάομαι I behold, see
θέλημα, θελήματος, τό will
θεμέλιον, τό foundation
θεός, ὁ God
θεραπεύω I heal
θεωρέω I look at, behold
θλῖψις, ἡ affliction, tribulation
θρόνος, ὁ throne
θύρα, ἡ door

ἴδιος one's own
ἱερόν, τό temple

ἱμάτιον, τό garment
ἵνα in order that
ἵστημι I stand, place

κάθημαι I sit
καθώς as, even as
καί and
καινός, ον, η new
καιρός, ὁ time
κακός, ον, η bad, evil
καλέω I call
καλός, ον, η beautiful, good
καρδία, ἡ heart
καρπός, ὁ fruit
κατά according to (with accusative); down from, against (with genitive)
καταβαίνω I go down
κατοικέω I inhabit, dwell
κεῖμαι I lie, recline
κεφαλή, ἡ head
κηρύσσω I proclaim, preach
κλαίω I weep
κόσμος, ὁ world
κράζω I cry out, call
κραυγάζω I cry out, shout
κρίνω I judge
κρίσις, ἡ judgment
κύριος, ὁ lord, Lord

λαλέω I speak
λαμβάνω I take, receive
λαός, ὁ people
λέγω I say, speak
λείπω I leave
λίθος, ὁ stone
λόγος, ὁ word
λοιπός, ον, η remaining; subst. the rest; adv. henceforth
λύω I loose, destroy

μαθητής, ὁ disciple
μακάριος, ον, α blessed, happy
μᾶλλον rather, more
μαρτυρέω I witness, testify
μαρτυρία, ἡ testimony, witness
μέγας, μεγάλου great
μείζων, ον, ων greater; comparative of μέγας (3rd decl.)
μέλλω I am about to
μένω I remain, abide

μέσος, ον, η middle, in the midst of
μετά with (with gen.); after (with acc.); becomes μετ' befor a word beginning with a vowel; μεθ' before a rough breathing
μή not (with moods other than ind.)
μηδέ but not, nor, not even
μήτηρ, μητρός, ἡ mother
μικρός, ον, α small, little
μισέω I hate
μνημεῖον, τό tomb, grave
μόνος, ον, η alone; as adverb (μόνον) only
μυστήριον, τό mystery

ναός, ὁ temple
νεανίας, ὁ young man
νεκρός, ον, α dead
νικάω I overcome, gain victory
νίπτω I wash
νόμος, ὁ law
νῦν now
νύξ, νυκτός, ἡ night

ὁ the masculine article, the
ὁδός, ἡ way, road
οἶδα I know
οἰκία, ἡ house
οἶκος, ὁ house
οἶνος, ὁ wine
ὅλος, ον, α whole
ὅμοιος, ον, α like
ὁμολογέω I confess
ὄνομα, ὀνόματος, τό name
ὀπίσω after, behind; also prep.
ὅπου where
ὅπως in order that, that
ὁράω I see
ὄρος, ὄρους, τό mountain
ὅτε when
ὅτι that, because
οὐ, οὐκ, οὐχ not (the second form is used before a word beginning with a vowel with smooth breathing, the third before one with a rough breathing)
οὐδέ and not, not even (οὐδέ. . . οὐδέ) neither. . . nor
οὐκέτι, μηκέτι no longer
οὖν therefore, then (postpositive)

231

οὔπω not yet
οὐρανός, ὁ heaven
οὔτε. . . οὔτε neither. . . nor
οὔτως thus, so
οὐχί not (strengthened οὐ)
ὀφθαλμός, ὁ eye
ὄχλος, ὁ crowd

παιδίον, τό infant, child
πάλιν again
πάντοτε always
παρά from (with gen.); beside,
  in the presence of (with dat.);
  alongside of (with acc.)
παραβολή, ἡ parable
παρακαλέω I beseech, exhort,
  console
παρρησία, ἡ openness, confidence
πάσχα, τό Passover
πατήρ, πατρός, ὁ father
πείθω I persuade
πέμπω I send
πέραν beyond
περί concerning, about (with
  gen.); around (with acc.)
περιπατέω I walk
πιάζω I lay hold, arrest
πίνω I drink
πιστεύω I believe
πίστις, πίστεως, ἡ faith, belief
πιστός, ον, η faithful, believing
πλείων, ον, ων; πλείονος larger,
  more
πληρόω I fill, fulfill
πλοῖον, τό boat
πνεῦμα, πνεύματος, τό spirit,
  Spirit, wind
πόθεν whence
ποιέω I do, make
ποιμήν, ποιμένος, ὁ shepherd
πόλις, πόλεως, ἡ city
πονηρός, ον, α evil
πορεύομαι I go
ποῦ where
πούς, ποδός, ὁ foot
πρεσβύτερος, ον, α elder; used
  as subs. also
πρό before (gen.)
πρόβατον, τό sheep
πρός to, toward, with (with

acc.)
προσεύχομαι I pray
πρόσωπον, τό face
προσκυνέω I worship
προφήτης, ὁ prophet
πρῶτος, ον, η first
πῦρ, πυρός, τό fire
πῶς how

ῥαββί rabbi, master
ῥῆμα, ῥήματος, τό word

σάββατον, τό Sabbath
σάρξ, σαρκός, ἡ flesh
σεαυτοῦ yourself (sing.)
σημεῖον, τό sign
σκοτία, ἡ darkness
σός, σόν, σή your (sing.)
σοφία, ἡ wisdom
σπείρω I sow
σπέρμα, τό seed
σταυρός, ὁ cross
σταυρόω I crucify
στρατιώτης, ὁ soldier
στόμα, στόματος, τό mouth
σύ you (sing.)
σύν with (with dative)
συνάγω I gather together
συναγωγή, ἡ synagogue
συνίημι I understand
σῴζω I save
σῶμα, σώματος, τό body
σωτήρ, σωτῆρος, ὁ Savior
σωτηρία, ἡ salvation

ταράσσω I trouble, disturb
τεκνίον, τό little child
τέκνον, τό child
τέλος, τέλους, τό end
τηρέω I keep
τίθημι I put, place, lay down
τιμάω I honor
τίς, τί who? what? which? (The
  first form is masculine and feminine, the last neuter. The neuter
  is translated "why?" as well;
  without the accent, it means,
  someone, something (indef. pron.)
τοιοῦτος, ουτον, αυτη such
τόπος, ὁ place
τότε then

τρεῖς, τρία three
τρίτος, ον, η third
τυφλός, ον, η blind

ὑγιής, ες, ης sound, well, healthy
ὕδωρ, ὕδατος, τό water
υἱός, ὁ son
ὑπάγω I depart
ὑπάρχω I am, exist
ὑπέρ in behalf of (with gen.);
  above (with acc.)
ὑπηρέτης, ὁ servant, officer
ὑπό by (with genitive); under
  (with accusative)

φανερόω I reveal, make known
φέρω I carry, bear
φημί I say
φιλέω I love
φίλος, ὁ friend
φοβέομαι I fear
φόβος, ὁ fear
φωνέω I call, invite
φωνή, ἡ voice, sound
φῶς, φωτός, τό light

χαίρω I rejoice
χαρά, ἡ joy
χάρις, χάριτος, ἡ grace
χείρ, χειρός, ἡ hand
χρόνος, ὁ time

ψυχή, ἡ soul

ὧδε hither
ὥρα, ἡ hour
ὡς like, as